REFORMING CL

REFORMING CLASSICAL EDUCATION:
TOWARD A NEW PARADIGM

Proceedings of the 8th Annual
Convivium Irenicum
Presented June 2–5, 2021

Edited by Rhys Laverty and Mark Hamilton

Copyright © 2022 The Davenant Press

All rights reserved.

ISBN: 1-949716-12-0

ISBN-13: 978-1-949716-12-2

Cover image is "The Allegory of Grammar" by Laurent de La Hyre (1650)

Cover design by Rachel Rosales, Orange Peal Design

Typeset and proofread by Mikael Good

"My son, if you receive my words
and treasure up my commandments within you,
making your ear attentive to wisdom
and inclining your heart to understanding,
if you seek it like silver
and search for it as for hidden treasure,
then you will understand the fear of the LORD,
and find the knowledge of God."

—Proverbs 2:1–5

CONTRIBUTORS

Bradford Littlejohn is President of the Davenant Institute and Fellow in Evangelicals in Civic Life at the Ethics and Public Policy Center. His research interests include Christian ethics, church history, and political theology. He is the author of *The Two Kingdoms: A Guide for the Perplexed* (Davenant Press, 2017), *The Peril and Promise of Christian Liberty: Richard Hooker, the Puritans, and Protestant Political Theology* (Eerdmans, 2017), and *Richard Hooker: A Companion to His Life and Work* (Cascade Books, 2015).

Gene Edward Veith is Professor of Literature Emeritus at Patrick Henry College (Purcellville, VA). He is well-known in Christian, conservative, and homeschooling circles through his writing and speaking on various aspects of Christianity and culture. Dr. Veith is the author of twenty books on topics involving Christianity and culture, classical education, literature, and the arts.

Colin Chan Redemer is Vice-President of the Davenant Institute, Poetry Editor of *Ad Fontes*, and Adjunct Associate Professor at St. Mary's College of California. He is currently pursuing a Ph.D. at the University of Aberdeen, exploring the philosophy of friendship.

Joshua Patch is a Ph.D. candidate in Literature at the University of Dallas. He teaches English in the Rhetoric School at The Covenant School in Dallas, Texas.

Gregory Wilbur is President and Dean of New College Franklin. He has lectured on a wide range of topics including music, geometry, cosmology, moral philosophy, and poetics. He is the author of and contributor to several books as well as numerous articles, and he speaks regularly on the arts, worship, and education. He contributes to The Christward Collective and the CiRCE Institute Blog. He has composed award-winning works for choir, orchestra, film, and corporate worship.

Nathan Johnson is a Professor of Moral Philosophy and the Trivium at New College Franklin. He previously taught humanities and composition at Greyfriars Classical Academy in Matthews, North Carolina. He is currently working on a Ph.D. in Humanities (with an emphasis in literature) at Faulkner University.

Michael J. Lynch teaches Classical Languages, Theology, and Humanities at Delaware Valley Classical School. He holds a Ph.D. from Calvin Seminary. His dissertation was published as *John Davenant's Hypothetical Universalism: A Defense of Catholic and Reformed Orthodoxy* (Oxford University Press, 2021).

Eli West teaches Humanities at Covenant High School in Tacoma, Washington. He studied History at Hillsdale College and holds a Master's of Arts in Teaching (MAT) from Templeton Honors College.

Brandon Spun is Dean of Academics and a Senior Fellow at New College Franklin, and is a Ph.D. candidate in Humanities at Faulkner University. His research interests include literature, literary theory, ancient philosophy, ethics, personalism, metaphysics, natural philosophy, and the liberal arts.

CONTENTS

    Introduction – On Naming the World: A Protestant Vision for
Training in Wisdom   iii
Bradford Littlejohn, The Davenant Institute

I   The Liberal Arts and the Art of Service: Protestantism's Challenge to
Classical Education   1
Gene Edward Veith, Patrick Henry College

II   On Corrupting the Youth: A Platonic Education   21
Colin Chan Redemer, St. Mary's College of California

III   Teaching Books, Teaching Arts: A View of Classical Christian Literary
Training   39
Joshua Patch, Ph.D. candidate at University of Dallas

IV   In Search of Virtue: Why the Quadrivium Matters   59
Gregory Wilbur, New College Franklin

V   Cosmic Wisdom: How the Quadrivium Serves Theology and Ethics   79
Nathan Johnson, New College Franklin

VI   Form, Content, and Purpose: Reflections on Early Modern Education
for Today   105
Michael Lynch, Delaware Valley Classical School

VII   A Confessional Education: Abraham Kuyper, J. Gresham Machen, and
the Christian Academy   123
Eli West, Covenant High School

VIII   Subalternation and the Liberal Arts: Vocation and Friendship with God   139
Brandon Spun, New College Franklin

INTRODUCTION
On Naming The World:
A Protestant Vision for Training in Wisdom

Bradford Littlejohn, The Davenant Institute

CALLING THE WORLD BY NAME[1]

WHEN I walk into my living room each morning, the first thing that greets me (assuming I've awoken early enough to enjoy some solitude) is the mesmerizing spectacle of the Blue Ridge Mountains, tinged with violet and pink in the first rays of the sun, dominating the horizon outside my windows in a great arc from West to North. An awe-inspiring vista for anyone, but for me, the ridge is more than that. For me, each peak and trough in the great ridge line is not merely a pretty sight, but an old friend. When I first moved my family back here to my old family stomping-grounds, my children wanted to know the names of the peaks. Thankfully, schooled by my father decades ago, I could still rattle them off: Hogback, Rocky Spur, Melrose, Little Warrior, Big Warrior, Round Mountain, Tryon Peak.

Naming, of course, comes naturally to small children: "What's this? What's that?" are usually among their earliest words as they poke their stubby index fingers in the direction of anything in sight. Too often, we run out of answers embarrassingly quickly: "It's a tree." "What kind of tree?" "Who knows? A big one." Naming, however, is the building-block of learning at every age. Even in describing complex processes, understanding comes when we are able to give things a name and rightly understand that to which the

---

[1] I would like to acknowledge my fellow teachers of Davenant's "How to Read the Bible and the World" course for helping to stimulate many of these thoughts over the years: Peter Escalante, Alastair Roberts, Joe Minich, and Nathan Johnson.

name applies. We learn not only to distinguish turtles from tortoises and annuals from perennials but also to distinguish the moderate Enlightenment from the radical Enlightenment and the benign tumor from the cancerous. As we reach out with the gift of language and lasso each new mystery with its own unique word or phrase, we render the murky transparent, the unfamiliar familiar.

Familiarity can breed contempt, as the saying goes; but familiarity can also engender love—one of the four loves that C. S. Lewis so memorably chronicled, in fact: *storge*, that is, affection. This love is not merely expressed through naming, it is also *activated* through naming: we call those whom we love by name. Moreover, I would argue, we come to love those things that we are able to call by name.

Why is this? Why is naming so important to us? If we turn to Scripture, we do not have to look far—no further than Genesis 2 in fact. When God planted Adam in the garden, the first task he gave him was to give every creature a name. Interestingly, God did not *command* Adam to name the animals; rather, "he brought them to the man to see what he would name them" (2:19)—he knows that Adam cannot help but name them.[2] Our own naming of the world is the way in which we participate in the Adamic task. This Adamic task is kingly and even *divine*. Consider Psalm 147:4: "[The LORD] determines the number of the stars; he gives to all of them their names." Naming things is a divine prerogative, and it is through our sub-creative power to name the world that we image the divine Creator who called the world into being through his Word.

This Adamic task must be at the heart of any Christian vision of education: we educate, above all, by equipping each new generation to name the world rightly. In this naming, I argue, lies one profound answer to the idea that we educate only to acquire concrete utility-maximizing skills—a reductionistic functionalism which characterizes so much of modern education. Within such a functionalist framework it becomes increasingly difficult to explain why everyone should be educated. After all, some function more highly than others. What is more, in a world of gadgets and search engines, machines function, for most purposes, more highly than any of us.

Increasingly, modern educators have been at a loss to explain why they should teach children to multiply instead of using a calculator, to spell

---

[2] Thanks to my colleague Rhys Laverty for this insight.

instead of using a spell-checker, and to know history instead of merely consulting Wikipedia. Why, indeed, not simply accept the fast-approaching utopia/dystopia of a small, highly educated, code-manipulating "creative class" able to design optimal experiences for a vast dependent underclass?

There's a favorite passage of mine from J. R. R. Tolkien's *Fellowship of the Ring* that gestures toward an answer, offering us profound insights into the purpose of education. The Fellowship are on their way south from Rivendell, and they awake one morning to find the Misty Mountains ahead of them rather than on their left. The following dialogue ensues:

> "'Dangerous or not, a real sunrise is mighty welcome,' said Frodo, throwing back his hood and letting the morning light fall on his face.
>
> 'But the mountains are ahead of us,' said Pippin. 'We must have turned eastwards in the night.'
>
> 'No,' said Gandalf. 'But you see further ahead in the clear light. Beyond those peaks the range bends round south-west. There are many maps in Elrond's house, but I suppose you never thought to look at them?'
>
> 'Yes I did, sometimes,' said Pippin, 'but I don't remember them. Frodo has a better head for that sort of thing.'
>
> 'I need no map,' said Gimli, who had come up with Legolas, and was gazing out before him with a strange light in his deep eyes. 'There is the land where our fathers worked of old, and we have wrought the image of these mountains into many works of metal and of stone, and into many songs and tales. They stand tall in our dreams: Baraz, Zirak, Shathur.
>
> 'Only once before have I seen them from afar in waking life, but I know them and their names, for under them lies Khazad-dum, the Dwarrowdelf, that is now called the Black Pit, Moria in the Elvish tongue. Yonder stands Barazinbar, the Redhorn, cruel Caradhras; and beyond him are Silvertine and Cloudyhead: Celebdil the White, and Fanuidhol the Grey, that we call Zirakzigil and Bundushathur.
>
> 'There the Misty Mountains divide, and between their arms lies the deep-shadowed valley which we cannot forget: Azanulbizar, the Dimrill Dale, which the Elves call Nanduhirion…

INTRODUCTION

'Dark is the water of Kheled-zaram,' said Gimli, 'and cold are the springs of Kibil-nala. My heart trembles at the thought that I may see them soon.'"[3]

Pippin here epitomizes your typical modern student—"Frodo has a much better head for such things." From the functionalist standpoint, why not let the high-functioning do the task of navigating for you? Or better yet, let your smartphone do it. The modern-day Pippin could've said, "Hey Siri, give me directions to Mordor." Of course, even from within a functionalist framework, Pippin's dismissal of the need for personal knowledge proves short-sighted. Occasionally, after all, you really will be left to your own resources and will regret not cultivating a basic knowledge of the path you may be called to tread—as Pippin later does in *The Two Towers*.

There is, however, a deeper critique here. Pippin's lack of education leaves him not merely useless as a route-finder; it makes him miss most of what makes this journey through Middle-earth more than mere drudgery. Contrast the clueless Pippin with Gimli and the "strange light" in his eyes. For Gimli, these mountains are not just impressive peaks on the horizon or points on a map. They are more like cherished friends; he does not simply *know about* them, he *knows* them intimately and personally. And this despite the fact that he has almost no direct experience of them! Rather, Gimli's knowledge is the result of what we might call a well-rounded dwarvish liberal-arts education. He has studied these peaks in geography and history; he has seen them in art, wrought in works of metal and stone; he has heard them in music, sung of in many songs, and studied them in literature, told of in many tales.

In short, we learn how to name the world, not merely for the sake of truth, but for the sake of beauty; not merely so that we can navigate the world, but so that we can *delight* in it. Such delight is an experience that we should aim to give to every son of Adam and daughter of Eve, according to their capacity. The vehicle for such delight, as Tolkien knew better than almost anyone, is language.

Tolkien's love affair with language is on bold display in the passage quoted above, as Gimli indulges in a dazzling and excessive display of

---

[3] J. R. R. Tolkien, *The Lord of the Rings: The Fellowship of the Ring* (Boston: Houghton Mifflin, 1988), 296.

polyglot pleonasm, calling each of the geographical features by three or four different names. From a purely functionalist standpoint, such multiplication of names and languages is a massive inefficiency. A world with only one language, like the world before Babel, is the dream of every global capitalist. The multiplication of languages, though, was not solely a divine punishment but a divine blessing, as the affirmation of a many-tongued people of God at Pentecost and in Revelation suggests. We need many languages to name the world because no single language can do so adequately. Reality is ever so much greater and richer than our words for it, and so, we need as many of them as possible. This is the purpose of poetry, which re-names creation in language and image that is ever-new, trying to capture in word the inexhaustible richness of the world, the "dearest freshness deep down things" that both transcends human speech and depends upon it.

GIVING VOICE TO THE VOICELESS CREATION

But why "depends upon it"? Why, indeed, was it so important for Adam to name the world? Couldn't the creatures have gotten along just fine without such a tedious ceremony? True, the catalyst for the naming of the animals is the need to illuminate Adam's need for a suitable helper. God, however, brings the animals "to see what he would call them" (Gen. 2:19), and so it seems that Adam cannot *but* name the creatures, wife-finding regardless. For a more developed answer, let's consider Psalm 19:1–4:

> The heavens declare the glory of God,
>   and the sky above proclaims his handiwork.
> Day to day pours out speech,
>   and night to night reveals knowledge.
> There is no speech, nor are there words,
>   whose voice is not heard.
> Their voice goes out through all the earth,
>   and their words to the end of the world.
> In them he has set a tent for the sun.

We are all, I imagine, familiar with these lines. We all intuitively recognize that this is an elaborate metaphor. The day does not *in fact* speak. Nor does the night. You can stand there straining your ears all day long, and you'll never hear the sun make a peep, much less communicate in any known language. Who does speak then? Well, the psalmist of course! Here in Psalm

INTRODUCTION

19, David *gives voice* to the voiceless heavens. He does the same in Psalm 104 at much greater length, describing the glory of God throughout the world.

Few of us pause to ask ourselves why God gave us the power of speech. No other creature has it, after all. Other creatures can *communicate*—they can send messages to one another, conveying their emotions, warning of danger, or signaling the presence of food or a mate. But they, however, cannot and do not attempt to describe the world around them except insofar as it relates directly to them. Even dolphins, so far as we know, while they can communicate a great deal to one another about the herring they are trying to catch, have no ability or desire to talk about what herring are *in themselves*—only as potential edibles. From this standpoint, we can see that modern education seeks to reduce us to the level of animals. It wants us to learn to talk about the world solely from the standpoint of its utility for our human purposes. We know carrots as food, oil as fuel, silicon as potential microchips.

This animalian level of communication is not, I would argue, why God gave us the power of speech. God gave us the power of speech because he *didn't* give it to the lower creation. The lower creation is shouting out God's glory, but inaudibly and inarticulately. It is waiting for man to give it voice. That is why God can say of creation on each day, "it is good," but only after the creation of man, "it is very good." Without man to name and describe the voiceless creation, the glory of God will go undeclared. Creation is so rich and manifold that one name will not do—we need a world's worth of languages to properly express creation's glory. The comet, the rose, the eagle, is waiting for the psalmist or poet to give it voice—like Gerard Manley Hopkins, who wrote:

> As kingfishers catch fire, dragonflies draw flame;
> As tumbled over rim in roundy wells
> Stones ring; like each tucked string tells, each hung bell's
> Bow swung finds tongue to fling out broad its name;
> Each mortal thing does one thing and the same:
> Deals out that being indoors each one dwells;
> Selves—goes itself; *myself* it speaks and spells,
> Crying *What I do is me: for that I came.*

"The world is charged with the grandeur of God," as Hopkins says in another famous poem, but it is waiting for us to discover and declare that glory. The same is true for mathematics. The triangle was waiting patiently and inarticulately for Pythagoras to announce his glorious theorem. The planets were waiting for Kepler's Law of Planetary Motion and Newton's Law of Universal Gravitation. By rightly naming the creation, man brings to completion, to fruition, to glory, God's work.

What about history and literature? The great deeds of men and women in ages past were great in themselves, but they are incomplete without a chronicler or a bard. They are waiting for their Homer or their Lord Macaulay to give voice to their voiceless deeds, and in so doing, to unfold the hidden glory of God's providential action. Indeed, the deeds of God's image-bearers do more than that—they point to Jesus Christ, "the express image of the invisible God." Hopkins continues his poem:

> I say more: the just man justices;
> Keeps grace; that keeps all his goings graces;
> Acts in God's eye what in God's eye he is—
> Christ. For Christ plays in ten thousand places,
> Lovely in limbs, and lovely in eyes not his
> To the Father through the features of men's faces.

CALLED TO MASTERY

And yet, much as we might like to, we cannot stop with poetry. We educate for delight, yes; we educate to glorify God, yes; but we educate also for a task that God has given the children of man: dominion. This means we educate in order to equip one another for mastery of the world. Such language is, of course, politically incorrect, since man's multiplying and filling the earth has increasingly shown how readily mastery can become domination, and domination exploitation. Still, we should not shy away from this kingly task.

Nonetheless, it matters deeply how we conceive of this mastery. There is a kind of mastery driven by hate and a kind driven by love. In the latter, we feel ourselves *mastered* in the midst of *mastering*; the world forms us even as we seek to impose form on it. This is indeed the classical Aristotelian understanding of knowledge according to which the already objective, already active form present in the matter of a thing impresses itself upon the mere potency of our organs of perception, compelling our minds to shape themselves in response to the reality of the world outside of our heads. Contrast this with the paradigmatically modern idea of knowledge, in which the ever-active intellect of man sallies forth to impose order on the formless and shapeless raw matter of the world; thus, creating a world in his own image and for his own purposes.

Most of us are still old enough to be familiar with that old euphemism of the King James Bible, "And Adam *knew* his wife." That euphemism was the product, not of prudish translators, but of a literal rendering of the Hebrew text in which *yada'* ("to know") could be used for the most intimate of human acts. To know, in biblical language, is to love: is to enter into intimate union with the thing known, a union of mutual indwelling. For modern man, however, the work of knowledge is more akin to rape than marriage. We have put the cosmos to death in order to know it properly—which is to say, to make better use of it for our purposes. As C. S. Lewis writes, "We do not look at trees either as Dryads or as beautiful objects while we cut them into beams: the first man who did so may have felt the price keenly, and the bleeding trees in Virgil and Spenser may be far-off echoes of that primeval sense of impiety. The stars lost their divinity as astronomy developed, and the Dying God has no place in chemical agriculture. . . From this point of view the conquest of Nature appears in a new light. We reduce things to mere Nature *in order that* we may 'conquer' them."[4]

The modern ideal of knowledge resembles what the medievals would have dismissed as the vice of *curiositas*. Medieval writers understood the love of knowledge, like any other wholesome love, could be disordered—warped toward wrong ends or pursued in a wrong way. On this basis, they distinguished the virtue of *studiosity*—which every educator should seek to inculcate—from the vice of *curiosity*. Among the many forms of curiosity was one that seems to particularly characterize our modern age, which we might call *impertinent curiosity*—impertinent in the sense of rude or disrespectful. This occurs when we seek to know things in a manner more certainly than they can be known, doing violence to the object of knowledge by forcing it into a Procrustean bed that will shave off all its mysteries. Rather than being animated by love of the object of knowledge, we are driven by hatred of the unknown.

As Paul Griffiths argues in his brilliant meditation *Intellectual Appetite*, this is the paradigmatically modern mode of knowing, which Griffiths calls *mathetic*: "Advocates of mathesis imagine a world of discrete objects arrayed spatially on a grid, each related to others causally in various ways, but each

---

[4] C. S. Lewis, *The Abolition of Man* (New York: HarperCollins, 2001), 70–71.

definable and knowable exhaustively in itself, each, that is, fully transparent to the appropriately catechized gaze and passive before that gaze, there to be gazed upon and addressed without itself returning or exceeding the gaze."[5] This sort of knowledge, he argues, prefers the visual, schematic, and atomized to the continuous interwoven text that is the paradigmatic mode by which the studious know.[6] Although easily confused with it, such mathesis is far from the Adamic vocation of naming, which understands that however much we might seek to provide a taxonomy of the world, the world as object always exceeds our gaze. Too often the curious modern believes he can know best of all through data arranged on a spreadsheet, while the studious seeker after wisdom understands that the object of knowledge must be grasped through a personal encounter, whether that object be a babbling brook or a profound theological truth. "The curious," observes Griffiths, "inhabit a world of objects, which can be sequestered and possessed; the studious inhabit a world of gifts, given things, which can be known by participation, but which, because of their very natures, can never be possessed."[7]

THE SEARCH FOR WISDOM

I have just used the word "wisdom" for the first time in this introduction. Wisdom is at the heart of the educational task, and a constant theme of our work at the Davenant Institute—but what does "wisdom" mean? I have ventured several definitions over the years, but here is one that I think captures the heart of the matter: wisdom is *a humble yet confident attunement to the order of reality that gives both delight and competence.* The wise man is humble, recognizing that he stands on the shoulders of giants, but also genuinely confident because he has come to possess the truth through hard-won personal encounter, rather than merely receiving it secondhand.

The essays comprising this volume, *Reforming Classical Education: Toward a New Paradigm*, were originally presented at a conference subtitled "A *Protestant* Vision for Training in Wisdom." What might we mean by such a sectarian adjective as *Protestant*? Well, many things might be said, and several of them will be said in the essays that follow. For now, it is worth stressing

---

[5] Paul Griffiths, *Intellectual Appetite: A Theological Grammar* (Washington, DC: Catholic University of America Press, 2009), 145.

[6] Griffiths, *Intellectual Appetite*, 151–54.

[7] Griffiths, *Intellectual Appetite*, 22.

that Protestantism has always had a certain democratizing impulse, challenging both the explicit elitism of ancient classical education and the implicit elitism of modern education. As William Tyndale said to the Roman clergyman of his day: "If God spares my life, ere many years, I will cause the boy that driveth the plow to know more of the Scriptures than thou dost!"

Thus a Protestant vision of wisdom stresses the hard-won personal encounter with truth and the confidence it engenders. My point is not to knock modern Roman Catholic education, which in many cases puts Protestant education to shame. At its inception, however, Protestantism set its face firmly against the intellectual elitism of the Roman church, and its doctrine of "implicit faith." On this medieval understanding (understandable, to be sure, in a society where books were scarce and education was a luxury), it did not much matter if the believer's faith had any clear grasp of the content of the Christian story and the hard truths of Christian teaching; so long as the believer trusted implicitly in his priest and his bishop, they could do the intellectual part of believing for him.

The Reformers hotly demurred, not least because this was a recipe for intellectual laziness on the part of priests and bishops as well, as Tyndale pointed out. Every believer must be trained, as much as possible, for a personal encounter with the Word of God—for a faith seeking understanding. Of course the Reformers recognized that there would still, of necessity, be an intellectual elite with special gifts and tasked with teaching. Contrary to Catholic caricatures then and now, the Reformers never sought to claim that every Tom, Dick, and Harry's reading of Scripture was equal to St. Augustine's. They did stress, however, that everyone had something to gain from reading the Scriptures for themselves and should be equipped accordingly.

From the beginning, it has been our contention at the Davenant Institute that this original message of the Reformation, this bold call for a society of sages, still needs vigorous restatement. In this, we cheerfully swim against the current of all of our age's fashionable laments about the death of expertise and out-of-control individualism. When we look at the modern landscape, we do not see too many people willing to think for themselves, but too few. American evangelicalism is increasingly characterized by a search for authority in a chaotic world. Such a search lends itself to a frenzied intellectual outsourcing, a "guru syndrome" that has been intensified by the disruptive technologies of the digital age. Instead of actually opening their eyes to the world around them, most Christians, fearful of the sea of uncertainty in which they have been called to swim, turn to their favorite answer-man pastors or political talk show hosts to provide them with a pre-packaged and pre-digested account of the world, which they can share comfortably with all of their fellow followers. We have seen this phenomenon vividly in the epistemic whirlwind of 2020 and 2021, as most Christians have allowed their tribal allegiances, rather than the minds that God gave them, to determine their judgments about a pandemic, about racial violence, about an election.

The solution, of course, is not "going it alone"—striking off across the desert like some intellectual Abraham in a Kierkegaardian romance—any more than the Reformers called for an intellectual levelling that would put the complete novice on the same level as the seasoned scholar. We obviously need experts, in the sense of master-craftsmen in the various arts and sciences. We depend upon them through the technologies we take for granted every hour. But we do not need gurus. What, then, is the difference?

The path of wisdom is one of imitation, not the imitation of the mere copycat or fanboy, not the carbon-copy mimicry of the follower who retweets his hero's every pithy insight or killer takedown. No, the path of wisdom is far narrower—there is no room upon it for the crowds that clamor after the guru. It is also far more difficult. The wise apprentice learns by closely observing and imitating the methods of a master craftsman—looking over his shoulder, as it were, as he works upon the world. The guru-follower fixes his enchanted gaze upon the face and lips of the guru, while the wise apprentice looks at his hands; or else follows the master's gaze, learning to fix his own eyes on the same objects that the master is studying. Every good human master will urge our attention back to the words and the world from which he himself has gained his skill and insight. Only the great Master, Jesus Christ, radiates enough wisdom that we are invited to fix our eyes on him.

The guru-follower, on the other hand, obsessively seeks to download the guru's every sermon, to read everything he has written, to memorize his canned slogans so he can recite them on every occasion. He tries to find the guru's every opinion, so as to make them (seemingly) his own. While the disciple of the master-craftsman has a decent shot at actually surpassing his master, improving on his work, the guru-follower will never be more than a follower—boring, tedious, and slavish in the full Aristotelian sense.

INTRODUCTION

WISDOM VS. WORLDVIEW

This brings me, at last, to the distinction between *wisdom* and *worldview*, a distinction central to the vision for renewing classical Christian education that the essays in this volume present, and one that has been a recurrent theme of our work here at Davenant. Reformed Evangelicalism's turn to worldview is an understandable response to modernity's separation of Word and world and fundamentalism's decision to hunker down in the bunker of the Word to avoid the taint of worldly knowledge. Realizing that Christians must stake some kind of claim to knowledge of the world if their God created it, a generation of late-twentieth-century Christian thinkers adopted the German idealist concept of a *Weltanschauung*, "world-view," as a kind of shortcut back to the holistic grasp of the world that the intellectual titans of an earlier Christian humanism had genuinely possessed. In most of its forms, however, this movement proposed simply to one-sidedly map Word onto world, conjuring from the pages of Scripture a comprehensive vision of reality that could then substitute for actual critical engagement with the world of nature and history, and often, one that could be weaponized against any insights that secular thought might dare to propose to the Church. The disconnect from earlier eras of Christianity, in which theologians had praised Plato and Cicero for both their wisdom and piety and leaned heavily on Islamic and Jewish philosophers to formulate their doctrinal systems, was jarring.

To be sure, the worldview concept can be used in helpful and nuanced ways, but much more often than not, it tends toward just the sort of pre-fabricated, pre-digested knowledge peddled by the guru, a Cliff's-Notes-version of reality that excuses you from the hard work and rich delight of really reading the world. Indeed, for all its fulminations against the evils of modernity, it is characteristically modern in its haste to transcend the fog of uncertainty endemic to the modern condition and in its "mathetic" mode of knowledge. "Advocates of mathesis," after all, as Griffiths notes, "imagine a world of discrete objects arrayed spatially on a grid," and anyone who has been to a Christian worldview seminar or bought a Christian worldview curriculum will know just how much the genre loves to use diagrams and schematics.

Christian-worldview training is like a map-reading seminar in Elrond's house—not useless, to be sure, and sometimes the best that you are going to get, but only a starting point, and deeply dangerous if you believe that the seminar has told you everything you need to know. Too often a "Christian worldview" becomes not an aid to, but a stand-in for, actually learning to *view* the *world*. There are tens of thousands of Christians who have been trained to walk around asking and telling each other what "the Christian worldview" has to say about any given subject, all the while never once pausing to actually observe the world to find out the truth of the matter.

But *can we* actually find out the truth of the matter? It's a fair question, given that the "worldview" metaphor is often employed more in the sense of a set of lenses through which we view the world (rather than a map by which we gain an overview of the world). In this usage, worldview is often used to emphasize bias and the unreliability of perspective. Unbelievers misconstrue some aspect of the world because they approach it from a "secular worldview." We, on the other hand, can look at the exact same issue and offer a radically opposed answer because we approach it from a "*Christian* worldview." More adventurous intellectual voyagers might want to stop in and try out more exotic sets of lenses, such as a Buddhist worldview, a nihilist worldview, or an existentialist worldview. One of the most popular books on this topic was tellingly titled *The Universe Next Door: A Basic Worldview Catalog*. Ironically, this style of thinking and speaking often goes hand-in-hand with un-self-conscious denunciations of "postmodern relativism."

Of course, such writers are not wrong to emphasize the importance of bias and perspective. It is true that each of us can see a radically different landscape depending on our point of view. I recall how disorienting it was when I visited a friend's house a few miles further along the Blue Ridge and he showed me his own stunning view of Melrose Mountain—but a Melrose Mountain all-but-unrecognizable from that to which my own eyes had been trained since childhood. Yet it is more important in our relativistic age to stress that, for all that, we are all looking at the same reality. How, then, do we see reality so differently? Well, many differences of perception owe to our divergent social locations and life experiences. There is no need to fancify all of these particular inflections of sight with the "-isms" so beloved by worldview diagnosticians. Other differences, however, do seem to go hand-in-hand with rigorous Christian belief, or lack thereof. There really do seem to be ways in which Christians are able to perceive the world differently (and better, we would argue) than unbelievers.

With these observations, we are on much firmer terrain than that of Kantian idealism. In Book I of his *Institutes*, John Calvin himself speaks of Scripture as providing "spectacles" for rightly reading the world and God's

INTRODUCTION

glory in it.[8] And Calvin is well-known for his rather dim view of unbelievers' knowledge, a knowledge that has been damaged by what theologians call "the noetic effects of sin." These effects are surely real—Romans 1 describes a terrifying (and terrifyingly familiar) pattern of mass self-delusion—but it is important to be clear about the source and nature of these effects. The Fall, after all, did not, as best we can tell, directly damage man's higher rational faculties in themselves; at any rate, the feats of mathematicians and logicians, fallen though they may be, remain dazzling. Sin's attack on our reason is more sneaky and subversive; it comes at us through the back door of our twisted will and depraved appetites. As a mentor of mine once put it memorably (if you'll pardon the vulgarity), "The Fall didn't so much impact our brains as our bellies and our balls." If knowledge is always a form of love, the Fall attacks our reason by making us love the wrong things and fix our eyes in the wrong places.

A closer look at the "spectacles" metaphor is quite illuminating in this regard. Although Calvin himself casually uses the example of the aged, unable to read (usually a result of farsightedness), I would suggest that the more usual form of bad vision—nearsightedness—is an apt metaphor for our fallen epistemic condition. The world is still the same, God's good creation, beautiful and ordered. And we are still capable of looking at it, and indeed, capable, in principle, of discerning its order and making sense of it. The problem is that there is so much of it, and we don't have the patience to look properly. Worse still, our eyes have become curiously unfocused, only able to see clearly those shiny, glittery goods in the foreground that cry out to our appetites. In the far distance behind them loom richer, truer goods, blurry and out-of-focus, and beyond them still, the craggy uplands of the heavenly country that is our final end, but lost to our fallen eyes in a blue haze. The best philosophers, willing to go to the hard work of getting up, walking around in the world, and peering beyond the juicy, distracting fruits in the foreground, have been able to gain some real, though fragmentary, knowledge of the truth, goodness, and beauty of the world. But only with the aid of Scripture, which sharpens our focus and restores our vision, will we have any hope of an authentic view of the world as it is.

Even here, however, the metaphor can mislead. For this corrective vision is not a one-time thing: "Just put on your biblical worldview glasses

---

[8] John Calvin, *Institutes of the Christian Religion*, I.6.1.

and everything will become clear." It's more like when you are in the optician's chair and they are incrementally improving your vision, constantly swapping out "Lens A" and "Lens B" until you are finally seeing every detail as a healthy person would. The task of Christian education is like a lifetime's worth of optician's appointments interspersed with field trips, as we return to the Word to have our vision sharpened a bit more and then head back out into the world to see what we can see. Of course, we speak here only of the role of Scripture in perfecting natural knowledge; as a source of supernatural knowledge, the spectacles of Scripture prepare our eyes to gaze straight at the Sun of Righteousness that illumines all else in creation.

This of course brings us back to my remarks about imitating craftsmen. Too many peddlers of Christian worldview hold up their worldviews as maps to be endlessly studied or lenses to be endlessly admired. They never seem to put the maps and the lenses to use in exploring the terrain. They forget that, useful as a good map or a good set of spectacles is when trying to follow old trails or blaze new ones, neither is a substitute for a good guide—especially if we want not merely to get from point A to point B, but to take dominion over all we see en route, naming and mastering the world. This we will do by learning to follow a master's gaze—focusing our attention on those features of the dizzyingly complex landscape that he knows how to pick out. By following his gaze, we learn to ignore the distracting foreground features that are apt to consume the attention of the unwary and to grasp the true shape of the reality we are seeking to know. By naming the world rightly, as the adept guide and explorer has himself learned to do from his mentors, we are enabled to join the ranks of the sons of Adam and daughters of Eve on a voyage of wonder through the cosmos, staking a claim to every square inch of creation in the name of our King. This, then, is the task of Christian education, the Protestant vision for training in wisdom.

I:
THE LIBERAL ARTS AND THE ART OF SERVICE: PROTESTANTISM'S CHALLENGE TO CLASSICAL EDUCATION

Gene Edward Veith, Patrick Henry College

INTRODUCTION

ONE OF the few fronts in the culture wars that Christians actually seem to be winning is education. As progressive education devolves into psychological conditioning and political indoctrination, churning out graduates with scarcely any knowledge or skills, Christians are rediscovering and implementing classical education. Though many Christians would be glad to simply protect their children from the baleful influence of the public schools, the new classical Christian schools and homeschools are outperforming their secularist counterparts *academically*. They are turning out young Christians who are learned, intellectual, and accomplished. They are the sort who will very likely outcompete their poorly educated peers and be in a position to exert a Christian influence on the culture once again.

Experience with the products of both progressive and classical education, on all educational levels, calls to mind the education of Gargantua, a story recounted in *The Works of Rabelais*.[1] The young giant had been educated for 53 years trying to master medieval commentaries. According to Rabelais, "At the last his father perceived, that indeed he studied hard, and that although he spent all his time therein, yet for all that did he profit

---

[1] François Rabelais (d. 1553) was a French Renaissance writer, physician, humanist, scholar, and monk. His status as a monk makes his educational satire here all the more pointed.

nothing: but, which is worse, grew thereby a fool, a sot, a dolt, and blockhead."[2] Whereupon a courtier suggested a comparative test with his twelve-year-old page who had studied for only two years in the new classical learning that was creating the Renaissance. The child delivered a learned and gracious discourse before the Giant King. As Rabelais puts it, "All this was by him delivered with such proper gestures, such distinct pronunciation, so pleasant a delivery, in such exquisite fine terms, and so good Latin, that beseemed rather a Gracchus, a Cicero, an Aemilius of the time past, than a youth of this age." Then it was Gargantua's turn to show what he could do. Reports Rabelais, "But all the countenance that Gargantua kept was, that he fell to crying like a cow, and cast down his face, hiding it with his cap."[3] Gargantua was sent to the page's schoolmaster, Ponocrates, who gave him a comprehensive education that turned him into Rabelais's comic model of a Renaissance Man, or, rather, a Renaissance Giant.

Ironically, though, the scholastic education that Rabelais lampoons was also a type of classical education. Classical education is a rich, multi-faceted tradition, which allows for many different variations and emphases. Those variations and emphases, in turn, reflect different philosophical, cultural, and theological commitments. The Reformation itself was a product of the Renaissance approach to classical education, and the schools that the Reformers established to teach the laity how to read the Bible were classical schools of a particular kind.

Gargantua's liberal education included listening to "sermons of evangelical preachers."[4] His daily regimen, overseen by his humanist teacher Panocrates, included Bible reading and worship. "There was read unto him some chapter of the Holy Scripture aloud and clearly," Rabelais writes. "According to the purpose and argument of that lesson, he oftentimes gave himself to worship, adore, pray, and send up his supplications to that good God, whose word did shew his majesty and marvelous judgment."[5] For all of his exuberant scatology and iconoclastic satire, Rabelais, a monk writing in

---

[2] François Rabelais, "Gargantua and Pantagruel," in *The Works of Rabelais*, trans. Thomas Urquhart and Peter Antony Motteux (Privately Printed, via Cornell University), https://warburg.sas.ac.uk/pdf/ebh565b2452783.pdf, 34.

[3] Rabelais, "Gargantua and Pantagruel," 35.

[4] Rabelais, "Gargantua and Pantagruel," 53. "Evangelical preachers" here likely means early Protestants.

[5] Rabelais, "Gargantua and Pantagruel," 48.

France in 1532, supported the reform of the Church. His ridicule of scholasticism and his rude and crude depictions of bishops and monks are little different from what the Reformers were turning out.

This essay will explore various approaches to classical education, both historically and as they manifest today. I want to focus on the kind of classical education cultivated by the Reformers and how it was distinct from other approaches. This, in turn, can help Christian educators today as we recover the rich heritage of classical Christian education, showing how we can ensure that it remain both classical and Christian.

THE VARIETIES OF CLASSICAL EDUCATION

Liberal Education in the Classical Era

What is classical or liberal, to use a more descriptive term, education? Although "liberal" has acquired unfortunate connotations owing to its American political association with progressivism, the word "liberal" in this context comes from the Latin *liberalis*, which means "befitting free men."[6] Originally, in ancient Greece and Rome, the distinction was between education in the liberal arts (*artes liberalis*)—the skills necessary for a free citizen—and education in the servile arts (*artes servilis*)—the skills necessary for a slave. Slaves needed to learn how to perform their crafts, do as they were told, and be productive functionaries of the economy. But the free citizens of the Greek democracies and of the Roman republic had to be educated so that they could be active participants in the deliberations and decisions of the *polis*. The free citizen needed to be able to use his mind at a very sophisticated level—he was responsible for receiving, applying, and transmitting the achievements and heritage of the past; he had to be able to express himself effectively in the forum so as to persuade others; he needed to conduct himself with honor and wisdom.

The specific list of liberal arts varied somewhat in the classical era. Plato gave a prominent role to gymnastics.[7] As Christians like Cassiodorus and Boethius appropriated classical education, seven liberal arts became the educational foundation: the trivium of grammar, dialectic or logic, and

---

[6] See the entry for "liberal" in *The Online Etymological Dictionary*: http://www.etymonline.com/index.php?term=liberal.

[7] Plato, *Republic*, Book II.

rhetoric (arts which would lead to the mastery and application of language) and the quadrivium of arithmetic, geometry, music, and astronomy (arts which would lead to the mastery and application of mathematics). Medieval educational theorists supplemented the "arts"—that is, skills—with the "sciences," that is, categories of knowledge. These liberal sciences were natural science (the knowledge of nature; that is, the objective creation); moral science (the knowledge of human beings and their interactions); and theological science (the knowledge of God). In effect, all knowledge could be included in these categories so that the classical curriculum studied a comprehensive range of subjects.

Other qualities and features of a liberal education would also emerge: the cultivation of the good, the true, and the beautiful; an emphasis on original sources; a concern for virtue; the imitation of excellence; reading good literature and cultivating creative and eloquent expression; study of the language and literature of the Greeks and Romans; Socratic questioning, so as to lead students to a personal discovery of truth.

The Rediscovery of Liberal Education

Some characteristics became clear when progressive education—beginning with the nineteenth-century German university model and continuing with Dewey and other modern theorists—reacted against the classical model. Whereas progressive education is highly specialized, liberal education introduces the student to a wide range of subjects in an attempt to develop all of the powers of the human being; progressive education emphasizes what is new and tends to denigrate the past, whereas liberal education values the achievements of the past and studies works that have stood the test of time; progressive education promotes change, whereas liberal education seeks to transmit the civilization to the next generation.

Today, many Christians and even non-Christians, in reacting against progressive education, have been rediscovering what is, in effect, the educational tradition of Western civilization. Much of this recovery has been piecemeal: Dorothy Sayers brings back the trivium; Mortimer Adler promotes the Great Books; Christian educators discover the *progymnasmata*, a powerful method of teaching writing; classical colleges bring back disputations, in which students publicly argue to support a thesis, as in Luther's academic exercise that sparked the Reformation. The classical Christian school movement, pioneered by Douglas Wilson and put into practice by hundreds of schools and thousands of homeschools, is bearing impressive fruit as it continues to grow.

In some instances, however, one element of the classical liberal arts has been mistaken for the whole. In the twentieth century, universities recognized that higher education on the German model could result in graduates who might know a great deal about a narrow field but remain essentially uneducated outside of that specialty. In response, universities crafted "liberal arts" requirements, ensuring that students sample a wide range of disciplines, including a dose of the "humanities." Unfortunately, those required classes were often just as specialized as every other program, with little effort to integrate the learning or to approach the different fields in a comprehensive, humane way.

At times, the elements of liberal education have been obscured by misconceptions. Dorothy L. Sayers was the catalyst for the current revival of classical education, but she did not get it completely right. She wrote perceptively about the importance of the trivium, but grammar, logic, and rhetoric are not simply developmental stages. There is a developmental element to them, as will be seen shortly in examining Johann Sturm's school, but the trivium refers more directly to discrete subjects and phases in the mastery of language. More profoundly, the trivium corresponds to the faculties of the mind as developed by St. Augustine: the memory (grammar), the understanding (dialectic), and the will (rhetoric). Thus, the trivium provides a blueprint for learning any subject in depth, with the entire mind, as the student progresses from knowledge through understanding to persuasion and creative personal application. While Sayers was very helpful in focusing on the trivium, she was simply wrong about the quadrivium. Arithmetic, geometry, music, and astronomy do not stand for the "subjects" (i.e., content) that students study in the upper grades. Rather, these are liberal *arts*. The knowledge that the arts are applied to are the natural, moral, and theological *sciences*; put differently, the quadrivium has to do with mathematics. The liberal arts comprise the two means of human learning: language and mathematics.

Forgetting that the liberal arts include mathematics, let alone that mathematics comprises four of the seven arts, has distorted classical education and damaged its appeal. Thus, in universities today, the term "liberal arts" has become synonymous with the "humanities." As a result, universities play off the "liberal arts"—often understood as literature, philosophy, history, and the like—against the much more desirable "STEM subjects" (Science, Technology, Engineering, and Mathematics). Such dichotomizing entirely overlooks the fact that Western science grew from the soil of the classical liberal arts. Today, science and the humanities are separated from each other, to the impoverishment of them both, whereas true classical education brings them together.

Classical educators need to recover the *quadrivium*, just as they have recovered the *trivium*. The opportunities are vast, since mathematics education is floundering in progressive schools, and there is an ever-growing need for professionals trained in STEM. However, a greater need from the Church's perspective is the role of mathematics in rebuilding Christian wisdom. Mathematics is a bracing tonic for those inclined to believe that there are no absolutes, that there are no objective truths, and that human beings construct their own realities. In both the "humanities" and the "sciences" today, separate though they are, it is commonly said that the universe is meaningless; and yet mathematics is a sheerly mental operation, which—amazingly—is found to describe, account for, and even predict the nature of the external, objective world, suggesting that there is a Mind that looms behind all physical reality.

The quadrivium employs mathematics not only in the numeric operations of arithmetic but in the spatial realm of geometry, the aesthetic realm of music, and the empirical observations of astronomy. As such, mathematics is an integrative discipline, just as language is. It teaches students to think objectively and to recognize the reality of forms and patterns and order. That recognition, in turn, has moral implications, as well as aesthetic ones. As classical educators explain the quadrivium, their students will see that arithmetic is about number; geometry is about number in space; music is about number in time; and astronomy is about number in space and time. Being able to think in terms such as these is an important legacy of the liberal arts.

Even when liberal education is clearly understood, there are still variations and options. In his history of liberal education, Bruce Kimball has shown how classical educators of different times and cultures have always vacillated in emphasis between logic and rhetoric.[8] The Greeks stressed

---

[8] Bruce A. Kimball, *Orators and Philosophers: A History of the Idea of Liberal Education* (New York: College Board, 1995).

dialectic, the pursuit of truth; the Romans stressed rhetoric, the formation of effective and influential citizens for the Roman Republic; in the Middle Ages, the conversational pursuit of dialectic was formalized into an emphasis on logic, leading to the rationalistic systems of scholastic philosophy and theology; the Renaissance version of classical education re-emphasized rhetoric, with its creativity and expressiveness.

To be sure, the genius of liberal education is integration—learning to embrace both the trivium and the quadrivium, rather than asserting one over the other. Why shouldn't a student be adept in both logic and rhetoric, language and mathematics, science and aesthetics? The highest achievement of liberal education is the "Renaissance Man," such as Leonardo da Vinci, a master of science, technology, engineering, and mathematics, who was also an artist of the highest order; or Sir Philip Sidney, the statesman and theologian, the soldier and poet. Such a level of integration is hard to achieve, of course, let alone sustain. Moreover, different worldviews manifest themselves in different kinds of education. Medieval Catholicism was rationalistic, and so, of course, its universities would put logic at the center. The Reformation, however, had a different basis and grew out of and promoted a different kind of liberal education.

CLASSICAL EDUCATION PLUS CATECHESIS

It is no exaggeration to say that the Reformation grew directly out of Renaissance classical education. It began at the University of Wittenberg, one of the new institutions built around the new learning. In accord with the educational methodology of *ad fontes* (meaning "to the sources" in Latin), the Renaissance curriculum focused on the reading of original sources instead of secondary scholarship. In the field of theology, whereas the scholastic universities studied commentaries and systematic treatises such as Peter Lombard's *Sentences*, the Renaissance universities studied the Bible. The catalyst for this new Renaissance classicism was the rediscovery in Western Europe of the Greek language. The great Renaissance humanist Erasmus edited and published his new edition of the Greek New Testament in 1516, which differed at many points from the Latin Vulgate. It was in the course of preparing lectures on the Bible that one Wittenberg professor, Martin Luther, realized the significance of the passage "the just shall live by faith" (Romans 1:17). Luther posted ninety-five theses for the purpose of holding an academic disputation–an exercise that was a staple of both medieval and

Renaissance universities—on the topic of indulgences. That disputation never took place, but others did, such as Luther's Heidelberg Disputation on the theology of the cross, and universities throughout Europe would be the forum for the theological debates of the Reformation. Later, Luther would use Erasmus's Greek New Testament and his colleague Philip Melanchthon's expertise in Hebrew to translate the Scriptures into the vernacular, the first translation of the whole biblical text from the original languages since the Latin translation of St. Jerome. The new Renaissance curriculum emphasized rhetoric, which carried over into the Reformation's emphasis on preaching. The new liberal learning stressed the formation of the free, individual human being, which carried over into the Reformation emphasis on personal faith.

Reformation and Renaissance

The Reformation, in turn, was a catalyst for the founding of new schools. The immediate goal was to teach everyone possible—not only clergy but laity, not only men but women, not only the socially privileged but peasants—how to read the Bible. The schools that the Reformation started were classical Renaissance schools.

The Reformation continued to employ classical education for centuries, though in a particular way. Thomas Korcok defines the Lutheran educational tradition as classical education plus catechesis[9]—that is, as the liberal arts combined with catechetical instruction.

In his history of Lutheran education (which likely also tracks with education in the Reformed tradition), Korcok shows that the theological conflicts of the Lutheran churches accompanied educational ones. The Enthusiasts wanted neither the liberal arts (considering them too worldly) nor catechesis (opposing the emphasis on doctrine rather than personal experience). They called for schools that simply taught students how to read the Bible. The Pietists likewise considered the liberal arts too worldly and catechism too doctrinal, calling for schools that taught the Bible and that prepared young people for a vocation. Later, the Rationalists opposed both the liberal arts and catechesis in favor of a "scientific" education. Throughout each controversy, however, the orthodox Lutherans insisted on liberal education plus Christian catechesis. Alternative approaches to

---

[9] Thomas Korcok, *Lutheran Education* (St. Louis: Concordia Publishing House, 2011), 57.

education—anti-intellectual fundamentalism, vocational training, and progressive scientism—persist today. Classical Christian educators must contend with them all, demonstrating that the classical Christian model is indeed the best alternative.

The Reformation schools also found themselves in conflict with other kinds of classical education. The first educational reforms put forward by the Reformation were in reaction against medieval scholasticism, a variety of classical education that put logic—along with Aristotle and Thomas Aquinas—at the center. Prof. Korcok summarizes the issues:

> In order for the Church to be free of these Thomistic and Aristotelian teachings, it was necessary to remove them from the classroom and replace them with a different approach to the liberal arts. This simultaneous need to reform the Church and education was apparent to Luther early on. In a letter to Jodocus Trutfetter in 1518, Luther said, "To explain myself further, I simply believe that it is impossible to reform the Church unless the canon law, scholastic theology, philosophy and logic, as they are now taught, are thoroughly rooted out and other studies put in their stead."[10]

The studies which took their place were the liberal arts as cultivated by the new Renaissance classicism, emphasizing rhetoric and accompanied by literature and other "humane" studies. Taking the lead in this project of educational reform was Melanchthon—Luther's friend, the author of the Augsburg Confession, and arguably the greatest humanist scholar next to Erasmus.

In time, tension grew between the Renaissance and the Reformation, a conflict that was both theological and educational. Renaissance educators such as Erasmus believed that a liberal education was sufficient in itself to shape its students in a life of virtue and spiritual enlightenment. Catechesis in the Law and Gospel was not, strictly speaking, necessary. The *artes liberalis* would result in a fully empowered human being who was "free." The exaltation of the "humanities" manifested itself in a high view of human potential, such that the so-called humanist learning tended to become "humanistic." Korcok again summarizes:

---

[10] Korcok, *Lutheran Education*, 20.

> While humanists like Erasmus were given to viewing the [liberal] arts as the starting point for a progressive life of moral improvement, Erasmus' contention that there was still a "scintilla of perfection" in a child led him to believe that the arts had the ability spiritually to reform a person. The Evangelicals could not accept that premise. For Luther, the corruption of the human soul was complete, voiding Erasmus' optimistic view.[11]

This controversy occasioned Luther's decisive break with Erasmus in his treatise *The Bondage of the Will*. Still, the Reformation schools did not abandon their commitment to the liberal arts. "The result," says Korcok, "was a new form of humanism: one which historian Josef Dolch calls a 'Confessional Humanism.' Unlike the humanism of the fifteenth and early sixteenth centuries, this 'Confessional Humanism' placed catechetical instruction as the first priority."[12] Catechetical instruction—with its grammatical memorizing, dialectical questions, and rhetorical confession—was itself an application of liberal pedagogy. Thus, humane learning was thought to fit well with a distinctly Christian framework. As Reformation historian Steven Ozment has said, "Humanities became for Protestant theologians what Aristotelian philosophy had been to the late medieval Catholic theologian, the favored handmaiden of theology."[13]

The Erasmian faith in classical liberal arts education as a self-contained religion persists today. Not all classical schools are classical *Christian* schools, though the very power of the liberal arts can vest them with a religious aura. Notice how the vocabulary of classical educational theory is replete with theological terminology. We have a "canon" of Great Books. For some, the Great Books—according to one canon or another—have precisely that kind of authority. Literary and philosophical masterpieces constitute secular scriptures, to which people can look for inspiration, guidance, and transcendence. While Christians may agree with such people about politics,

---

[11] Korcok, *Lutheran Education*, 32.

[12] Korcok, *Lutheran Education*, 33.

[13] Steven Ozment, "The Intellectual Origins of the Reformation," in *Continuity and Discontinuity in Church History*, ed. F. Forrester Church, George Huntston Williams, and Timothy George, *Studies in the History of Christian Thought* (Leiden: Brill, 1979), 9:147. Quoted in Korcok, *Lutheran Education*, 33.

the decadence of modern life, and the value of Western civilization, they remain humanists, and nothing more.

Having used the theological terms "transcendence" and "inspiration," we could add "creation," "epiphany," and "revelation." It is very easy to turn classical education into a religion. This is a testimony to the brilliance of classical education, but it is no substitute for Christianity. Wise Christians recognize this, and when the necessary distinctions are made, liberal education and the Christian faith can complement each other. But sometimes, an education that seems to provide all the answers, that offers pleasures instead of disciplines, that makes fewer demands, and that exalts the student beyond all measure can be twisted into a substitute for Christianity. It is entirely possible for Christians to send their children to excellent liberal arts colleges which cause them to lose their faith

A liberally educated person, even one externally disciplined by the classical virtues, can still be a desperate sinner. Indeed, an excellent and dangerously equipped sinner, whose education makes him capable of doing worse things than he otherwise would have been able to do. This is the lesson of classical education itself. Socrates's most brilliant disciple was Alcibiades, who would betray his native Athens first to the Spartans and then to the Persians. Aristotle's most notable pupil, Alexander the Great, conquered the known world and, yet, he shed rivers of blood and met his end because he could not control his own appetites. Thankfully, *Christian* classical education—the liberal arts plus catechesis—can give rise to another kind of empowered human being and another kind of freedom.

CLASSICAL EDUCATION PLUS VOCATION

Another important difference between the Reformation's classical schools and many liberal arts schools today deserves mention. Apologists for the liberal arts often distinguish between their approach, which pursues its subjects as ends in themselves, and "vocational" training, which aims at the pragmatic end of teaching young people an occupation, trade, or profession. The Reformation discussions of the liberal arts, however, nearly always related them to "vocation"—not in a contemporary, narrow occupational sense, but in light of the Reformation doctrine of vocation. That is to say, a liberal education as the Reformers conceived of it equips its students for *service* to their neighbors. This understanding of vocation and its relation to the liberal arts complicates the classic distinction between "liberal" and "servile" education, resulting in a different notion of the freedom that liberal education cultivates.

Luther's Commitment to Liberal Education

Luther's *Large Catechism*—one of the official confessions of faith for Lutherans—enshrines the Reformation's commitment to a classical liberal arts education. Luther's explanation of the commandment to honor one's father and mother ends with a discussion of parental responsibilities:

> For if we wish to have excellent and apt persons both for civil and ecclesiastical government, we must spare no diligence, time, or cost in teaching and educating our children, that they may serve God and the world, and we must not think only how we may amass money and possessions for them. For God can indeed without us support and make them rich, as He daily does. But for this purpose He has given us children, and issued this command that we should train and govern them according to His will, else He would have no need of father and mother. Let everyone know, therefore, that it is his duty, on peril of losing the divine favor, to bring up his children above all things in the fear and knowledge of God, and if they are talented, have them learn and study something, that they may be employed for whatever need there is [to have them instructed and trained in a liberal education, that men may be able to have their aid in government and in whatever is necessary]. If that were done, God would also richly bless us and give us grace to train men by whom land and people might be improved, and likewise well-educated citizens, chaste and domestic wives, who afterwards would rear godly children and servants.

Parents are charged to bring up their children in the fear and knowledge of God and also, according to the Latin translation, "to have them instructed and trained in a liberal education, that men may be able to have their aid in government and in whatever is necessary."[14]

---

[14] Martin Luther, *Concordia Triglotta*, trans. F. Bente and W. H. T. Dau (St. Louis: Concordia Publishing House, 1921), 631. The specification of a "liberal" education is present only in the official Latin version of the *Large Catechism*. Lutherans have

It would seem, then, that Lutherans would be confessionally bound—"on peril of losing the divine favor," no less—to give their children a classical liberal arts education. As it happens, though, confessional subscription must be to the German version, which leaves out the reference to a distinctly liberal education and speaks only of "formal study." So a commitment to the classical liberal arts, as such, though highly favored by the Reformers, is not an absolute confessional mandate. Nevertheless, a commitment to education is. It is the parents' "chief duty" to educate their children for both the spiritual and earthly kingdoms. The purpose of both the "formal study" in the German version and the "liberal education" in the Latin version is "service." That is, the purpose of education for Luther as well as his fellow educators and confessors is vocation.

The Two Kingdoms and Liberal Education

In other words, Luther is referring to the importance of parents equipping their children for both of God's two kingdoms: God's eternal kingdom (to bring them up "in the fear of knowledge of God") and God's temporal kingdom ("that men may have their aid in government and in whatever is necessary"). This two kingdom framework, described here as "both for civil and ecclesiastical government," explains why the Lutheran educational tradition consists of liberal education for the temporal kingdom and catechesis for the eternal kingdom. The competing approaches to education mentioned earlier, to which the Reformers were opposed, each neglected one of the two kingdoms in favor of the other: the humanists, in thinking a temporal education sufficient, neglected man's citizenship in the eternal kingdom; the Enthusiasts, in thinking an education for eternity sufficient, neglected man's citizenship in the temporal kingdom; although the Pietists understood the necessity for both kingdoms, their focus on economic callings narrowed the true scope of vocation and Christian service.

---

traditionally accepted the original German version as authoritative, which has opened the door to other approaches.

The Three Estates and Liberal Education

Luther taught that God reigns in His temporal kingdom through three "estates": the Church, the family, and the state. Christians have multiple vocations in all three of those estates: in the Church, as pastors, other church offices, and laypeople; in the family, as husband or wife, father or mother, son or daughter, and other positions in the extended family; in the state, as ruler, magistrate, soldier, or simply citizen. As for what people do to make a living—as in our contemporary meaning of "vocation"—Luther included it primarily as part of the family estate, calling it "the household," namely how the family supports itself. In the late medieval economy of peasant farmers, craft guilds, and feudal landholdings, most economic labor was inextricably tied to family. Luther also occasionally writes about vocations within the state, as with the offices of government, law, administration, and the military.

We must not miss that Luther's *Large Catechism* says that a liberal education is the best preparation for vocations in *all* of the estates. Luther specifically refers to "government," "well-educated citizens," and improving people in the state, as well as the vocations of the "household": those who improve land, servants (that is, employees), parents, and wives. He also highlights "chaste and domestic wives, who afterwards rear godly children and servants." Luther believed that women too should be educated—and with a liberal education—which he believed would help them not only as mothers but also as governors of their household servants.

Luther on Vocation as Service

Luther is not advocating "vocational" education in the modern sense. He explicitly rejects the notion, commonly-held today, that the purpose of education is to train young people so that they will obtain gainful employment and amass wealth. He tells parents, "we must not think only how we may amass money and possessions for them." God will provide these things. Rather, the role of parents is to give their children an education that equips them for *service* in both of God's kingdoms: "we must spare no diligence, time, or cost in teaching and educating our children, *that they may serve God and the world.*"

In his tract *To the Councilmen of All Cities in Germany, That They Establish and Maintain Christian Schools* (1524), Luther explains how liberal education equips young people for service. He discusses vocation and education in the same terms:

> Hitherto the sophists have shown no concern whatever for the temporal government, and have confined their schools so exclusively to the spiritual estate that it was well nigh a disgrace for an educated man to marry; he had to hear such remarks as, "Behold, he is turning secular and does not care to become a spiritual!" just as if their estate were alone pleasing to God and the secular estate, as they call it, were altogether of the devil and unchristian.[15]

Herein lies the pivotal insight which led to Luther's doctrine of vocation: a rejection of the notion that the spiritual orders are more holy than the temporal orders. The medieval church taught that a person who desires Christian perfection must become a priest, a monk, or a nun. This required taking vows of celibacy (thus forswearing participation in marriage and parenthood) and poverty (thus forswearing ordinary economic activity). In the medieval church, the word "vocation" referred solely to a call to the religious orders. Luther, however, extended the concept to the temporal orders. Thus, the Table of Duties in Luther's *Small Catechism* refers to being a husband, wife, parent, child, master, servant, day laborer, worker, and the like as being "holy orders," the same term used for those who have taken clerical vows.[16]

Luther's educational reforms promoted the "priesthood of all believers." The new Reformation schools went far beyond teaching lay people how to read the Bible. Rather, since vocation opened up the secular realm as the proper arena for the Christian life, they provided liberal education.

> "But," you say again, "granted that we must have schools, what is the use of teaching Latin, Greek, Hebrew, and the other liberal arts? We can still teach the Bible and God's Word in German, which is sufficient for our salvation." I reply: Alas! I know well that we Germans must always

---

[15] Luther, *Concordia Triglotta*, 631.

[16] Martin Luther, "Table of Duties," in *Luther's Small Catechism* (St. Louis: Concordia Publishing House, 2017), 33.

> remain brutes and stupid beasts, as neighboring nations call us and as we richly deserve to be called. But I wonder why we never ask: What is the use of silks, wine, spices, and strange foreign wares, when we have in Germany not only wine, grain, wool, flax, wood and stone enough for our needs, but also the very best and choicest of them for our honor and ornament? Arts and languages, which are not only not harmful, but a greater ornament, profit, honor and benefit, both for the understanding of Scripture and for the conduct of government, these we despise; but we cannot do without foreign wares, which we do not need, which bring us in no profit, and which reduce us to our last penny. Are we not justly dubbed German fools and beasts?[17]

Here we see the common notion of the liberal arts elevating human beings above their natural barbaric state. But Luther goes further, saying that these arts, particularly the ancient languages that were the foundation of a classical liberal arts education, are gifts of God: "Truly, if there were no other use for the languages, this alone ought to rejoice and move us, that they are so fine and noble a gift of God, with which He is now richly visiting and endowing us Germans, more richly indeed than any other land."[18]

Luther then relates the liberal arts to vocation:

> If then there were no soul, as I have said, and if there were no need at all of schools and languages for the sake of the Scriptures and of God, this one consideration should suffice to establish everywhere the very best schools for both boys and girls, namely, that in order outwardly to maintain its temporal estate, the world must have good and skilled men and women, so that the former may rule well over land and people and the latter may keep house and train children and servants aright. Now such men must come from our boys and such women from our girls. Therefore the thing to do is to teach and train our boys and girls in the proper manner.[19]

---

[17] Martin Luther, "To the Councilmen of All Cities in Germany, That They Establish and Maintain Christian Schools" (1524), accessed March 29, 2022, http://www.godrules.net/library/luther/NEW1luther_d9.htm.

[18] Luther, "To the Councilmen."

[19] Luther, "To the Councilmen."

What such an education can give both boys and girls is not specific job-training. In this same treatise, Luther states that such practical training for specific professions should be conducted outside of school, in apprenticeships. The kind of education he is envisioning, however, teaches the ability to "rule well" in the natural, social, family, and economic orders.

It is highly significant that the Reformation schools rejected a model of servile education and instead began providing a liberal education, designed specifically to equip human beings for freedom, for all classes of people, doing so even in a hierarchical sixteenth-century society, and for girls as well as boys. Once peasants received such an education, they did not stay peasants for long. The Reformation was soon accompanied by unprecedented social mobility. This was due in part to the churches' efforts to make all Christians not only literate but liberally educated. In time, this education for freedom would lead to the rise of social and political freedom as well. The liberal arts could liberate human beings precisely by cultivating their intellectual and creative powers and drawing out their individual talents. This, too, Luther related to vocation.

Luther recognized how liberal education cultivates original thought and independent thinking:

> If children were instructed and trained in schools or elsewhere where there were learned and well-trained schoolmasters and schoolmistresses to teach the languages, the other arts, and history, they would hear the happenings and the sayings of all the world and learn how it fared with various cities, estates, kingdoms, princes, men, and women; thus they could in a short time set before themselves, as in a mirror, the character, life, counsels and purposes, success and failure of the whole world from the beginning. As a result of this knowledge, they could form their own opinions and adapt themselves to the course of this outward life in the fear of God, draw from history the knowledge and understanding of what should be sought and what avoided in this outward life, and become able also by this standard to assist and direct others.[20]

---

[20] Luther, "To the Councilmen."

This education, for Luther, also had a moral dimension, akin to the First Use of the Law, in regulating "this outward life."[21] Here too, Luther relates liberal education to vocation, the equipping of Christians "to assist and direct others"; that is, to love and serve their neighbors, the purpose of every vocation.

CONCLUSION

Thus, for Luther, liberal education *was* vocational education—not in the sense of professional training, but in the sense of equipping young people to love and serve their neighbors in their families and societies. This does distinguish Luther, to a certain extent, from perhaps the best-known theorist of the liberal arts, Cardinal John Henry Newman. A liberal education, in his view, involves knowledge pursued for its own sake, as opposed to mechanical "instruction," which employs knowledge for other ends, that is, to be "useful."[22] Cardinal Newman's idea of the university as a realm unto itself for the pursuit of the higher good, unsullied with the demands of the world—making the university a sort of secular monastery—may owe something to the ancient Catholic tradition. It goes back further, though, to Luther's philosophical nemesis, Aristotle. In his *Politics*, the great philosopher not only develops the notion that knowledge pursued for its own sake is a higher good, but specifically rejects the concept of service: "The object also which a man sets before him makes a great difference; if he does or learns anything for his own sake or for the sake of his friends, or with a view to excellence, the action will not appear illiberal; but if done for the sake of others, the very same action will be thought menial and servile."[23]

While Aristotle believed that doing things for others is not fitting for a free man and, thus, that education that benefits others is inferior to that pursued for its own sake, Luther had a very different view—not only of

---

[21] Article VI of the Book of Concord defines the first use of the law as "that thereby outward discipline might be maintained against wild, disobedient men [and that wild and intractable men might be restrained, as though by certain bars]." The Formula of Concord – Epitome, *The Book of Concord*, accessed March 29, 2022, https://bookofconcord.org/epitome/third-use-of-the-law/.

[22] John Henry Newman, "Discourse 5," *The Idea of a University*, accessed March 29, 2022, http://www.newmanreader.org/works/idea/discourse5.html.

[23] Aristotle, "Politics," in *Classic and Contemporary Readings in the Philosophy of Education*, ed. Steven M. Cahn (New York: McGraw Hill, 1997), 138.

education but of freedom. In his treatise "On the Freedom of a Christian," Luther said that true freedom manifests itself in vocation; that is, in love and service to one's neighbor:

> A Christian… ought to entertain this view and look only to this object—that he may serve and be useful to others in all that he does; having nothing before his eyes but the necessities and the advantage of his neighbor.… And as our heavenly Father has freely helped us in Christ, so ought we freely to help our neighbour by our body and works, and each should become to the other a sort of Christ, so that we may be mutually Christs, and that the same Christ may be in all of us; that is, that we may be truly Christians.[24]

If freedom for the Christian is expressed in service, it would follow that the kind of education associated with freedom—that is, the liberal arts—would also exist to serve the neighbor.

---

[24] Martin Luther, *On the Freedom of a Christian* (1520), trans. R. S. Grignon, accessed March 29, 2022, http://www.ctsfw.edu/etext/luther/freedom/.

BIBLIOGRAPHY

Aristotle. "Politics." In *Classic and Contemporary Readings in the Philosophy of Education*, edited by Steven M. Cahn. New York: McGraw Hill, 1997.

Book of Concord. Accessed March 29, 2022. https://bookofconcord.org/epitome/third-use-of-the-law/.

Kimball, Bruce A. *Orators and Philosophers: A History of the Idea of Liberal Education*. New York: College Board, 1995.

Korcok, Thomas. *Lutheran Education*. St. Louis: Concordia Publishing House, 2011.

Luther, Martin. *Concordia Triglotta*. Translated by F. Bente and W. H. T. Dau. St. Louis: Concordia Publishing House, 1921.

———. *On the Freedom of a Christian*. Translated by R. S. Grignon. 1520. Accessed March 29, 2022, http://www.ctsfw.edu/etext/luther/freedom/.

———. "Table of Duties." *Luther's Small Catechism*. St. Louis: Concordia Publishing House, 2017.

———. "To the Councilmen of All Cities in Germany, That They Establish and Maintain Christian Schools." 1524. Accessed March 29, 2022. http://www.godrules.net/library/luther/NEW1luther_d9.htm.

Newman, John Henry. "Discourse 5." *The Idea of a University*. Accessed March 29, 2022. http://www.newmanreader.org/works/idea/discourse5.html.

Plato. *Republic*. Translated by Benjamin Jowett. Accessed April 7, 2022. http://classics.mit.edu/Plato/republic.3.ii.html.

Rabelais, François. *The Works of Rabelais*. Translated by Thomas Urquhart and Peter Antony Motteux. Privately Printed, via Cornell University. https://warburg.sas.ac.uk/pdf/ebh565b2452783.pdf.

II:
ON CORRUPTING THE YOUTH: A PLATONIC EDUCATION[1]

Colin Redemer, St. Mary's College of California

A CRITICAL ENGAGEMENT WITH THE POPULAR PERSPECTIVE

READ Plato from the popular perspective and his theory of education is thought to go as follows: "Plato's works describe and deploy a pattern of education which is applicable to all education, not just successful or ideal education. He accepts the outcome of being a good citizen as a worthwhile end, which encompasses and includes many other good outcomes."[2] Given

---

[1] This essay was originally delivered as a response to a paper by Dr. Al Harmon entitled "Plato's Logic of Education," which was the first address in a public discussion entitled "Plato's Theory of Education." The original audio of the exchange can be found at https://soundcloud.com/user-240690980/discussion-on-platos-theory-of?in=user-240690980/sets/national-convivium-2021.

[2] Paraphrased from "Plato's Logic of Education" by Dr. Al Harmon. Harmon's argument in that paper is a robust restatement of the authoritative interpretation of Plato on the issue of education. And he cites several passages which support his position. I summarize it in larger form as follows: Socrates promises in several places that the art he teaches is "the political art" by which one can manage both their household and the city itself (cf. *Protagoras* 318e–a7; *Meno* 91a3–6). But it isn't a tyrannical art because it also requires the student to learn to be ruled if they are to be a good citizen—to rule and be ruled in turn (cf. *Laws* 643e3–644a2). And a major component of ruling and being ruled is itself having the piety and self-regard to want to pass on the education which the city offered you to future generations—an education in the form of life conducive to life in the city (cf. *Laws* 653a5–c4). As such, the education which Plato describes is also the one he offers his readers; it is all inclusive of the other goods of the city. This argument is particularly convincing

this reading, it is no secret that many schools in the classical Christian education movement consider Plato an integral part of their curriculum. Such schools are spreading like fire—which is, we should note, one of the most hopeful developments in modern educational theory and practice. Reading Plato in such schools, they say, allows Plato to instruct schoolmasters on how to get educated and, in so doing, he educates. Students learn to ask questions "socratically," trading the strong and proper noun in for the weak and slack adverb. They think about, and discover, real virtue and become good little boys and girls. And on and on rolls the defense of the teaching of Plato in secondary schools. All the while these Plato boosters think such a defense is a defense of Christianity. And so they teach Plato.

They should not.

We can preface our response to this popular reading by stating agreement with the above argument on every point. Plato does, in fact, describe a process of education which purports to create good citizens and a happy, peaceful, civic order. There is, however, a sizable gap between the reading of Plato offered in this essay and the one outlined above. I can summarize this as follows: if Plato's theory of education is merely to produce good citizens, who are activating their natural capacities and becoming useful to themselves and their fellow man, then it would seem that we do not need Plato at all. Surely there are manifold works which can teach us these lessons—works more accessible and more effective at accomplishing these goals. The Bible alone will do quite nicely, as will more contemporary works—perhaps the *Autobiography of Ben Franklin* combined with a quick course on financial literacy and modern tax law. Surely such a course of study will be more pragmatic for our students. Such a proposal may sound like putting Socrates on trial a second time. This is not the case. Rather, it is to

---

if one reads Plato's theory as developing over time into something fundamentally at peace with his world and temporal situation and downplays the comparatively rare, terse statements which arrest the attention of characters and readers. Readers can engage my argument as a response to his, but this essay is also intended to stand on its own as a more general engagement with the question of Plato's role in classical Christian education. For other literature to see that our argument is in disagreement with a broader position held in the modern Church see Louis Markos's recent book *From Plato to Christ* (Downer's Grove, IL: IVP Academic, 2021), which we will quote favorably later on. It serves as a good example of the kind of book which trades in broadly similar arguments to Harmon, even if Markos, on the edges, is aware that the reading of Plato is a deal more complex than it may at first appear.

ask an innocent question: what, if anything, does Plato's theory of education in particular have to offer us? What, if anything, does Plato offer us beyond producing good citizens?

THE NATURE OF THEAGES'S EDUCATION: AN EXAMINATION

To begin our investigation, we will eschew a sweeping summary of all of Plato's works, and look instead to one specific dialogue and then consider the rest of the corpus in light of it. Rarely read nowadays, the dialogue to which we turn our attention is titled the *Theages*.[3] This is Plato's dialogue on wisdom. The dialogue opens in a highly irregular fashion with Socrates being approached by a pillar of respectable Athenian democracy named Demodocus. Demodocus, a successful farmer, approaches Socrates because he is looking for help in raising his son Theages. Theages, it seems, wants something from his education that he claims his father cannot provide. The

---

[3] A discussion of the authenticity of the *Theages* is probably best reserved for a footnote. Since Friedrich Schleiermacher's *Introductions to the Dialogues of Plato* it has been fashionable to consider *Theages*'s authenticity as, if not fraudulent, at least suspect. It should be noted how novel this claim is to Schleiermacher and his heirs. The appendix of Seth Benardete's *The Daimonion of Socrates: A Study of Plato's* Theages answers a chorus of these critiques. (To see just how recently the accusations of *Theages* authenticity are, consult: John M. Rist, "Plotinus and the 'Daimonion' of Socrates," *Phoenix* 17, no. 1 [January 1963]: 13–24.) To summarize the pedigree of scholarship which considers *Theages* not only worthy of scholarly interest but also thoroughly Platonic here we note that the nearly forgotten scholar Thrasyllus of Mendes included *Theages* to lead off his fifth tetralogy; Diogenes Laertius, a man who showed interest in debunking spurious "Platonic" dialogues, considered *Theages* authentic; Plutarch quotes Socrates with a citation from *Theages*; Albinus, the student of Gaius the Platonist, tells us there are scholars of Plato who begin their classes on Plato by lecturing on this dialogue; even our near contemporary Nicholas D. Smith in his introduction to the dialogue in *Plato: Complete Works* (where, by the way, it is included) tells us that while there is "virtual unanimity among modern scholars [that *Theages* is not of Platonic origin]," the arguments *against* including it in the corpus are "circumstantial," before going on to state his position that the dialogue was likely written by a now-forgotten student of Plato. And so the modern quest for the historical Plato continues. It perhaps says more about modern readers than it does about the dialogue per se that two hundred years of effort have been poured forth to prevent us from reading it. The testament of history often prevents us from having the history we desire. And, after all, it is still a question open to future historians to uncover whether those passages in *Introductions to the Dialogues of Plato* were really written by Schleiermacher.

father and son have set out, apparently, to enlist the help of Socrates in this "vexing" problem of education. The given theme makes *Theages* the perfect place to start for our purposes. Where better to uncover the secret of Platonic education than in this dialogue in which a father seeks the secrets of education from Socrates?

At the outset, Demodocus assures us that he has taught his son the art of farming and the related useful arts and the arts of citizenship. We assume such useful arts have in mind the things one needs on an Athenian farm of that era; carpentry, husbandry, leatherworking, but perhaps also such things as apiculture or viticulture or magirology, and certainly it would have involved the social art of the management of workers. But Theages wants more. What more? The more of wisdom itself. Socrates interrogates them, asking what is meant by this "wisdom" until he uncovers what Theages truly wants: to be a tyrant. It seems Theages is not hoping to be educated by Socrates but rather to be educated by a tyrant. Socrates knows nothing of tyranny, having been an *idiot* his whole life.[4] Theages, further, does not seem to be too promising of a pupil. He fails to see the relevance of the questions that Socrates tosses his way in the form of metaphors: the ship, the chariot, the doctor, the cook, etc. Theages can't hold his own opinion long enough to be honest about his tyrannical desire. Theages intuits that the wisdom he seeks is likely "wisdom of the city" and follows the argument just far enough to gather that wisdom is a form of knowledge. But he can't see beyond that. He wants what his father has, but also to be clever like the other boys who spend time with Socrates. He can't perceive that wisdom *is* of the city, and the city being like the man is thus an exposition of the knowledge of himself to himself. This is the point at which Delphic and Platonic wisdom unite, and readers are invited to wonder at it. But we are left wondering instead at what Theages missed. Try not to blink. Socrates now changes tactics and makes every effort to send Theages away, in as polite a way as possible (after all, his influential father is standing right there). Any insult could cause harm to the listeners as they may unjustly harm him. Truths are dangerous that way. "How do I look in this

---

[4] That is, he was labeled an *idiotes*—the term in Greece for those who did not get involved in public life, meaning literally "private person." These origins are more accurately reflected today in English words such as "idiom" or "idiosyncratic." In modern Greece, *idiotes* is used to describe those employed in the private rather than public sector. Greece was noted to have the lowest standard of living in Europe as recently as 1981. However, the modern use of *idiotes* is likely not meant as a commentary on the relative economic prospects of such workers.

outfit?" is often not a question earnestly asked, and Socrates seems to see that the reaction to the truth may cause those who hear it to overreact. If they harm him they would do so unjustly, and yet he would be, in part, to blame. To these gentlemen of Athens he is gentlemanly. In the end, Socrates reluctantly agrees to allow Theages to spend time with him, after having given a stern warning: "pups like you often feel like they're getting cleverer when they're in my presence, but once they leave me they go back to the way they were. This contact-high might satisfy you, or might not, but it is all *you* will get from me." From the perspective of Theages and Demodocus, this is enough; after all, "education" is about sitting in class, obeying the teacher, and *doing the work*. Socrates is willing to do this for Theages but he hides his real teaching. The subtextual truth is hidden to Theages at least, but discernible for the attentive reader: Socrates is saying that Theages is uneducable—a blasphemous statement to modern educational ears, and one we do not want to hear. We feel guilty even entertaining the idea. Of course, times change and Socrates is as much a man of his time and place as we are of ours. Socrates's ancient standard of education is so radically different from ours that we hardly know what to make of a dialogue like this. In the modern system we lack "the ancient standard of excellence that can be had only by hierarchy, judgment, and eccentricity."[5] Now we deal in the opposite: equality, feedback, and homogeneity.

An outline of this difference is then necessary for us to clarify what was meant by education as Plato conceived it. And here we will turn to that supreme reader of Plato, Leo Strauss.[6] In his essay "Persecution and the Art of Writing," Strauss deals with the problem of our conception of education as it relates to our epistemology and our anthropology. Some select passages can serve as a guide to rereading the *Theages*.

> What attitude people adopt towards freedom of public discussion, depends decisively on what they think about popular education and its limits. Generally speaking,

---

[5] Donald Phillip Verene, *The Art of Humane Education* (Ithaca: Cornell University Press, 2002), xii.

[6] Strauss and his students, often referred to as "Straussians," have pioneered a recovery of Plato and of Great Books education more generally starting roughly from the 1950s.

premodern philosophers were more timid in this respect than modern philosophers.[7]

The timidity which we see in Socrates's engagement with Theages hinges on something which is practically invisible to us but was all too clear to Plato and his earlier readers—the problem of persecution. Do not forget that Plato watched his beloved teacher die at the hands of the just and pious Athenians. In an era, like ours, where we are free to speak, and uninhibited in publishing our thoughts, the natural consequence is a belief in education which is (or ought to be) universal. Plato depicts Socrates as shy towards Theages because he doesn't want to expose himself; he knows there is a danger in certain truths which are not politically neutral, even if they are morally salutary. Thus, his investigation of the boy is cryptic. That is not something we even have to consider in modernity—certainly not in an era when we speak of an "enrollment crisis." Our language itself exposes our unexamined assumption of the educability and edification of all.

> [The philosophical architects of modernity] looked forward to a time when, as a result of the progress of popular education, practically complete freedom of speech would be possible, or—to exaggerate for purposes of clarification—to a time when no one would suffer any harm from hearing any truth…The attitude of an earlier type of writers was fundamentally different. They believed that the gulf separating "the wise" from "the vulgar" was a basic fact of human nature which could not be influenced by any progress of popular education: philosophy or science was essentially a privilege of "the few." They were convinced that philosophy as such was suspect to, and hated by, the majority of men.[8]

In proof of this suspicion we can look briefly outside of the *Theages* to Plato's *Phaedo* 64b, where the masses laugh at the philosopher—the necessarily rare, because supreme type of, man—while a murderous rage seethes under their grins (though Plato is quick to add that they laugh in this way without knowledge). Or we can look to *Republic* 520b2–3 where Socrates

---

[7] Leo Strauss, *Persecution and the Art of Writing* (Glencoe: The Free Press, 1952), 33.
[8] Strauss, *Persecution and the Art of Writing*, 33–34.

claims that there is a superior type of man—once again the philosopher—who "grows up spontaneously against the will of the regime" regardless of where they are. Earlier, in 494a4–10, Plato notes how, through envy and avarice, the whole city is as likely to turn on the rare youth of a true philosophic nature in its potency as they are to respect and nurture it. Most of us are familiar with the salutary sounding aspects of Plato's theory of education, such as that which Aristotle cites: that the beginning of education is teaching the young what they ought to love and what they ought to hate.[9] This salutary platitude, however, masks deeper, more uncomfortable truths, in light of which the benign statements take on a new meaning. For example, consider Plato's seventh letter.[10] He writes: "For this knowledge [of education] is not something that can be put into words like other sciences; but after long-continued intercourse between teacher and pupil, in joint pursuit of the subject, suddenly, like light flashing forth when a fire is kindled, it is born in the soul and straight away nourishes itself."[11] This light being kindled may happen and may not, but there is no technique by which it can be made to take place reliably and predictably. It is a secret fire. There are no words to describe it; there is no guaranteed way to execute it. The love we hear Aristotle talk about is impressed upon us because we are impressionable. But the dark truth Plato is hiding is that *we* are the stuff impressed upon. It is *our nature* which is key, not the technique or the content or the subject.[12] And once that is seen, we see further that, to Plato, our natures *differ*. Just as a wax seal pressed into stone does no good, so too some are clay and some are bronze and others gold. In the light of this fire, the myth of the metals from

---

[9] See Aristotle, *Nicomachean Ethics*, 1104b.

[10] For readers who may doubt the veracity of the letters' provenance I ask them to see the scholarly introduction to the letters by someone I always respect even when I sometimes disagree: John M. Cooper, who describes Letter VII as "the least unlikely to have come from Plato's pen...If not by Plato, *Letter VII* must have been written when it says it was—not long after Dion's death in 354 [BC]—and by someone close enough to Plato to be confident of writing about philosophy in a way that could convince a discriminating audience that included Greek philosophers in Southern Italy that the author was indeed Plato." "The Seventh Letter," in *Plato: Complete Works*, ed. John M. Cooper (Indianapolis: Hackett Publishing Company, 1997), 1635.

[11] Plato, "The Seventh Letter," 1659.

[12] Certainly not the learning outcomes…

the *Republic* takes on a new, strange meaning.[13] And it takes eyes to see when a myth which is confessed as a myth disguises a truth too dangerous to admit to. A cutting comment which is then named as "a joke" is sometimes clearly no such thing.

In light of this teaching, we see that Socrates's exoteric offer to educate Theages is a lie. But, of course, Plato has the gentlemanly grace to admit it is a lie. However, he only admits this to those who are perceptive readers. Theages has no potential to become a philosopher. He is *uneducable by nature*, and Socrates alludes to as much in passing when Theages is mentioned in the *Republic*. In an admittedly cryptic passage, *Republic* 496b clearly indicates that Theages sticks with Socrates because there's something wrong with him, perhaps a physical disability. Allan Bloom is correct in his interpretive essay that the thrust of the passage regards reasons why philosophers are so rare.[14] As those young men whose potential enables them to do anything, their miseducators are the masses who pull them with their applause into war, politics, and business. Theages is listed as one who has resisted these temptations—but only because he seems never to have been applauded for abilities at any of those trades in the first place. The reader of *Republic* is left to ask if the defect extends beyond the body and into the intellect or soul, thus precluding Theages from the category of philosopher altogether. The teaching that there are uneducable people in an ultimate sense, and further that this must be kept hidden from them, is perhaps clearer in other passages of Plato. In the *Republic*, Plato claims the philosophical nature is necessarily among the rarest human types.[15] Further, he claims education cannot be forced and should always come about through play and be driven by the interests of the young; the young, however, being interested in various things,

---

[13] The Myth of the Metals is presented in Book III of the Republic. Socrates relates how, supposedly, God created three types of human beings, each mingled with a different kind of metal: those made to rule society (the guardian class) were mixed with gold; those made to protect society (the auxiliaries) were mingled with silver; and those made to produce for society (the workers) were mingled with brass. The Myth is famously known as "the Noble Lie" which gives order to society. It also serves as an allegory for the structure of the soul in Plato's philosophy.

[14] Plato, *The Republic of Plato*, trans. and ed. Allan Bloom (New York: Basic Books, 2016), 400; 456.

[15] Roslyn Weiss, *Philosophers in the "Republic": Plato's Two Paradigms* (Ithaca: Cornell University Press, 2012). See particularly the chapter titled "Philosophers by Nature."

will end up in different places.¹⁶ The combination of these claims means that mass education cannot work because the undistracted love of learning is *rare*. Plato intends to keep it that way since learning in the hands of the masses is as likely to lead to evil as well as good (if not evil more often than good, given that virtue is a form of knowledge).¹⁷ Education, from the perspective of the state, is mostly about hiding the fact that only some of them are philosophers born, and thus that liberal education is wasted on most people, all while allowing those who rule or teach to observe and identify those with philosophical natures, separating them from the masses in the same way that farmers separate female from male chicks.

CHRISTIANITY HAS SUNDAY DINNER WITH SOCRATES'S DEMON

Strauss wrote that "[e]very decent modern reader is bound to be shocked by the mere suggestion that a great man might have deliberately deceived the large majority of his readers."¹⁸ Yet, he argued, this deception is key to understanding Plato. And we must be sure to understand Plato rightly if we are to answer our initial question. So, to return to that question: what, if anything, does Plato's theory of education have to offer us? Let us ask this by first reviewing the popular perspective on Plato with which we opened and searching for its source in the tradition of Christian engagement with Plato to determine its provenance. If the popular perspective of Plato is correct then we come up with one answer which is predetermined for us. This perspective has a long pedigree, dating at least to the Enlightenment-era humanists' re-appropriation of ancient Greek philosophy. However, anyone trying to search for its source earlier than that would discover significant complications. It dates back, perhaps, to the time of Justin Martyr (and his contemporaries) of the first and second century, in whose eyes, we tell ourselves, the Platonic teaching was uncomplicated and straightforward. To them, Socrates (and probably Plato) was a Christian by dint of his interest in

---

¹⁶ Armand D'Angour, "Plato and Play: Taking Education Seriously in Ancient Greece," *American Journal of Play* 5, no. 3 (Spring 2013): 293–307.

¹⁷ T. S. Eliot makes much the same point in "Notes toward the Definition of Culture," in *Christianity and Culture* (New York: Houghton Mifflin Harcourt, 2014), 179–80.

¹⁸ Strauss, *Persecution and the Art of Writing*, 35.

the *logos* and his disinterest in the conventional gods of his day. As Justin says in Chapter 46 of his *First Apology,* all those who lived by the *logos* were Christians even if they were thought atheists by their pagan peers.[19] Justin in particular, as demonstrated in his *Dialogue with Trypho*, spent a young lifetime studying philosophies of various schools, not least the Stoics, the Peripatetics, and the Pythagoreans, over the course of which he did not become a Christian but neither was his intellect satisfied. After moving on to Plato he began to be interested in the contemplation of God. Plato did not deliver the pure vision of God to Justin, however, as that required the hearing of the Word delivered to him by an old man whom he happened to meet on the seashore one day. Thus philosophy might be recovered, but not as a straightforwardly Christian practice, even in the hands of Justin.[20] It is thus not clear that we can establish the popular perspective from Justin Martyr since he establishes himself as being of two minds about the issue at hand. But, on the other hand, there may be other sources worthy of examination. Origen also was influenced by Plato from his time studying with Ammonius Saccas, who was later to become teacher of Plotinus. We cannot know exactly what Origen's Platonic education entailed, as he mostly left us with biblical commentaries, and no direct statements on his learnings at the feet of Saccas. However, Origen's understanding of Christianity is not without controversy.[21] Origen's most redeeming quality appears to be his near total ambivalence in public statements towards Plato in particular and philosophy in general.[22] However, even here one need not wade deep into the scholarly

---

[19] Justin Martyr, *The First Apology*, New Advent, accessed April 15, 2019, https://www.newadvent.org/fathers/0126.htm.

[20] T. J. Lang, "Intellect Ordered: An Allusion to Plato in Dialogue with Trypho and Its Significance for Justin's Christian Epistemology," *The Journal of Theological Studies* 67, no. 1 (2016): 77–96.

[21] Henry Chadwick, "Origen," in *The Cambridge History of Later Greek and Early Medieval Philosophy*, ed. A. H. Armstrong (Cambridge: Cambridge University Press, 1967), 182–92.

[22] But worth quoting at length here that in Chadwick's eyes Origen "is wholly without trace of any inferiority complex…Origen is not one of those apologists who derived encouragement from similarities to Christian ideas in Plato or Chrysippus. He is completely free of the notion that there is a mystique of authority attaching to the great classical philosophers, and is without the least desire to claim the protection of their name for any statement. Nothing for Origen is true because Plato said it, though he thinks that Plato, being a clever man, said many things that are true. What Origen

literature to conclude that Origen, when at his most Platonic, is "heterodox at best."[23] This is, on some level, to be expected; after all, it should not be forgotten what Socrates Scholasticus, in his *Historia Ecclesiastica*, says happened to the brilliant but misled Porphyry. At some point after Porphyry was exposed to Plato he lost his faith and began writing his *Adversus Christianos*, a work so caustic and evil that Theodosius II had to outlaw it.[24] This story about Porphyry is also attested by that pride of Protestantism, Augustine, who would be yet another source most readers would reach towards to establish the popular perspective, and here again the trail leads in fascinating directions. Like Justin, Augustine spent a young life searching for secrets to divinity. Among the sources he looked to, he lists, in his *Confessions*, Manichaeanism, astrology, sexual hedonism, proto-romanticism, and worldly success, until he met the great Bishop Ambrose.[25] Ambrose was not only a saintly and well-ordered man but also wise beyond Augustine's ken. However, in Augustine's telling, Ambrose is not what answers his questions; rather, it is not until Augustine reads the philosophy of Plato that he begins to feel a philosophical settling in his life. Casual readers may stop here to think we have uncovered the view most amenable to the popular position, but to Augustine this philosophical life is simply the last and greatest temptation impeding the straight road to heaven. He has not yet taken up and read the Word which can draw him into God. It is the story of one learned Neoplatonist, Victorinus, who converts after years of study, that helps Augustine see the limits of Plato's school. However, this is all simply to summarize the man's biography, and we ought to give Augustine space to speak for himself. It is known he was influenced by Plato and Platonic philosophy, but comparably less attention gets paid to his comments that, while the Platonists might not be as wrong as, say, the Manichaeans, they are

---

claims is not an affinity with this or that philosophy, but the right to think and reason from a Christian standpoint." Chadwick, "Origen," 185.

[23] Louis Markos, *From Plato to Christ: How Platonic Thought Shaped the Christian Faith* (Downer's Grove, IL: IVP Academic, 2021), 158.

[24] Philip Schaff and Henry Wace, *A Select Library of Nicene and Post-Nicene Fathers of the Christian Church*, Second Series (The Christian Literature Company, 1890), Vol. II, Book III, Chapter XXIII.

[25] Augustine, *The Confessions*, trans. Maria Boulding (New York: New City Press, 1997), Part I, Vol. 1, Books II–IV.

nevertheless wrong.[26] Or, further, that to Augustine the failing of the philosopher is a moral failure as much as an intellectual one: the moral failure of pride. The philosophers think, in their pride, that they can find the ultimate good in this life, and "so does pride perversely copy God."[27] In thinking that by their own power they have raised themselves up, they have in fact fallen below their nature as the *flammifer* had before them. Finally, and for our purposes most definitively, as Augustine says, "philosophers have much to say on this subject, but one does not find among them true affection, that is, true worship of the true God, to which all the activities of right living ought to be directed. This arises chiefly, as I understand it, because they wanted to construct their own happiness for themselves, in one way or another, and they thought this was more a matter of doing than of receiving, whereas God is its only giver. "Only He who made man makes man's happiness."[28] After which he, again, implores his readers to "cast off" the vanities of the philosophers. He goes so far as to call them liars.[29] To risk repetition, this is not a unique move which Augustine, in his genius, came up with. He sounds like no one so much as his now-forgotten near-contemporary Shenoute the Great, friend and colleague of Cyril of Alexandria, who advises us to be wary of not just Plato, not just philosophers, but "all books outside the scriptures, whether belonging to the pagans, or belonging to all godless peoples, or belonging to the heretics, they are erring spirits that are in them…When they proclaim the name of God in them or say similar words, all the evils that are written in them destroy even the one that is good."[30] We have seen that the conversion of the pagan Platonist Victorinus was essential for Augustine's own journey towards faith: the path of the public pagan *rhetor* converting to,

---

[26] Gerald G. Walsh and Grace Monahan, "Book Fourteen. Chapter 5," in *The City of God, Books VIII–XVI*, in *The Fathers of the Church* (Washington, DC: Catholic University of America Press, 1952), 4:356–58.

[27] Gerald G. Walsh and Daniel J. Honan, "Book Nineteen," in *The City of God, Books XVII–XXII*, in *The Fathers of the Church* (Washington, DC: Catholic University of America Press, 1954), 24:198, 215.

[28] Augustine, "155 To Macedonius," trans. Wilfrid Parsons, in *Letters, Volume 3 (131–164)*, in *The Fathers of the Church* (Washington, DC: Catholic University of America Press, 1953), 20:305.

[29] Augustine, "155 To Macedonius," 310.

[30] Shenoute the Great, *Selected Discourses of Shenoute the Great: Community, Theology, and Social Conflict in Late Antique Egypt*, ed. David Brakke and Andrew Crislip (Cambridge: Cambridge University Press, 2015), 64.

and then defending, faith in Jesus. But turning for only a moment to Victorinus, we see that even a thinker as committed to Plato as he had to reject the full implications of Neoplatonism once he came to the light of truth in Christ.[31] And, lest we think the matter settled in the time of Augustine, orthodox readers need look no farther than that east facing sun-worshiper Proclus to see that Neoplatonism and the challenge of philosophy in general (and of Plato in particular) continues side by side with Christianity, leading many astray, often hiding in plain sight behind dubious authorship.[32] We can clearly see that each generation must take up the battle anew. The now forgotten John Philoponus had to refute Proclus's heresies and Maximus the Confessor stepped in to offer correction to his brother in Christ, Philoponus.[33] As I. P. Sheldon-Williams has made clear, uncritical acceptance of pagan philosophy has been ruled out of bounds from the earliest days of the Church, and the above partial review of the Church's history with Plato confirms that view (even if Sheldon-Williams is overly pessimistic with regard to modern Protestant philosophy), which leaves us room to engage Plato but not to baptize him, and certainly not to thrust him upon any and all who wander into a Church or Christian educational space as if he were a panacea.[34]

---

[31] R. A. Markus, "Marius Victorinus and Augustine," in *The Cambridge History of Later Greek and Early Medieval Philosophy*, ed. A. H. Armstrong (Cambridge: Cambridge University Press, 1967), 334.

[32] Ben Schomakers, "An Unknown *Elements of Theology*? On Proclus as the Model for the Hierotheos in the Dionysian Corpus," in *Proclus and His Legacy*, ed. Danielle Layne and David B. Butorac (Walter de Gruyter GmbH, 2017).

[33] Timur Shchukin, "Matter as a Universal: John Philoponus and Maximus the Confessor on the Eternity of the World," *Scrinium* 13, no. 1 (2017): 361–82.

[34] I. P Sheldon-Williams, "Introduction: Greek Christian Platonism," in *The Cambridge History of Later Greek and Early Medieval Philosophy*, 421–31. Note that he does say "some modern protestantism [*sic*]" on page 425, "some" not "all," and thus saves himself for the careful reader. We further say, in a footnote that is perhaps *nicht notwendig*, that Sheldon-Williams agrees that the earliest Christian position was a rejection of Hellenistic learning. In a choice quote discussing Gregory of Nyssa in the following chapter titled "The Cappadocians," the point is sharpened thusly on page 440 while discussing and quoting from Gregory: "reason derives its value from faith and the Platonic achievement is of no avail unless it is subordinated to faith and acknowledges its limits: 'Take for your guide faith rather than reason; from the realization of your weakness in regard to the things that are nearest to you judge the value of your reason and understand that there are things that are beyond it.'" Later approaches are said to be substantially different than this, but it is far from clear that

So, so much for the popular perspective. If, on the other foot, our reading of Plato is correct, then we come to a different answer. The answer can only be a teaching which classical Christian education must reject.

As someone who has spent time in the classical Christian education world I have to conclude that we cannot use Plato as a model for our educational institutions. At present, lip service is paid to him in our "socratic discussions" and by keeping him in the curriculum in a minimal way—a sprinkling 0f *Apology* here, a dash from the *Republic* there, the fairy dust of *culture*. We do not take him seriously enough to engage him robustly, nor do we fear him. He exists as an aged uncle invited to dinner out of an abundance of piety. He shows up, and sups, and speaks, and we nod as we studiously ignore him and return to our meal. But such uncles must be watched as they are not universally benign. Contemporary educators who assign Plato for homework are leaving their charges in a vulnerable position. They should not.

None of this is to sit in judgment over Plato, but we cannot advise that he be taught by the masses for the masses. As pious Christians, it would violate our consciences, and as Americans it would violate our sacred laws— our consciences because we believe in every single human as an image bearer of the same God; our laws because we believe all are equal citizens of the same republic. Socrates made every effort to send Theages away so that he could live the life of a pious Athenian; or, if Theages wouldn't leave, then Socrates knew well enough not to teach him anything at all, and to prepare him in advance with the knowledge that, in his course of study, he wouldn't learn much. The classical Christian educators of the modern era who keep Plato in the curriculum are in much the same relationship to him: he is interesting, but not much use. In his presence we feel intelligent, but when we leave him we continue on as if we'd never heard him. In truth, we simply *cannot* hear him, as we believe in education for every citizen, and in the formation of our children into useful human beings who are engaged in continual self-betterment from one generation to the next. We believe in the inherent dignity of each soul created in the image of God. And these are values we cannot and should not give up. Plato himself advises us not to let young people study philosophy until age thirty.[35] We would do well to heed

---

such is the case inside orthodox catholic Christianity. As the saying goes, Philosophy must be the handmaiden of Theology.

[35] Plato, *Republic*, Book 7.

that advice, or perhaps even to up the age to three-hundred, though that may be going too far. Let classical Christian educators read Plato themselves to contend with what he is saying in all his caustic brilliance, but let them turn to other texts to accomplish their educational goals with the young.[36] At best, reading Plato with children will be a needless diversion you make use of as you teach the truly essential elements of Logic, Grammar, and Rhetoric. Plato is a mere, useless adjunct. At worst, compulsory reading of Plato may cause young persons to lose their faith and bring the end of the Church in our land closer.

---

[36] Assuming such educators share our desire to keep those spirited young ones living in the path of righteousness, hidden in the heart of God.

BIBLIOGRAPHY

Augustine. "155 To Macedonius." Translated by Wilfrid Parsons. In *Letters, Volume 3 (131–164)*, in *The Fathers of the Church*, vol. 20. Washington, DC: Catholic University of America Press, 1953.

———. *The Confessions*. Translated by Maria Boulding. New York: New City Press, 1997.

Chadwick, Henry. "Origen." In *The Cambridge History of Later Greek and Early Medieval Philosophy*, edited by A. H. Armstrong. Cambridge: Cambridge University Press, 1967.

D'Angour, Armand. "Plato and Play: Taking Education Seriously in Ancient Greece." *American Journal of Play* 5, no. 3 (Spring 2013): 293–307.

Eliot, T. S. "Notes toward the Definition of Culture." In *Christianity and Culture*. New York: Houghton Mifflin Harcourt, 2014.

Justin Martyr. *The First Apology*. New Advent. Accessed April 15, 2019. https://www.newadvent.org/fathers/0126.htm.

Lang, T. J. "Intellect Ordered: An Allusion to Plato in Dialogue with Trypho and Its Significance for Justin's Christian Epistemology." *The Journal of Theological Studies* 67, no. 1 (2016): 77–96.

Markos, Louis. *From Plato to Christ: How Platonic Thought Shaped the Christian Faith*. Downer's Grove, IL: IVP Academic, 2021.

Markus, R. A. "Marius Victorinus and Augustine." In *The Cambridge History of Later Greek and Early Medieval Philosophy*, edited by A. H. Armstrong. Cambridge: Cambridge University Press, 1967.

Monahan, Grace, and Gerald G. Walsh. "Book Fourteen. Chapter 5." In *The City of God, Books VIII–XVI*, in *The Fathers of the Church*, vol. 4. Washington, DC: Catholic University of America Press, 1952.

Plato. *Plato: Complete Works*. Edited by John M. Cooper. Indianapolis: Hackett Publishing Company, 1997.

———. "Republic." Translated by G. M. A. Grube, revised by C. D. C. Reeve. In *Plato: Complete Works*, edited by John M. Cooper, 971–1223. Indianapolis: Hackett Publishing Company, 1997.

———. "The Seventh Letter." Translated by Glenn R. Morrow, introduced by John M. Cooper. In *Plato: Complete Works*, edited by John M. Cooper, 1634–67. Indianapolis: Hackett Publishing Company, 1997.

———. *The Republic of Plato*. Translated and edited by Allan Bloom. New York: Basic Books, 2016.

Schaff, Philip, and Henry Wace. *A Select Library of Nicene and Post-Nicene Fathers of the Christian Church*. Second Series. The Christian Literature Company, 1890.

Schomakers, Ben. "An Unknown *Elements of Theology*? On Proclus as the Model for the Hierotheosin the Dionysian Corpus." In *Proclus and His Legacy*, edited by Danielle Layne and David D. Butorac. Walter de Gruyter GmbH, 2017.

Shchukin, Timur. "Matter as a Universal: John Philoponus and Maximus the Confessor on the Eternity of the World." *Scrinium* 13, no. 1 (2017): 361–82.

Sheldon-Williams, I. P. "Introduction: Greek Christian Platonism." In *The Cambridge History of Later Greek and Early Medieval Philosophy*, edited by A. H. Armstrong. Cambridge: Cambridge University Press, 1967.

Shenoute the Great. *Selected Discourses of Shenoute the Great: Community, Theology, and Social Conflict in Late Antique Egypt*. Edited by Davi Brakke and Andrew Crislip. Cambridge: Cambridge University Press, 2015.

Strauss, Leo. *Persecution and the Art of Writing*. Glencoe: The Free Press, 1952.

Verene, Donald Phillip. *The Art of Humane Education*. Ithaca: Cornell University Press, 2002.

Walsh, Gerald G., and Daniel J. Honan. "Book Nineteen." In *The City of God, Books XVII–XXII*, in *The Fathers of the Church*, vol. 24. Washington, DC: Catholic University of America Press, 1954.

Weiss, Roslyn. *Philosophers in the "Republic": Plato's Two Paradigms*. Ithaca: Cornell University Press, 2012.

III:
TEACHING BOOKS, TEACHING ARTS: A VIEW OF CLASSICAL CHRISTIAN LITERARY TRAINING

Joshua Patch, University of Dallas

IN THE first book of his *Confessions*, Augustine weighs the value of his early training in the liberal arts. Though an avid student of the Latin literature taught by the *grammatici*, he recalls, he had no taste as a boy for the rudiments of Latin language taught in the primary schools, and an outright aversion to Greek (1.20). The mature Augustine finds this preference for literature over language arts foolish and disturbing. In a passage famous for its denigration of Vergil, he clarifies the distinction:

> At any event, those rudiments are better, because they're more solid. Through them developed in me, and came to fruition, and remains in my possession, the ability to read any piece of writing I come across and to write something if I want to; that's better than the training in which I was forced to memorize the wanderings of some Aeneas or other, while I had no sense of my own wanderings; and to bewail the death of Dido, because she "died for love," when all the time I endured dry-eyed the utter misery of myself dying away from you, God, my life.[1]

Augustine feels the ability to read is a treasure of genuine value, as opposed to familiarity with a work of fiction like the *Aeneid*, whose value is dubious.

For one thing, literacy is a power native to the mind: it develops internally and is permanently lodged in the memory. Knowledge of a fiction,

---

[1] Augustine, *Confessions*, trans. Sarah Ruden (New York: Modern Library, 2017), 1.20.

meanwhile, is a foreign element that must be "forced" into the memory; and, once it is present, it offers, at least in Augustine's experience, no standpoint from which to understand one's own life. Though Augustine surely never read Aristotle's *Poetics*, his salvo against Virgil here could be read as a counterargument to Aristotelian *mimesis* and *catharsis*. In Augustine's experience, poetry does not present life under a universal aspect or effect a purification of emotions, as Aristotle says a good tragedy should. Instead, despite clear analogies between the *Aeneid*'s "wanderings" and "deaths" and Augustine's inner life, Virgil's poetry drowns his ethical sense in overwhelming emotion. In the culminating school-exercise of declaiming a passage from the *Aeneid*, described just after this, a prize goes to the student "whose emoting stood out as more like aggrieved rage, as befit the worthiness of the character he was sketching" (1.27). Poetry (at least of Virgil's sort) encourages the reader to imitate a destructive emotion not even his own.

Perhaps, consequently, knowledge of literature is inferior to simple literacy also because it is more easily forgotten. "I'm far more apt," says Augustine, "to forget the wanderings of Aeneas and everything else of the kind than to forget to read and write" (1.22). Reading and writing, as arts native to the mind, are ever-present and capable of manifold applications—including spiritually vital ones like studying the Scriptures—whereas the plot of an epic poem is mere superficial content, easily lost.

I begin with Augustine's rigoristic view of poetry in order to highlight a distinction in literary education. Mastery of the art of reading in general is one thing, and familiarity with the content of certain texts is another. The distinction need not be agonistic, as Augustine makes it here, since, of course, reading is an art always practiced on some specific text. It is generally understood in our American academy that composition and language arts, along with literature, are the joint province of the English department. But what does it mean to learn literature as distinct from language arts? Whereas the latter study has a clear, applicable purpose, the former is more difficult to explain. One might well wonder with Augustine what claim a fictional narrative has upon our attention and memory, such that it belongs in a required curriculum. English teachers frequently speak of literary works as objects of knowledge in themselves: "I am teaching *Paradise Lost* in the spring." This unqualified formulation is not usually applied to, say, works of art or music. "I am teaching Schubert's 29th piano sonata." Such a statement would seem to imply that the class is learning to perform Schubert's work, not merely surveying it, as students do with literature. Music appreciation is its own subject, where students might learn *about* Schubert's piece, but the art of playing or singing is clearly the proper content of a musical education. Famous compositions provide the matter for the cultivation of an art.

THE CONTENT OF LITERARY EDUCATION

What is the proper content of literary education? The question ought to interest those involved in the Christian classical education movement, which aspires to renovate not only the methods of modern American education, but also the very ends it serves. The "classical" aspect of the movement indicates loyalty to a traditional ideal, one that has been lost with modern developments. Such a stance necessarily implies commitment to rigorous research in order to recover that ideal. The "Christian" aspect seems to imply even more circumspection. As can be seen from Augustine alone, the Christian tradition has not always been perfectly amicable to the aims of liberal education. Considerable struggle produced the great syntheses of the Middle Ages and early modernity. Relatively new as the Christian classical movement is, its research in the historical sources and effort to apply its findings to the modern classroom are still in their early stages. In the meantime, a lack of specific standards, paired with a disposition of anti-modernism, creates the temptation to embrace ideas merely for their savor of antiquity, or because they run contrary to the educational mainstream.

This danger of this temptation is often discussed in reference to academic subjects that fall outside the traditional liberal arts, e.g., biology. But literary study, often thought of as the heart of the classical curriculum, is no less exempt from missteps. My purpose in this essay is to consider some trends in classical literary education, largely from a historical standpoint. In particular, I will consider contemporary classical pedagogy's commitment to the Great Books, both in light of the history of the Great Books movement in the United States, and in light of older theories of literary canons and the *auctores*. I will focus on praxis in primary and secondary education, where the Christian classical movement has mostly made its name, though trends in university education necessarily come into play. It is impossible to go beyond a sampling of these topics now, and much work will need to be done by way of implementation, but it will suffice to raise questions and sketch a way forward for scholars and educators. The heart of the issue, I believe, is the disjunct, articulated in the *Confessions*, between literature as a body of knowledge and the art of reading—or, more precisely, the three arts of the trivium.

THE PRINCIPLES OF GREAT BOOKS PROGRAMS

A handful of texts exert an immense influence on the educational philosophy of classical schools. One of them is Charles Evans's and Robert Littlejohn's *Wisdom and Eloquence: A Christian Paradigm for Classical Learning*. This book helped propel the Christian classical movement out of a period of overdependence on Dorothy Sayers's fascinating but idiosyncratic essay, "The Lost Tools of Learning," which served at first as a kind of creed for the classical renaissance. Instead of treating grammar, as the "Sayers model" does, as a stage in child development, *Wisdom and Eloquence* rightly treats it as an actual subject, namely "the study of the structure of language."[2] In their "modern trivium" paradigm, Evans and Littlejohn use the three traditional trivial arts as loose subcategories to organize a variety of subjects within the larger category of "the language arts."[3] Under the traditional heading of "grammar" fall basic phonics and spelling, English and classical grammars, and literature, among other subjects.

On the purpose of literary education, the authors express two different principles. On the one hand, they promote great literature as containing the "ingredients for the delightful exercise of grammatical, dialectical, and rhetorical skills."[4] This is essentially the classical idea, to which I will return later, that the ancient authors provide sources of the liberal arts. Augustine's declamation assignment illustrates how the *Aeneid* was used for training in rhetoric, another of the arts of the trivium. To learn to speak persuasively, one learns a famous speech from antiquity, which provides a model for imitation. The same goes for grammar and dialectic, insofar as ancient texts offer standard examples of correct language and of argumentation. The texts serve as tools for learning the arts. As Evans and Littlejohn put it, "great readers are made by great books."[5]

---

[2] Charles Evans and Robert Littlejohn, *Wisdom and Eloquence: A Christian Paradigm for Classical Learning* (Wheaton, IL: Crossway, 2006), 89.
[3] Evans and Littlejohn, *Wisdom and Eloquence*, 87.
[4] Evans and Littlejohn, *Wisdom and Eloquence*, 97.
[5] Evans and Littlejohn, *Wisdom and Eloquence*, 98.

But the choice of specific "Great Books" for the school curriculum relies on a second principle as well. Note how the authors frame this question: "What canon of literature do we want our students to master by the time they graduate?"[6] The object of knowledge in this question is the canon of books itself. The authors recommend the Bible, Homer, Virgil, Dante, and Milton, by whom, they say, "the literary foundation of our civilization is formed." Homer in particular should be assigned by "ninth grade at the latest," the literature courses at lower levels being properly graded so that students are prepared. Familiarity with the entirety of the Bible and the epics, as well as an awareness of "the importance of those stories to our cultural identity," are described as steps to "becoming a well-educated person."[7] Without casting any judgment on the truth of this claim, one can discern that it differs from the claim that ancient books furnish ideal material for practicing the arts of the trivium. At least part of the reason why certain books are recommended for the curriculum is that they are cultural monuments, works of genius that a cultured person simply must know.

The latter idea can be found in other classical education texts. Kevin Clark and Ravi Jain, in their influential book, *The Liberal Arts Tradition,* devote no chapter to literature as a subject, but mention it in connection with other topics. Drawing on Quintilian, they explain how a canon of texts serves the art of grammar by establishing "the meanings of words and their etymologies."[8] That is, these texts ground a study of the conventions of language, necessary to read, write, and speak well. They serve as sources for the arts. But Clark and Jain elsewhere speak of classical works as objects of knowledge in themselves. In their argument for the study of Latin and Greek (summarizing an excerpt from W. H. D Rouse), they write, "[T]he foundational ideas of Western civilization are originally Greek and Roman; these ideas arise from texts written in Greek and Latin; translations of these texts offer access to the original meaning, but with diminished access to original associations, beauty, and context; therefore to engage fully with this tradition—which is our tradition—one must return to Greek and Latin."[9] It is, again, unnecessary to assess the soundness of this argument. What matters

---

[6] Evans and Littlejohn, *Wisdom and Eloquence*, 98.

[7] Evans and Littlejohn, *Wisdom and Eloquence*, 98.

[8] Kevin Clark and Ravi Jain, *The Liberal Arts Tradition: A Philosophy of Christian Classical Education*, 2nd ed. (Camp Hill, PA: Classical Academic Press, 2019), 40.

[9] Clark and Jain, *Liberal Arts Tradition*, 49.

is that it attributes innate value to reading certain texts because of their cultural influence, grand ideas, and irreducible beauty. Simple familiarity with them is an essential pedagogical goal.

Such claims for classic literature are likely familiar to most of us. Very few in our culture share Augustine's deep ambivalence toward poetry and fiction as such. The passages cited above feature standard defenses of the so-called Great Books, which are now ubiquitous in American traditionalist education. A blog post from Memoria Press, a publisher in the Christian classical sphere, defines a Great Book by three criteria: "The first is universality. A great book speaks to people across many ages—affecting, inspiring, and changing readers far removed from the time and place in which it was written. Second, it has a Central One Idea and themes that address matters of enduring importance. And third, it features noble language. A great book is written in beautiful language that enriches the mind and elevates the soul."[10] Note the emphasis on affect in this definition, as well as on influential ideas. Aesthetic beauty, along with relevance for what E. D. Hirsch has called "cultural literacy" (see his book by that title), are hallmarks of the Great Books. They are texts that, by virtue of wide influence and aesthetic quality, everyone should know.

But the category of Great Books is not simply timeless, as traditionalist educators sometimes assert. It has a definite history in American education. Littlejohn and Evans cite Mortimer Adler as one of their authorities on literary studies.[11] Adler, a philosopher at the University of Chicago in the first half of the twentieth century, may be the defining figure in the development of the modern concept of Great Books. Together with Robert Maynard Hutchins, then president of the University of Chicago, Adler spearheaded a program of educational reform that influenced universities as well as high schools throughout the country. Hutchins and Adler also edited the fifty-four-volume *Great Books of the Western World* series in 1952, accompanied at the time by an adult education initiative focused on the formation of Great Books discussion-groups, at first around Chicago and ultimately nationwide.[12] Though Hutchins's and Adler's plan to reform the university

---

[10] David M. Wright, "Why Read Literature?" *Memoria Press*, accessed March 15, 2022, https://www.memoriapress.com/articles/why-read-literature/.

[11] Evans and Littlejohn, *Wisdom and Eloquence*, 98.

[12] William McNeill, *Hutchins' University: A Memoir of the University of Chicago, 1929–1950* (Chicago: University of Chicago Press, 2007), 122.

curriculum was never fully realized, the University of Chicago's liberal arts approach became famous and other hubs of Great Books learning, such as the arts program at St. John's College, were established under its influence.

Adler brought the idea for Great Books pedagogy to Chicago from Columbia, where he took (and later taught) an honors course on classic texts from John Erskine.[13] Erskine's course was denigrated by many of Columbia's faculty for including non-anglophone texts, both ancient and modern, in English translation alongside English ones. Works that had hitherto been the separate specialties of philosophers, historians, and classical philologists Erskine assigned indiscriminately, with the expectation that students prepare to discuss "whatever ideas the reading provoked."[14] Mortimer Adler was transformed by this experience, especially by reading the works of Aristotle and Thomas Aquinas, whose metaphysics he embraced almost wholesale, despite remaining a non-observant Jew.[15] Study of old authors seems to have struck a chord with Adler, who even as an undergraduate had been displeased with contemporary trends in philosophy, such as the fashionable pragmatism of John Dewey.[16] He emerged from his graduate studies at Columbia convinced of the indispensable wisdom of the ancients and "disdainful of courses that relied on textbooks."[17] His vision was of an educational model where students came into unmediated contact with the foundational ideas expressed in classic works, without the hindrance of specialized interpretation.

William McNeill, in his work *Hutchins' University: A Memoir of the University of Chicago 1929–1950,* gives an account of Adler's alliance with John Maynard Hutchins to reform the Chicago curriculum. Whereas Adler was compelled by the actual arguments of the classic authors he read, McNeill views Hutchins as having found in the Great Books idea itself a kind of elusive vision of absolute truth. According to McNeill, "The proposition that the core of a liberal education ought to rest in firsthand acquaintance with books that had shaped Western literary culture seemed completely convincing to Hutchins even before he had made his own acquaintance with

---

[13] McNeill, *Hutchins' University*, 35.

[14] McNeill, *Hutchins' University*, 35.

[15] McNeill, *Hutchins' University*, 34, 37.

[16] McNeill, *Hutchins' University*, 35.

[17] McNeill, *Hutchins' University*, 35.

a suitable selection of such books."[18] Hutchins's implicit belief in the Great Books idea was perhaps quasi-religious. McNeill considers it crucial to understand Hutchins in light of his devout Presbyterian upbringing: "Having abandoned the Bible as a reliable guide to truth and righteousness in his youth…he sought for the rest of his life to find other texts that could satisfy his yearning for metaphysical and moral truth."[19] It must be significant that—at least in the view of McNeill (a faculty member under Hutchins' regime)—one of the most important early proponents of the Great Books considered them a potential alternative to the biblical canon.

The first volume of *The Great Books of the Western World*, written by Hutchins and entitled *The Great Conversation*, argues for Great Books education in a modern setting. Hutchins views the Great Books as a safeguard of democracy, able to inoculate readers against propaganda by introducing them to a variety of basic and well-articulated ideas and thence training their powers of "independent judgment."[20] The strength of Great Books is that, taken together, they present all sides of the important issues. They are therefore well-suited to educating citizens of a democracy, who must learn to judge between a variety of options in order to self-govern. To give an example of Hutchins's argumentation, he responds to the objection that modern education must center on experimental science, not literature. His response is that this very objection stems from the ideas of David Hume, himself a part of the Great Conversation.[21] Should we accept Hume's ideas without giving his opponents a hearing? "The Great Conversation, in short," says Hutchins, "contains both sides of the issue that in modern times is thought to have a most critical bearing on the significance of the Great Conversation itself."[22] Hutchins's and Adler's presentation of the Great Books as a conversation implies a final reservation of judgment, certainly on the part of the teacher, regarding the issues discussed within the canon. An individual reader might, as Adler did with Thomas Aquinas, assent finally to the point of view of one great author. But the educational program, if it is to avoid eventual collapse, seems to require a detached, "overhead" view of the

---

[18] McNeill, *Hutchins' University*, 36.

[19] McNeill, *Hutchins' University*, 36.

[20] Robert Hutchins, *The Great Conversation: The Substance of a Liberal Education*, The Great Books of the Western World (Chicago: Encyclopedia Britannica, 1952), xiii.

[21] Hutchins, *Great Conversation*, 34.

[22] Hutchins, *Great Conversation*, 35.

whole canon—a commitment to the notion that truth is lodged irreducibly in a series of disparate writings. Training in such detachment seems very close to what Hutchins means by "the liberal arts."

Though much more could be said in regards to Hutchins and Adler, it is worth mentioning briefly another influential brand of Great Books thinking, which arises from a different quarter. Harold Bloom's *The Western Canon* purports to collect the greatest Western texts, judged not by their participation in a conversation of great ideas, but by their aesthetic value.[23] Bloom, for all his railing against modern schools of criticism, is not a traditionalist. He contends that "[t]he West's greatest writers are subversive of all values."[24] In fact, "If we read the Western Canon in order to form our social, political, or personal moral values…we will become monsters of selfishness and exploitation."[25] Education in the Great Books for Bloom is not a preparation for responsible citizenship, but an education in inwardness, an encounter with sublime genius that produces an individualized wisdom for coping with life.[26] Bloom elsewhere speaks of the Western canon as the key to navigating modern "literary culture," by which he means a sort of decadent society that has lost trust in its religious and civic institutions, so that it falls back on monuments of aesthetic beauty as a prop.[27] Bloom and Hutchins both, though in different ways, conceive of the canon of Great Books as a fundamentally secular tool for confronting a secularized world. Both view it as a canon in a quasi-religious sense, to be deployed following the failure of religion. Their precursor in this is Matthew Arnold, the nineteenth-century author and educator who championed the study of literature—of "the best that has been thought and said"—as a bulwark of meaning after the recent cataclysm of Darwinian biology, which destabilized the factual claims of Christianity.[28]

---

[23] Harold Bloom, *The Western Canon: The Books and School of the Ages* (New York: Riverhead Books, 1995), 2.

[24] Bloom, *Western Canon*, 29.

[25] Bloom, *Western Canon*, 29.

[26] Bloom, *Western Canon*, 29–30.

[27] Antonio Weiss, "Harold Bloom: The Art of Criticism No. 1," *Paris Review* 118 (Spring 1991): accessed March 16, 2022, https://www.theparisreview.org/interviews/2225/the-art-of-criticism-no-1-harold-bloom.

[28] Matthew Arnold, "Literature and Science," in *Matthew Arnold: Prose and Poetry*, ed. Archibald Bouton (New York: C. Scribner's Sons, 1927), 73–75.

GREAT BOOKS AND LIBERAL ARTS IN CHRISTIANITY

Naturally, the question arises how this conception of Great Books fits into a Christian educational scheme. Patrick Deneen raised it, once in a 2010 post on *Minding the Campus*,[29] and again in 2013 in *First Things*, in an opinion piece brusquely titled "Against Great Books."[30] In the latter, Deneen points out what Hutchins already noted in *The Great Conversation*, that there are some voices in the Western tradition—specifically modern ones—that are opposed to any deference to the Western tradition. Instead of taking Hutchins's route and maintaining these dissident voices within the canon by a principle of detachment, Deneen recommends siding with what he calls the "humble books," those that affirm the wisdom of antiquity and Christendom, against the innovations of modern *auctores* like Bacon and Descartes. In his *Minding the Campus* piece, Deneen explicitly suggests that the reading curriculum be normed by "the standards that the Catholic tradition would provide." Whether one agrees with Deneen or not, it seems evident that sincere commitment to Christian claims would at least prompt hesitancy to embrace the Great Books model, especially since Christian classical education is a conscious departure from modern, secularized educational philosophies. The Great Books approach, while admittedly a fellow-traveler in diverging from the progressive educational mainstream, has often assumed a philosophical framework closer to that of its progressive opponents than to orthodox Christianity. At the very least, Christian educators would seem to be under less constraint to invest all hope for the preservation of meaning and wisdom in an "alternative canon."

But what is the relationship of the Great Books movement to the classical liberal arts? According to McNeill, Hutchins, *et al.* worked to revise high school and early college curricula to offer "coherent training in the liberal arts of grammar, logic, and rhetoric" through the Great Books.[31] There

---

[29] Patrick Deneen, "Why the Great Books Aren't the Answer," *Minding the Campus*, accessed May 20, 2021, https://www.mindingthecampus.org/2010/03/31/why_the_great_books_arent_the/.

[30] Patrick Deneen, "Against Great Books: Questioning Our Approach to the Western Canon," *First Things*, January 2013, https://www.firstthings.com/article/2013/01/against-great-books.

[31] McNeill, *Hutchins' University*, 66.

is reason to think that Adler, along with his Thomist associates like Sister Miriam Joseph, did consider the canon as a workshop for the arts. But the presentation of "liberal arts" learning in *The Great Conversation* emphasizes far more the goal of freethinking through engagement with great ideas, rather than the arts as traditionally understood. Some consideration of the traditional presentation of the trivium, and its relationship with literature, will provide a grounds for comparison, and perhaps a paradigm for future reforms.

The Middle Ages and Literary Canons

The notion of a literary canon, peopled by *auctores* or venerable authors, is a product of the Middle Ages, and the lists of *auctores* studied by medieval students are somewhat surprising. Ernst Robert Curtius, in his *European Literature and the Latin Middle Ages*, conducts a study of medieval curricula, reproducing lists of *auctores* assigned by grammarians. Here is an early list: "When Walter of Speyer was in school about 975, he read Virgil, 'Homer' (that is, the so-called *Ilias latina*, a crude condensation of the *Iliad* in 1070 hexameters, of the first century AD), Martianus Capella, Horace, Persius, Juvenal, Boethius, Statius, Terence, Lucan."[32] Curtius explains that this is not an anomalous, but a normative list. The authors are not what we normally think of as "great," not, for the most part, conveyors of foundational ideas. As Curtius puts it, "The Middle Ages make no distinction between 'gold' and 'silver' Latinity. The concept 'classical' is unknown to it. All authors are, as it were, authorities."[33] He further notes that, for the medieval grammarians, the importance of authors we now consider classics—Cicero, Horace, Virgil—was "conceived to lie almost exclusively in their ethical influence."[34] For many *auctores*, even apart from the crude abridgment of Homer, their now-revered works were not the works studied. Cicero was known as the author of *On Friendship* and *On Old Age*; Horace primarily of the *Ars Poetica*; Ovid of the *Fasti* and the *Ex Ponto* and, eventually, the *Remedia Amoris*, not of the salacious *Metamorphoses*. A great many more *auctores* were added as time went

---

[32] Ernst Robert Curtius, *European Literature and the Latin Middle Ages*, trans. Willard Trask (Princeton, NJ: Bollingen Foundation, 1953), 49.

[33] Curtius, *European Literature*, 49.

[34] Curitus, *European Literature*, 49.

on, all considered timeless and of roughly the same value.³⁵ The authors include allegorists, writers of didactic fables, love elegists, grammarians, and chroniclers. These were read primarily as models to aid students toward an understanding of parts and figures of speech, and ultimately toward mastery of Latin reading, writing, and speaking.³⁶

John of Salisbury, a twelfth-century scholar and grammarian, describes in his *Metalogicon* the use of *auctores* in the classroom. The *auctores*, he explains, "when they would take the crude materials of history, arguments, narratives, and other topics, would so copiously embellish them by the various branches of knowledge, in such charming style, with such pleasing ornament, that their finished masterpiece would seem to image all the arts."³⁷ The role of the teacher, then, is, in the presence of his students, to "'shake out' the authors, and, without exciting ridicule, despoil them of their feathers, which (crow fashion) they have borrowed from the several branches of learning in order to bedeck their works and make them more colorful."³⁸ The teacher must take apart the book, which is a work of collage composed of pieces of grammar, logic, and rhetoric, and give the pieces to his students as tools for composition.³⁹ Reading and writing go together, since the detection of linguistic techniques in the *auctores* is complementary to the selection of those same techniques for use in one's own discourse. In medieval education, then, the main role of the *auctores* was to supply a model and a source for the arts of language, faculties inherent in the mind of the learner and active both in reception and transmission of language. The *auctores* were certainly considered great, but they were not to be sifted for kernels of aesthetic or intellectual greatness; they were to be reaped from as abundant harvests of grammatical and rhetorical figures, poetic ornaments, and argumentative structures.

---

³⁵ Curtius, *European Literature*, 51.

³⁶ Curtius, *European Literature*, 43.

³⁷ John of Salisbury, *The Metalogicon of John of Salisbury: A Twelfth-Century Defense of the Verbal and Logical Arts of the Trivium*, trans. Daniel McGarry (Mansfield Centre, CT: Martino Publishing, 2015), 66–67.

³⁸ John of Salibury, *Metalogicon*, 66.

³⁹ John of Salisbury, *Metalogicon*, 69.

Thomas More and Christian Humanism

We turn now to the early modern era, which can be thought of as a period of resurgence in the arts of grammar and rhetoric as reaped from *auctores*, though with two new elements. First, due to a prejudice against the previous era, it selected its *auctores* more carefully, mostly from antiquity and not the Middle Ages. Second, it tended to consider the liberal arts in light of their relevance to the good of a commonwealth. Thomas More's writings exemplify the Northern Humanist zeal to recover the full array of liberal arts in the service of public duty. In his *Dialogue of Sir Thomas More, Knight*, he praises the much-maligned study of poetry: "And albeit poets be with many men taken for but painted words, yet do they much help the judgment, and make a man, among other things, well furnished of one special thing, without which all learning is half lame…a good mother wit."[40] "Wit," a word for governing intelligence or power of invention, is exercised by the reading of poetry. We see in More's letters to his children his concern for their ability to compose both epistles and poetry with "pure Latinity," communicating clearly while making use of tropes and embellishments.[41] For More, the arts were to be oriented toward piety, virtue, and, perhaps above all, civic duty.[42] The study of Great Books without an eye to the proper use of the arts can be illustrated in the *Life of Pico*, which More translated. The young Pico della Mirandola, bored with studying canon law, "full of pride, and desirous of man's glory and praise," makes an in-depth study of all ancient philosophy and hermeticism with the goal of synthesizing it.[43] Eventually he repents, forsakes these fruitless studies, and devotes himself to Scripture and projects useful to the Church.[44] Thomas More's version of Christian humanism is devoted, not primarily to certain texts, but to the recovery of liberal arts and their employment for the good of the commonwealth.

---

[40] Thomas More, "A Dialogue of Sir Thomas More, Knight," in *The Essential Works of Thomas More*, ed. Gerard Wegemer and Stephen Smith (New Haven, CT: Yale University Press), 581.

[41] More, *Essential Works*, 317.

[42] More, *Essential Works*, 289.

[43] More, *Essential Works*, 65.

[44] More, *Essential Works*, 69.

Philip Melanchthon on the Liberal Arts

A seminal figure for early modern reforms in education is Philip Melanchthon. Called the *Praeceptor Germaniae*, the "Teacher of Germany," he revised the arts curriculum at the University of Wittenberg and, through his pamphlets and textbooks, set the agenda for schools throughout Germany (*Orations* loc. 41).[45] Melanchthon's Protestant vision for literary training in the arts, as expressed in his public orations, will be the final stop in our historical overview.

Melanchthon views schools as integral to man's communal nature—his status as a "political animal" in Aristotle's terms. He says that all human arts, whether the liberal arts or those of rulers, farmers, craftsmen, or soldiers, unite in the service of the commonwealth. But what, he asks, is that ultimate purpose? The commonwealth, says Melanchthon, is itself like a school. "Men are formed," he says,

> for fellowship to such a degree that the knowledge of God shines in this gathering, and God is praised and invoked, and one is imbued by the other with that doctrine that opens access to eternal joy and to the presence of God. Consider this fellowship of men similar to a school, in which men have to occupy their minds with God and with virtue more than with anything else. The homes of that assembly are the states. And we hold that the government—the leaders, the army, the farmers, the craftsmen, in short all the ranks of life—serves the highest work, that is the propagation of doctrine.[46]

God puts man in fellowship in the first place so that the doctrine of eternal life can be taught by one to another. Therefore all estates of society are ordered toward the proper teaching of the Scriptures. Indeed, it befits the textual nature of God's revelation that schools be attached to churches, and that those schools teach the arts necessary for accurate reading and

---

[45] Philip Melanchthon, *Orations on Philosophy and Education*, Cambridge Texts on the History of Philosophy, trans. Christine Salazar, ed. Suchiko Kusukawa (Cambridge: Cambridge University Press, 1999)

[46] Melanchthon, "On the Role of Schools," in *Orations on Philosophy and Education*.

interpretation.[47] The classical arts of the trivium are more than ornaments of learning or tools for problem-solving—they are nothing short of means of grace, since God in his providence has shown his will in Scripture. Hence the liberal arts, as well as moral philosophy, which teaches duties proper to life in a commonwealth, should be fostered by the Church along with the study of Scripture.[48]

Within this scheme Melanchthon discusses the study of literature, of which he says, "apart from the Gospel of Christ this world holds nothing more splendid nor more divine."[49] He is especially effusive in his praise for Homer. Homer represents for Melanchthon the Renaissance ideal of the poet who teaches virtue by way of delight. He writes, "If it is true that, as they say, studies are transformed into manners…by contact with the most humane and delightful poet, minds also grow gentle and become more humane and peaceful."[50] Literary education may aid the young in the acquisition of virtue, especially if, like Homer, the poet expresses ethical principles in beautiful language. But Melanchthon also notes that this education through beauty is available only to "noble and inquiring minds."[51] Any teacher of literature knows that the most beautiful passage of poetry is lost on the student who does not know how to read it. Melanchthon enumerates some of the virtues "noble minds" can find in Homer:

> There are countless passages intended and devised as if by divine providence…and throughout they are all created with incredible elegance and pleasantness, diversified by various moods, chiefly the dispositions, however, and by many splendid and pleasant accidents—indeed arranged with such order and economy of things that I would consider anyone who is not charmed by reading Homer lacking in any sense of humanity: an animal, not a man.[52]

---

[47] Melanchthon, "Role of Schools."
[48] Melanchthon, "Role of Schools."
[49] Melanchthon, "Preface to Homer," in *Orations on Philosophy and Education.*
[50] Melanchthon, "Preface to Homer."
[51] Melanchthon, "Preface to Homer."
[52] Melanchthon, "Preface to Homer."

Moods, dispositions, accidents, and economy are among Homer's foremost beauties. Melanchthon is speaking of poetic conventions that are part of the art of grammar. It is the student trained in the trivium who is suited to revel in Homer and to learn the virtues from him. Though it is hard for us to accept, Melanchthon believed that Homer's poems were written by following rules that can also be taught to children. Certainly they are inimitable—but this is because he lacked Homer's genius, rather than because we lack his tools. The arts of language connect us with the great authors. They teach us the arts by example and we are able to use the arts to interpret, enjoy, and in small ways imitate them by using language ourselves.

CONCLUSION

From this somewhat uneven study, we can draw some conclusions applicable to Christian classical schools. The main conclusion is that the curricular goal of teaching a large canon of literary works prior to the university level is dubious. It relies on a conception of Great Books that a) originated in the context of university education, b) is traditionally secular in its approach, and c) differs from the traditional notion of the role of literature in teaching the liberal arts. It is not uncommon for schools to pack their reading lists with Great Books on the assumption that these particular texts render an education "classical" merely by students' being introduced to them. It is deemed necessary always to teach ancient books in their entirety, never through excerpts, since the intent is to acquaint students thoroughly with the foundational ideas of the authors. This state of affairs can create immense difficulties for students, especially in reading pre- and early modern works, if they have not developed the necessary reading ability. This may seem obvious, but consider for instance *Paradise Lost*. What skills are needed to read it well? Not only what we think of as a broad vocabulary, but a sense of etymology, a mastery of scansion, a knowledge of tropes, schemata, rules of English syntax and punctuation, Roman history and mythology, Bible narratives including apocrypha, Ptolemaic cosmology, basic Greek metaphysics, etc. In classical terms, these are all elements of grammar. We have not even mentioned dialectical and rhetorical aspects of Milton's poem. Many students are introduced to difficult works without having received the requisite training to read them, and they leave the experience with a lasting distaste for these works rather than any appreciation of their beauty or importance.

The tradition of the liberal arts gives educators permission to narrow their reading lists and focus more on training the skills of good reading. After all, in the medieval grammar schools the literary curriculum was a training ground for arts, whose purpose was not to prepare students for any specific text, but to read and write in general. The *auctores* are themselves teachers of an ability we share with them—the ability to think rationally and to express our thought with symbols. We should note in that the arts of the trivium are not reducible to the modern concept of "critical thinking," a wide-ranging capacity for discrimination and judgment of ideas. If anything, critical thinking is a small part of the trivium, which must be learned in part from convention, since language is never purely rational. The trivium is better thought of as a course in deep familiarity with all that pertains to the mind, both its inner workings and its outward expression. To learn it requires patience and submission to tradition, but its fruit is a sensitive and receptive intellect, able to engage truly in a "great conversation" across time.

C. S. Lewis, in his *Experiment in Criticism*, poses the idea that the measure of a good book is how much it can delight a good reader. This hypothesis captures the spirit of a literary education grounded in the liberal arts. What matters first is the cultivation of good readers, who, if they are well taught, will be attracted to good books instead of needing to be led to them by force. Curriculum designers would conform better to the liberal arts tradition if they assigned shorter and fewer readings at the pre-university stage, but ensured that those readings were exemplary of the principles of the trivium—especially grammar—and also fit the learning level of the students in question. Many Very Good Books can serve as sources for the arts without overwhelming students, and many of the Great Books can be excerpted to good effect years before they can be reasonably assigned in their entirety. Indeed, to strike a final Augustinian note, classical educators might ask themselves if in the refusal to follow this course and cull some of the "greatness" from their curricula there is not a small hint of what Augustine called the fountainhead of all other sins: pride.

BIBLIOGRAPHY

Arnold, Matthew. "Literature and Science." In *Matthew Arnold: Prose and Poetry*, edited by Archibald Bouton, 70–76. New York: C. Scribner's Sons, 1927.

Augustine. *Confessions*. Translated by Sarah Ruden. New York: Modern Library, 2017.

Bloom, Harold. *The Western Canon: The Books and School of the Ages*. New York: Riverhead Books, 1995.

Clark, Kevin, and Ravi Jain. *The Liberal Arts Tradition: A Philosophy of Christian Classical Education*. 2nd ed. Camp Hill, PA: Classical Academic Press, 2019.

Curtius, Ernst Robert. *European Literature and the Latin Middle Ages*. Translated by Willard Trask. Princeton, NJ: Bollingen Foundation, 1953.

Deneen, Patrick. "Against Great Books: Questioning Our Approach to the Western Canon." *First Things*. January 2013. https://www.firstthings.com/article/2013/01/against-great-books.

———. "Why the Great Books Aren't the Answer." *Minding the Campus*. Accessed May 20, 2021. https://www.mindingthecampus.org/2010/03/31/why_the_great_books_arent_the/.

Evans, Charles, and Robert Littlejohn. *Wisdom and Eloquence: A Christian Paradigm for Classical Learning*. Wheaton, IL: Crossway, 2006.

Hirsch, E. D. *Cultural Literacy: What Every American Needs to Know*. 1st ed. New York: Vintage Books, 1988.

Hutchins, Robert. *The Great Conversation: The Substance of a Liberal Education*. The Great Books of the Western World. Chicago: Encyclopedia Britannica, 1952.

John of Salisbury. *The Metalogicon of John of Salisbury: A Twelfth-Century Defense of the Verbal and Logical Arts of the Trivium*. Translated by Daniel McGarry. Mansfield Centre, CT: Martino Publishing, 2015.

McNeill, William. *Hutchins' University: A Memoir of the University of Chicago, 1929–1950*. Chicago: University of Chicago Press, 2007.

Melanchthon, Philip. *Orations on Philosophy and Education*. Cambridge Texts on the History of Philosophy. Translated by Christine Salazar, edited by Suchiko Kusukawa. Cambridge: Cambridge University Press, 1999.

More, Thomas. "A Dialogue of Sir Thomas More, Knight." In *The Essential Works of Thomas More*, edited by Gerard Wegemer and Stephen Smith, 525–734. New Haven, CT: Yale University Press, 2020.

———. "The Life of John Pico." In *The Essential Works of Thomas More*, edited by Gerard Wegemer and Stephen Smith, 61–94. New Haven, CT: Yale University Press, 2020.

Weiss, Antonio. "Harold Bloom: The Art of Criticism, No. 1." *Paris Review* 118 (Spring 1991). Accessed March 16, 2022. https://www.theparisreview.org/interviews/2225/the-art-of-criticism-no-1-harold-bloom.

Wright, David. "Why Read Literature?" *Memoria Press*. Accessed May 22, 2021. https://www.memoriapress.com/articles/why-read-literature/.

IV:
IN SEARCH OF VIRTUE:
WHY THE QUADRIVIUM MATTERS

Gregory Wilbur, New College Franklin

IN THE winter of 1793, Samuel Miller came before the Presbytery of New York. Eventually, Miller would help found Princeton Theological Seminary and teach there for more than thirty-five years. On this particular occasion, however, the New York Presbytery examined Miller for the purpose of licensure in order for him to accept a call from a church within their jurisdiction. Miller's exam took place over three separate meetings. As reported in presbytery minutes, in order to be approved to preach, Miller, and all other candidates, were tested in the area of personal spiritual life and sense of call to the ministry. He was further examined in "Latin and Greek, in geography, logic, rhetoric, natural philosophy, astronomy, moral philosophy, divinity, ecclesiastical history, and church government."[1] The foundation of gospel ministry assumed thorough knowledge of the liberal arts. This is not an isolated example of such thinking. Historically speaking, this is consistent with the understanding that a study of the trivium and the quadrivium was preparation for the study of theology and philosophy. For, how one should think about such a breadth of ideas bore significantly on how thinkers once attributed meaning and purpose to the created cosmos. To this end, in what follows, this essay argues that the quadrivium formed an essential part of education for centuries as a means for understanding number, for growing in virtue, and for encountering the attributes of God in the created world. Before venturing a more refined definition of the

---

[1] C. Van Rensselaer, *The Presbyterian Magazine 2* (Philadelphia, PA: Wm. H. Mitchell, 1853), 182.

quadrivium, let us consider several additional, historical examples akin to the educational foundation of Miller.

Henry Chadwick, for example, summarizes Boethius's thoughts on number and music and the importance of the quadrivium not only as a means of study but also because of its moral component:

> Arithmetic directs the mind towards immutable truths unaffected by the contingencies of time and space. But music advances even further towards that 'summit of perfection' for which the *quadrivium* is a prerequisite. The theory of music is a penetration of the very heart of Providence's ordering of things. It is not a matter of cheerful entertainment or superficial consolation for sad moods, but a central clue to the interpretation of the hidden harmony of God and nature in which the only discordant element is evil in the heart of man.[2]

Among medieval educational discourses, perhaps the most well-known is the *Scholia enchiriadis*. In this educational treatise from the ninth century, students are encouraged and directed as to the goal of the quadrivium:

> [T]hese quantities, further, are variously considered in Arithmetic, in Music, in Geometry, and in Astronomy. For these four disciplines are not arts of human invention, but considerable investigations of divine works; and by most marvelous reasons they lead ingenious minds to understand the creatures of the world; so that those who through these things know God and His eternal divinity are inexcusable if they do not glorify Him and give thanks.[3]

The purpose of these disciplines is understanding about creation as well as the Creator, which leads to gratitude.

As these were salient features of education among the medieval tradition, so too were they features among the Reformers. For example, when

---

[2] Henry Chadwick, *Boethius: The Consolations of Music, Logic, Theology, and Philosophy* (Oxford: Clarendon Press, 1981), 101.

[3] W. Oliver Strunk, *Source Readings in Music History*, revised ed., ed. Leo Treitler (London: W. W. Norton & Company, 1998), 134–35.

Martin Luther says that "music is next to theology," he is likely recalling his own education in the seven liberal arts at the University of Erfurt and acknowledging that music, as a final study in the quadrivium, leads to theology—it was literally "next to" the continued study of theology.[4] John Calvin too spends a whole section in the *Institutes* on the knowledge of God in creation. In the following section, which is deservedly quoted at length, Calvin speaks directly as to the advantage of a liberal arts education:

> First, then, whichever way we turn our eyes, there is no part of the world, however small, in which at least some spark of God's glory does not shine. In particular, we cannot gaze upon this beautiful masterpiece of the world, and all its length and breath, without being completely dazzled, as it were, by an endless flood of light. Accordingly, in Hebrews, the Apostle aptly calls the world the mirror of things invisible, because the structure of the world serves as a mirror in which we behold God, who otherwise cannot be seen (Heb. 11:3). This too is why the prophet ascribes to the heavenly bodies a language familiar to every nation, since their witness to divinity is so clear that it is not unknown even to the most simple and barbarous men (Psa.19:1–4). Paul puts it still more plainly when he writes that "what needed to be known about God was made manifest, since the invisible things concerning him—his eternal power and deity—are clear to us when we consider the world which he has made" (Romans 1:19–20).
>
> There are countless proofs, both in heaven and earth, which testify to his marvellous wisdom. Nor are these only proofs which are hard to comprehend, and intelligible only through the study of astronomy, medicine and natural science. They are visible even to the dullest and most ignorant, so that the eye, once opened, is constrained to witness these things. It is of course true that people who are schooled in the liberal arts or who have had some taste of them are especially helped to plumb the secrets of divine wisdom. Yet ignorance of these things does not stop anyone

---

[4] The placement of music and astronomy differ among thinkers. Luther notably believed that music should be understood as the final study in the quadrivium.

> observing much skillful design in God's works, and being led as a result to marvel at the skill of the worker.[5]

Calvin is here affirming that creation speaks of God's eternal power and deity to everyone, but those who have studied the liberal arts have an advantage in interpreting and grasping the testimony of creation. This is how it can be said that the language of creation is numbers. As Michael S. Schneider writes, "Numbers are a map of the beautiful order of the universe, the plan by which the divine Architect transformed undifferentiated Chaos into orderly Cosmos."[6] The study of numbers in the context and disciplines of the quadrivium directly pertains to the knowledge of God. To gain a theological and pedagogical understanding of the quadrivium, it is necessary to further define what it is and, what is more, what those who employ it are attempting to accomplish.

DEFINING THE QUADRIVIUM AND ITS PURPOSE

The word quadrivium literally means the "four paths" or the "four ways." Historically, the study of the quadrivium was a means to explore the nature of the cosmos. It was understood that number—the meaning of number, numbers in relation, numerical relations in time, temporal numerical relations in space—was the mode of discovery. Thus, the disciplines of arithmetic, geometry, *harmonia* (music), and cosmology (astronomy) developed as a means to discover and explore the work of God in creation. This is how Paul can write in Romans 1:20 that God's "invisible attributes, namely, his eternal power and divine nature, have been clearly perceived, ever since the creation of the world, in the things that have been made" (ESV), and so, by virtue of this natural revelation, mankind is without excuse. As Christopher Ruckdeschel aptly explains,

> God created the universe "in order that His goodness might be communicated to His creatures," that He might show forth His glory according to the order of wisdom, which is the best mode of communicating. He addressed this

---

[5] John Calvin, *Institutes of the Christian Religion: Calvin's Own Essential Edition*, trans. Robert White (London: Banner of Truth Trust, 2014), V.1–2.

[6] As quoted by Stratford Caldecott in *Beauty for Truth's Sake: On the Re-enchantment of Education* (Grand Rapids: Brazos Press, 2009), 54.

extraordinary work to mankind, "that they might praise the name which he hath sanctified, and glory in His wondrous acts." Since His goodness could not be sufficiently represented by a single creature, "He produced many and diverse creatures, that what was wanting to one in the representation of the divine goodness might be supplied by another." This goodness that is "simple and uniform" in God must be "manifold and divided" in creation because while "God alone has the whole plenitude of His Being in a certain unity…every other thing has its proper fullness of being in a certain multiplicity…." This distinction is twofold: "one is a formal distinction as regards things differing specifically,…" concerning the *Trivium*, and "the other is a material distinction as regards things differing numerically only," which is the foundation of the *Quadrivium*.[7]

God has revealed himself in the things that He has made, and the universe is upheld by Christ, the Word of his power (Hebrews 1:3). The echo of this is likewise contained in C. S. Lewis's *English Literature in the Sixteenth Century*, which asserts that the medieval understanding of the world, as inherited from the ancients and translated through the lens of Christianity, assumed a divine hand at work in an ordered world that is imbued with meaning. Lewis describes it as "tingling with anthropomorphic life, dancing, ceremonial, a festival not a machine."[8]

From a post-Enlightenment perspective, the universe is a system or machine that runs by laws rather than a reflection of the goodness of the Lord. In *Redeeming Mathematics*, Vern Poythress writes,

> Christians have sometimes adopted an unbiblical concept of God that moves him one step out of the way of our ordinary affairs. We ourselves may think of 'scientific law' or 'natural law' or mathematics as a kind of cosmic mechanism or impersonal clockwork that runs the world most of the time, while God is on vacation. God comes and acts only rarely through miracle. But this is not biblical. "You cause the

---

[7] Christopher Ruckdeschel, *On the Nature of the Classical Liberal Arts* (BookBay, 2019), 15–16. Ruckdeschel is quoting freely from Thomas Aquinas.

[8] C. S. Lewis, *English Literature in the Sixteenth Century, Excluding Drama* (Oxford: Clarendon Press, 1954), 4.

grass to grow for the livestock" (Psalm 104:14). "He gives snow like wool" (Psalm 147:16). Let us not forget it.[9]

If thinking about the cosmos starts from a mechanistic viewpoint, this influences the very nature, purpose, and process of discovery by focusing on disconnected pieces. However, by looking at the universe as interconnected and structured, we find its root in the creative order of an almighty God who made the heavens and the earth. For thousands of years, this was the dominant idea and foundation of intellectual and theological thought. Since God created an orderly world, by studying this world through the means of number, we would not only learn more about the creation but we would also learn about the Creator.[10]

COSMOS AND *SHALOM*

The concept of *harmony* brings together disparate ideas and parts, and makes sense of creation through the idea and manifestation of numbers. In theological terms, we might consider harmony in terms of the idea of *cosmos* (or order) and the blessing of *shalom* (or peace). Adam's sin in the Garden of Eden brought disorder to the cosmos, a chaos consisting of broken relationships with God, nature, and fellow humans, and within oneself. The redemptive work of Christ brings peace, *shalom*, by the blood of the cross (Colossians 1:15–23) and reconciliation in both earth and heaven. This is a restoring work of bringing harmony to discord.

Shalom is the way things were meant to be: wholeness, right ordering, harmony. It is expressed in the Trinity, redemption, and the created order sustained by divine harmony—for in Christ all things hold together (Col. 1:17). Harmony is displayed in God's creation in right relationship with him, with others, and in the world that he has made—the soul, body, *polis*, and cosmos. Sin wrecked that order and added a discordant tuning to that which God had made. Steven Guthrie discusses that idea by including the concept of ratio with regard to the disruption that sin causes:

---

[9] Vern S. Poythress, *Redeeming Mathematics: A God-Centered Approach* (Wheaton: Crossway, 2015), 26.

[10] Gregory Wilbur, "The Quadrivium and the Character of God," *Forma Journal* 5 (Winter 2017): 16–27.

> The fundamental human dilemma is that by aspiring to equality with God (Genesis 3:5) humanity has abandoned its well-ordered place within God's Song of the Universe [*carmen universitatis*]. There has been a universal loss of ratio. We no longer stand in right relation to God. We no longer stand in right relation to the non-human creation ("Cursed is the ground because of you, through painful toil you will eat of it." Genesis 3:17), and we no longer stand in right relation to one another. More than this, we no longer stand in right relation to ourselves. (And so Paul for instance can speak of the members of his body waging war against the law of his mind, making him a prisoner of his own members. [Romans 7:23.]) As Augustine recognizes, though body and soul are part of a differentiated unity, our experience in this life is often that of a hostile and mutually antagonistic plurality: body and mind, affections, appetites, and imaginations, resisting, refusing, and tormenting one another. In each of these arenas, we see that Satan is the Father of separation; that the dynamic of sin is division; that the hallmark of corruption is the distortion of relation.[11]

Abandoning its ordered place, humanity has sown the discord of sin and disobedience which destroys the harmony and peace that inhabited the pre-fallen Eden.

The Apostle Paul connects and highlights harmony, peace, and music as indicators of right relationships. *Harmonia* (ἁρμονία) comes from the Greek word "to fit together, to join" and refers to objects, ideas, or realities that are in correct relationship, agreement, or concord, leading to balance, order and peace. Thus, the study of number in the quadrivium centers on the greater concepts of harmony and order: personally, ethically, and cosmically. In Colossians 3:12–16, Paul describes the redeemed body of Christ as one in which love binds everything together in perfect harmony, in which the peace of Christ rules in one body, and where the Word dwells in music and by singing which in turn teaches and admonishes. Paul writes,

> Put on then, as God's chosen ones, holy and beloved, compassionate hearts, kindness, humility,

---

[11] Steven R. Guthrie, "Carmen Universitatis: A Theological Study of Music and Measure" (Ph.D. thesis, University of St. Andrews, 2000), 277.

> meekness, and patience, bearing with one another and, if one has a complaint against another, forgiving each other; as the Lord has forgiven you, so you also must forgive. And above all these put on love, which binds everything together in perfect harmony. And let the peace of Christ rule in your hearts, to which indeed you were called in one body. And be thankful. Let the word of Christ dwell in you richly, teaching and admonishing one another in all wisdom, singing psalms and hymns and spiritual songs, with thankfulness in your hearts to God.

Being called to peace and having peace rule in your heart concerns personal order/harmony/peace.[12] Compassion, kindness, humility, meekness, patience, and forgiveness, as well as the call to be one body, are all ethical concerns regarding how to live with one another in order/harmony/peace.[13] Love that binds everything together in perfect harmony with thanksgiving and dwelling richly in the Word of Christ, the *logos*, are cosmic concerns of living in relationship to the Creator God.[14] For this reason, Church Fathers, reformers, theologians, philosophers, artists, writers, astronomers, etc. consistently refer to the idea of order and the harmony of the world as those things worthy of study. Consider the following, rather diverse, examples.

---

[12] This is consistent with Augustine's idea of "rightly ordered loves."

[13] Consider, for example, Romans 12:15–16: "Rejoice with those who rejoice, weep with those who weep. Live in harmony with one another. Do not be haughty, but associate with the lowly [or give yourself to lowly tasks]. Never be wise in your own sight" (ESV); and Romans 15:5–6, "May the God of endurance and encouragement grant you to live in such harmony with one another, in accord with Christ Jesus, that together you may with one voice glorify the God and Father of our Lord Jesus Christ."

[14] Quentin Faulkner explains these categories from Boethius's text on music in *Wiser than Despair: The Evolution of Ideas in the Relationship of Music and the Christian Church* (Westport, CT: Greenwood Press, 1996), 77: "The source of all beauty, all order, is God, who has created cosmic order and harmony (*musica mundana* in Boethius's terminology, the music of the universe). The world is a reflection of that beauty in order, as is human beauty (Boethius's *musica humana*—not merely physical beauty, but the perfect harmony of body and soul), and all of these beauties may be expressed mathematically in the form of numerical ratios. Those ratios in turn may be perceived by the ear as Boethius's *musica instrumentalis*, sounding music (both vocal and instrumental)."

FURTHER EXAMPLES OF ORDER AND HARMONY

In the late first century to early second century, Clement of Rome (d. 99 AD) wrote a letter to the Corinthians in which he speaks of God as the Master Craftsman who ordered all of creation. He uses language of liturgy, boundaries, order, and harmony to describe the created cosmos:

> The heavens, rolled around in his diocese, obey him in peace. Both day and night finish the course assigned by him, neither impeding the other. Sun, moon, and stars, according to his direction, unroll in harmony in the courses assigned them.
>
> The earth, pregnant according to his will in its own seasons, gives birth to every kind of food for men, wild animals, and everything that lives. The earth does not withstand or edit anything he has decreed.
>
> Even the abyss, unsearchable and fathomless, in its ineffable judgments concurs with his ordinances. The hollow of the impenetrable sea, gathered by the Master-Craftsman into congregations, does not break the bars placed around it. No, as he ordered it, so it does. For he said, "this far you may go, and then your waves will be halted in you." The ocean, impassable by men, and the worlds beyond it are conveyed by the same commands of the Master.
>
> The seasons—springtime and summer and autumn and winter—yield to one another in peace. The winds from their dwellings fulfill their liturgies in their proper time though blind.
>
> The ever-flowing springs, crafted for pleasure and health, give their breast without fail for the life of men. Even the smallest living things are brought together in harmony and peace.
>
> The Great Craftsman and Master of all these things has ordered them to exist in peace and harmony. He works all things beautifully, but especially to us who are refugees hiding in His compassion through our Lord Jesus Christ. To him be glory and Majesty to the ages of the ages. Amen.[15]

---

[15] Clement of Rome, "I Clement 20," trans. Jamie Crampton (unpublished manuscript, 2021).

Athanasius (c. 296–373 AD) too writes of the order of creation as an apologetic for God in his *Oratio contra gentes* 38. Using logic and experience, he presents a musical example to speak about the necessity of recognizing that an orderly world can only exist from the hand of God who reigns and directs His creation. Accordingly, Athanasius writes,

> Just as when one hears from afar a lyre, made up of many different strings, and wonders at their harmonious symphony, that not only the low one produces a sound, not only the high one, and not only the middle one, but all sound together in balanced tension, and one concludes from all this that the lyre neither operates by itself nor is played by many, but rather that there is one musician who by his art blends the sound of each string into a harmonious symphony—even though one fails to see him—so too, since there is an entirely harmonious order in the world as a whole, without things being at odds with those below, and those below with those above, but one completed order of all; it follows that we know there is one leader and king of all creation, not many, who illuminates and moves everything with his own light.[16]

With regards to *shalom*, harmony, and order, Augustine (354–430 AD) writes beautifully in *The City of God* about how these three ideas coalesce. In a densely rich section, he repeats the concept of peace as applied to a wide variety of spheres from the body, the soul, spiritual life, relationships, and culture, and the essence of true harmony, as the tension of "equal and unequal things." He says,

> The peace of the body, therefore, lies in the balanced ordering of its parts; the peace of the irrational soul lies in the rightly ordered disposition of the appetites; the peace of the rational soul lies in the rightly ordered relationship of cognition and action; the peace of the body and soul lies in the rightly ordered life and health of a living creature; peace between mortal man and God is an ordered obedience, in faith, under an eternal law; and peace between men is an ordered agreement of mind with mind. The peace of a

---

[16] Athanasius, *Oratio contra gentes* 38, quoted in James McKinnon, *Music in Early Christian Literature* (Cambridge: Cambridge University Press, 1987), 55–56.

household is an ordered concord, with respect to command and obedience, of those who dwell together; the peace of a city is an ordered concord, with respect to command and obedience, of the citizens; and the peace of the Heavenly City is a perfectly ordered and perfectly harmonious fellowship in the enjoyment of God, and of one another in God. The peace of all things lies in the tranquility of order, and order is the disposition of equal and unequal things in such a way as to give to each its proper place.[17]

As I pointed out previously, Martin Luther often introduced the concept of music and the harmony of creation in his many writings. At one point, he writes, "[L]ooking at music itself, you will find it from the beginning of the world it has been instilled and implanted in all creatures, individually and collectively. For nothing is without sound or harmony [literally 'sounding number']."[18] Elsewhere, he says, "Music is a gift and largesse of God, not a human gift. Praise through word and music is a sermon in sound."[19]

Similarly, poet and Anglican priest John Donne (1572–1631) used the idea of world harmony and the analogy of music in one of his sermons that he preached about the tuning of the world and redemption, saying,

> God made this whole world in such an uniformity, such a *correspondency*, such a *concinnity* of parts that it was an *Instrument, perfectly in tune*: we may say, the trebles, the highest strings were disordered first; the best understandings, angels and men, put this instrument *out of tune*. God rectified all again, by putting in *a new string, semen, mulieris*, the seed of the woman, the Messias: And onely by sounding that string in your ears, become we *musicum carmen*, true *musick*, true *harmony*, true peace to you. [The world harmony, destroyed by origin sin and the fall of the angels, was restored by Christ, the 'new string,' to the world lute.][20]

---

[17] Augustine, *The City of God against the Pagans*, ed. and trans. R. W. Dyson (Cambridge: Cambridge University Press, 1998), XIX, xiii, p. 938.

[18] Martin Luther, quoted in Faulkner, *Wiser than Despair*, 139.

[19] Martin Luther, quoted in James R. Gaines, *Evening in the Palace of Reason* (New York City: Harper Collins, 2005), 43.

[20] John Donne, quoted in Leo Spitzer, *Classical and Christian Ideas of World Harmony* (Baltimore: Johns Hopkins Press, 1963), 135–36.

This brief survey of thinkers reveals that references to and symbolism of order, harmony, and peace pertaining to the liberal arts, education, theology, literature, music, and science were prolific and variously used. Indeed, there was a universal assumption that the universe had meaning, that it was created, knowable, and filled with repeating patterns and intentionality. In turn, this means that life has meaning, purpose, context, responsibility, and the opportunity for discovery of not only the things that God has made but also of God himself. Metaphysical realities intermingle with the physical and what is done on earth has echoes in eternity. The study of number and order through the quadrivium existed as the means to do just that. Not only does the study of the quadrivium explore the beauties of the order of creation, but the disciplines of the studies themselves serve a formative and spiritual dimension. They remind us of the coinherence of the physical and spiritual and that the demise of the metaphysical through the Enlightenment impoverished our knowledge of God and his works.

THE QUADRIVIUM AS FORMATIVE

Kevin Clark and Ravi Scott Jain's *The Liberal Arts Tradition* is a helpful and comprehensive approach to classical education that places the quadrivium in the broader context of a fully realized vision for Christian classical education. They write that the original role of the quadrivium was "to lead the mind to the realm of eternal and unchanging truths," but that this was "eventually displaced by the amazing power of mathematics to describe the physical world."[21] Both are necessary: "the useful and the formative."[22] However, as Clark and Jain recall, Plato speaks in the *Republic* about the importance of the formative aspect of mathematics above its usefulness: "Plato believed that the study of mathematics leads the mind toward pure reason and cultivates the true love of wisdom (the origin of the term philosophy). By training one's thoughts on the perfections of mathematics, the mind learns to transcend the level of changing opinions to identify objective truth."[23] This wisdom and truth is found in none other but God himself.

---

[21] Kevin Clark and Ravi Scott Jain, *The Liberal Arts Tradition: A Philosophy of Christian Classical Education* (Camp Hill, PA: Classical Academic Press, 2013), 52.

[22] Clark and Jain, *Liberal Arts Tradition*, 52.

[23] Clark and Jain, *Liberal Arts Tradition*, 50.

In a 1988 article in *The Journal of Pastoral Care*, David Duncombe discusses the nature of learning that the classical seven liberal arts were intended to provide and how this learning connects to pastoral care. He writes that educators considered the "intrinsic subject matter" of these studies "to have an ennobling effect on the learner," but "it was the discipline of the study itself that was given greater credit for broadening the mind, deepening the soul, and strengthening the character. Educators of the classical period assumed that the mind and heart were somehow stretched and formed by the rigors of mastering these disciplines, whether or not the subject matter had any practical application." [24] One could argue that the deepening of souls and stretching of characters is the practical application and the studies in the quadrivium were beautiful ways to encourage that path.

CONCLUSION

Martin Luther famously wrote: "Music I have always loved. He who knows music has a good nature. Necessity demands that music be kept in the schools. A schoolmaster must be able to sing; otherwise, I will not look at him. And before a young man is ordained in the ministry, he should practice music in school."[25] Luther assumed that the study of theology flowed from the study of music as part of the trivium and quadrivium. Returning to the example of Samuel Miller and his presbytery licensure exams, the Presbyters, like Luther, considered a full seven liberal arts education as a prerequisite for gospel ministry, for its depth and breadth as well as its formative attributes.

Charles Taylor, channeling Max Weber, has written about the effect of "disenchantment" stemming from the forces of secularism that have dominated modern culture and thought—within and without the Church.[26]

---

[24] David C. Duncombe, "The Trivial Nature of Clinical Pastoral Education," *The Journal of Pastoral Care* 42, no. 1 (Spring 1988): 46–47.

[25] Robin A. Leaver, "Music and Lutheranism," in *The Cambridge Companion to Bach*, ed. John Butt (Cambridge: Cambridge University Press, 2000), 42.

[26] "[Pre-modern people] lived in an 'enchanted' world. This is perhaps not the best expression: it seems to evoke light and fairies. But I am invoking here its negation, Weber's expression 'disenchantment' as a description of our modern condition. This term has achieved such wide currency in our discussion of these matters, that I'm going to use its antonym to describe a crucial feature of the pre-modern condition. The enchanted world in this sense is the world of spirits, demons, and moral forces

Rod Dreher rightly explains how disenchantment changes our very view of creation, saying,

> Christians of the Middle Ages took Paul's words recorded in Acts—'in Him we live and move and have our being'—and in his letter to the Colossians—'He is before all things and in Him all things hold together'—in a much more literal sense than we do. Medieval man did not see himself as fundamentally separate from the natural order; rather, the alienation he felt was an effect of the Fall, a catastrophe that, as he understood it, made it difficult for humans to see Creation as it really is. His task was to join himself to the love of God and harmonize his own steps with the great cosmic dance. Truth was guaranteed by the existence of God, whose Logos, the divine Principle of order, was made fully manifest in Jesus Christ but is present to some degree in all Creation.[27]

The trivium is essentially important for the development of the mind and spirit, but so is the quadrivium. These seven arts were always conceived as working in tandem and in conjunction with another. Although the recovery and renewal of Christian classical education has flourished in the past decades, the quadrivium still lags behind. There are multiple reasons for this, but perhaps the most significant lies in the way in which the world is perceived. While a biblical foundation for speaking, writing, logic, philosophy, and history seems like an obvious endeavor, the ill-effects of the Enlightenment and the scientific revolution have narrowed and focused the study of mathematics to pragmatic and quantitative purposes only. One of the reasons that the Church and science can sometimes seem to be at odds is that the Church has forgotten her richer inheritance of studying the cosmos as the reflection of its Creator. As Quentin Faulkner writes, "The Enlightenment was at heart a denial of the mystical, spiritual dimension of existence. Leading thinkers were disposed to consider religion, especially

---

which our ancestors lived in." Charles Taylor, *A Secular Age* (Cambridge, MA: Harvard University Press, 2007), 25–26.

[27] Rod Dreher, *The Benedict Option: A Strategy for Christians in a Post-Christian Nation* (New York: Penguin Random House, 2017), 25.

Christian religion, as superstition, and in criticizing, indeed, ridiculing it they hastened the evaporation not only of superstition, but also of spirituality."[28]

The separation between the physical and the metaphysical is a casualty of that evaporation. Because of this, the Church has had a more difficult time explaining and preserving ritual and ceremony, sacrament, and the idea that bodily posture has a spiritual component—in fact, it has had a difficult time explaining at all that what is done in and by the flesh has significant spiritual repercussions. This has also had a deleterious effect on the idea of covenants; Faulkner continues, saying, "The idea of covenant presumes an unshakable belief in the omnipotence of God and God's ability to act in the world. The various enlightenment conceptions of God (e.g., Deism, divine subservience to reason and natural law) tended to limit that belief; such conceptions could not help but dilute the immediacy of the idea of covenant."[29] The disciplines of the quadrivium help to lead students back to a re-enchantment of the cosmos.

In this overview and defense of the quadrivium the point is not to propose a curriculum but to open the possibility of what past generations knew for millennia and what has been neglected, forgotten, or rejected in the past few centuries. The purpose is the glory of God and knowledge of what He has made and how He has revealed Himself. Historically, the quadrivium has been the preferred method to undertake those studies and to train affections and virtues towards delight and gratitude for Almighty God.

Clark and Jain explain, "While grounded in wonder, respecting work, and leading to wisdom, natural philosophy also situated its endeavor in the context of worship. The entire medieval vision of reality was conceived from the perspective of an ordered unity—a cosmos comprised of both whole and parts. While the ancient Pre-Socratics and Pythagoreans developed the concept of an ordered cosmos, the medievals understood it as creation ordered by Christ, the *logos*, under the creative impulse of God."[30] Steven Guthrie sums up this idea, starting with music as his premise:

> In fact (as the Pythagorean tradition acknowledges), the very acoustical and harmonic foundations of music reflect principles of mathematical proportion and balance—

---

[28] Faulkner, *Wiser than Despair*, 165.

[29] Faulkner, *Wiser than Despair*, 166.

[30] Clark and Jain, *Liberal Arts Tradition*, 97.

principles expressed in every aspect of the universe, animate and inanimate. While one of the purposes of the cosmos is the creation of music, the ultimate purpose of all things, including music, is the glory of God. It is this common *telos* which unifies creation and invests every act and object with purpose and meaning. All things are good and significant, because they all may contribute to the Highest Good. Additionally, there is unity to the cosmos, because all things have been created for one purpose and end.[31]

The heavens declare the glory and the beauty and the splendor and the infinite variety of God, and we are called to dance in that creation. Christ is glorified as the Word of God—everything in existence was called forth by him, is held together by him, and is itself the communication of God: in number, in space and relationship, in *harmonia* and the music of the spheres, in time and space. God is all in all: sovereign over all, creating all, employing all for his glory and beauty. Arithmetic points us to the Trinity; geometry shows the need for mediation; *harmonia* displays redemption and reconciling peace; cosmology calls us to move in sanctifying submission to the steps of the Lord of the Dance.

In his *Divine Comedy*, Dante traveled through the seven spheres of heaven from sun and moon and planets and stars to encounter the living light of Divine Love "that moves the sun and the other stars."[32] The Unified Theory of Everything is Christ and the Word of his power. As we begin to apprehend this with knowledge, we are led to wonder and awe and worship.

In Ephesians 3:17–19, Paul gives us a geometry lesson and calls us to be rooted and grounded in love, to have the strength to comprehend the breadth and length and height and depth, to know the love of Christ, and to be filled with the fullness of God. A line, a triangle, a tetrahedron—from one dimension to three dimensions. But Paul doesn't stop there: by adding depth he moves us into the fourth dimension—to new discovery and to greater fullness of Divine Love. The purpose of education is love—to see God in such a way as to love him—to see the King in his beauty and the craftsman in his work. The cosmos is filled with the workings of Divine Love in the order, beauty, patterns, majesty, and glory of creation. He set the spheres in

---

[31] Guthrie, "Carmen Universitatis," 80.

[32] Dante Alighieri, *Paradiso*, trans. Anthony Esolen (USA: Random House, 2014), 33.144–45.

motion and our hearts are restless until they find their rest (their peace, their *shalom*) in him.

BIBLIOGRAPHY

Alighieri, Dante. *Paradiso*. Translated by Anthony Esolen. USA: Random House, 2014.

Augustine. *The City of God against the Pagans*. Edited and translated by R. W. Dyson. Cambridge: Cambridge University Press, 1998.

Caldecott, Stratford. *Beauty for Truth's Sake: On the Re-enchantment of Education*. Grand Rapids: Brazos Press, 2009.

Calvin, John. *Institutes of the Christian Religion: Calvin's Own Essential Edition*. Translated by Robert White. London: Banner of Truth Trust, 2014.

Chadwick, Henry. *Boethius: The Consolations of Music, Logic, Theology, and Philosophy*. Oxford: Clarendon Press, 1981.

Clark, Kevin, and Ravi Scott Jain. *The Liberal Arts Tradition: A Philosophy of Christian Classical Education*. Camp Hill, PA: Classical Academic Press, 2013.

Clement of Rome. "I Clement 20." Translated by Jamie Crampton. Unpublished Manuscript, 2021.

Dreher, Rod. *The Benedict Option: A Strategy for Christians in a Post-Christian Nation*. New York: Penguin Random House, 2017.

Duncombe, David C. "The Trivial Nature of Clinical Pastoral Education." *The Journal of Pastoral Care* 42, no. 1 (Spring 1988): 46–56.

Faulkner, Quentin. *Wiser than Despair: The Evolution of Ideas in the Relationship of Music and the Christian Church*. Westport, CT: Greenwood Press, 1996.

Gaines, James R. *Evening in the Palace of Reason*. New York: Harper Collins, 2005.

Guthrie, Steven R. "Carmen Universitatis: A Theological Study of Music and Measure." Ph.D. thesis, University of St. Andrews, 2000.

Leaver, Robin A. "Music and Lutheranism." In *The Cambridge Companion to Bach*, edited by John Butt. Cambridge: Cambridge University Press, 2000.

Lewis, C. S. *English Literature in the Sixteenth Century, Excluding Drama*. Oxford: Clarendon Press, 1954.

McKinnon, James. *Music in Early Christian Literature*. Cambridge: Cambridge University Press, 1987.

Poythress, Vern S. *Redeeming Mathematics: A God-Centered Approach*. Wheaton: Crossway, 2015.

Ruckdeschel, Christopher. *On the Nature of the Classical Liberal Arts*. BookBay, 2019.

Spitzer, Leo. *Classical and Christian Ideas of World Harmony*. Baltimore: Johns Hopkins Press, 1963.

Strunk, W. Oliver. *Source Readings in Music History*. Revised edition. Edited by Leo Treitler. London: W. W. Norton & Company, 1998.

Taylor, Charles. *A Secular Age*. Cambridge, MA: Harvard University Press, 2007.

Van Rensselaer, C. *The Presbyterian Magazine 2*. Philadelphia, PA: Wm. H. Mitchell, 1853.

Wilbur, Gregory. "The Quadrivium and the Character of God." *Forma Journal* 5 (Winter 2017).

V:
COSMIC WISDOM:
HOW THE QUADRIVIUM SERVES
THEOLOGY AND ETHICS

Nathan Johnson, New College Franklin

IN THE past several decades, America has witnessed a resurgence in what has become known as "classical education." Spurred on by Mortimer Adler, Dorothy Sayers, and others, private schools, homeschool families, and even some colleges are adopting liberal arts curriculums that emphasize reading the great texts of the Western tradition and engaging in the kind of liberal education that many of the great thinkers and statesmen of the past received. In most of these classical schools, the emphasis has been on teaching the trivium—the three ways of grammar, logic, and rhetoric—as a precursor to philosophical and theological study. While it is true to the spirit of the classical liberal arts to master the written word and read classic texts in literature, history, and philosophy, the accompanying "four ways" of the quadrivium have been neglected: arithmetic, geometry, music, and astronomy. If classical education is to continue to conform to the historic pattern of the seven liberal arts, it must reconsider the place of the quadrivium in classical education, for the ancients considered these four ways as the logical prerequisite to wisdom and virtue.

At its most basic, the quadrivium is the study of the underlying *stoicheia* (that is the elements, rudiments, or principles) of the cosmos, for number is that by which the cosmos is ordered. As such, ancient philosophers understood the quadrivium to be the entryway into metaphysics and, by extension, ethics. The fundamental assumption of the quadrivium is that the cosmos is ordered and intelligible, that it bears within its nature structures, harmonies, and elements that can be understood by the rational mind. One of the fundamental reasons that the natural world is intelligible is because it is patterned according to *number*, one of the fundamental elements of being. As John Locke says, "Number applies itself to men, angels, actions, thoughts; everything that either does exist, or can be imagined....Every object our senses are employed about; every idea in our understandings; every thought of our minds, brings this idea along with it. And therefore, it is...in its agreement to all other things, the most universal idea we have."[1] The order, due proportion, and beauty of the cosmos testifies to the reality of wisdom, goodness, and the presence of a Creator after whom the cosmos was patterned. Because of this, the study of number in its various forms can be an entryway into ethics and theology.

As education has gradually turned away from the metaphysical and ethical dimension of the mathematical arts and turned them solely into mechanical and utilitarian arts, various Western societies have lost their trust in the presence of an underlying order, structure, and purpose to life and human action. The mathematical arts, which were studied under the heading of the quadrivium, used to be seen as a mediating art between the physical and metaphysical. As such, it is not merely useful in understanding and manipulating the physical universe; it also points to the deeper metaphysical realities that stand under and above the material world: realities such as being, unity, goodness, beauty, truth, and first cause.

Simply put, when one speaks of natural wisdom, natural law, and natural theology, one is operating in the domain of the quadrivium in one form or another. Devoid of the revealed law of God in Scripture and conscience, ethical, philosophical, and theological explorations operate through the paradigms revealed in the quadrivium. This chapter will explore the ways in which the quadrivium was historically understood in the ancient and medieval world as an essential foundation for theology, metaphysics, and ethics.

---

[1] John Locke, quoted in Mortimer Adler, "Quantity," in *The Syntopicon of the Great Books of the Western World*, ed. Mortimer Adler, 2nd ed. (USA: Encyclopedia Britannica, 1993), 2:229.

NUMBER AND MATHEMATICS

For many of the ancient Greeks, mathematics was a "speculative art" distinct from examination and manipulation of the physical makeup of the world. Arithmetic is first concerned with number as an abstraction, not primarily with things one numbers. Geometry is first concerned with figures on a plane, not with magnitudes of physical shapes. Music can be studied according to numerical ratios rather than notes and sounds; astronomy can be studied according to geometrical configurations rather than "visible celestial motions."[2] The study of quantity, then, became the starting point of philosophy, for magnitude and multitude are the first two forms of being.[3] And because the study of number leads to the study of philosophy, it leads to wisdom and happiness. This is explored in depth by Nichomachus in his *Introduction to Arithmetic*.

Nichomachus

Nichomachus (c. 60–c. 120 AD), who was of the Pythagorean school, begins his *Introduction* by giving a justification for the study of number by relating it to wisdom and happiness. He contends that arithmetic helps man reach his *telos*, for happiness is the goal of life and it is only accomplished through philosophy; philosophy is the love of wisdom, and wisdom is gained first through the study of mathematics.

The quadrivium investigates the "first two forms of being" (1.3.4). Thus, the mathematical arts are the essential prerequisite for philosophy, for "without the aid of these, then, it is not possible to deal accurately with the forms of being nor to discover the truth in things, knowledge of which is wisdom" (1.3.3). Nichomachus further justifies the essential link between number and philosophy by referencing Plato's *Laws*, in which philosophy is directly related to the problem of the one and many:

> Every diagram, system of numbers, every scheme of harmony, and every law of the movement of the stars, ought

---

[2] Adler, "Quantity," 230.

[3] Nichomachus, *Introduction to Arithmetic*, trans. Martin L. D'ooge, in *The Great Books of the Western World*, ed. Mortimer Adler, 2nd ed., vol. 10 (USA: Encyclopedia Britannica, 1993), 1.3.4.

to appear one to him who studies rightly; and what we say will properly appear if one studies all things looking into one principle, for there will be seen to be one bond for all these things, and if any one attempts philosophy in any other way he must call on Fortune to assist him. For there is never a path without these.[4]

In light of the changing realities and disparate elements of the world, philosophy seeks after knowledge of the fundamental unity and substance that grounds and upholds all things. The study of number is the means of grappling with the first problem of metaphysics, and by means of number, we come to better understand all that is. In the history of philosophy, the exploration of unity and being leads to an exploration of the nature of God Himself, who is Absolute Being and Absolute Unity. This can be seen in the method Thomas Aquinas uses in the *Summa* 1.11 to study the Unity of God through the historical and philosophical exploration of the meaning and interrelation of unity, multiplicity, and being.[5]

Nichomachus claims that the study of number can be done through the material world, because the universe has been ordered according to it. All things share in number (1.6.1). Hence, the study of number is a mediating endeavor that sheds light on the nature of the material universe as well as the immaterial forms that abide alongside it, unchanging in their very being. And since God is Creator and Being-in-Itself, the study of number leads to the knowledge of God, and this knowledge is the end of man. This idea is developed further in Plato, with reference both to the blissful knowledge of God and the ethical implications of the study of number.

Plato

Of all the ancient philosophers, Plato (428/427 or 424/423–348/347 BC) most famously advocates for the study of the mathematical arts as a means to reaching metaphysical knowledge, wisdom, and virtuous action. Plato explores the significance of the quadrivium through several different lenses, emphasizing the quadrivium's connection to metaphysics, ethics, epistemology, and, most ultimately, the knowledge and love of the Good.

---

[4] Plato, *Laws*, quoted in Nichomachus, *Introduction*, 1.3.5.
[5] Thomas Aquinas, *Summa Theologica*, 1.11.

Philebus

In *Philebus*, Plato outlines in brief the metaphysical implications of the study of number. In a conversation mostly centered on ethics and the good life—and whether the good and the pleasurable are the same thing—Socrates insists on a more fundamental exploration of the natures of pleasure (one candidate for the good life) and knowledge (another possible means to the good life). The conversation centers on mathematical—and ultimately metaphysical—questions related to the "one" within the "many" forms of pleasure and knowledge, and what a unity of pleasure and knowledge might look like. Hence, the question of the good life becomes a mathematical question leading to a metaphysical question. Here, Socrates claims that one must study the mathematical arts to be equipped to answer these questions, for it is "the discipline concerned with being and with what is really and forever in every way eternally self-same [and is] by far the truest of all kinds of knowledge."[6] According to Socrates, the study of the quadrivium is the entryway into philosophy and particularly metaphysics, because it studies things eternal and unchanging (i.e., being) rather than simply things in this material world (i.e., becoming), which are more the subject of opinion, rather than knowledge (58d–59b). Because of this, knowledge of the quadrivium can help answer fundamental questions about what things truly are.

Symposium

The first step in learning to imitate the Good is to learn to love the Good, a love that can be taught through study of the order of the cosmos. In *Symposium*, Eryximachus says that love directs everything that happens in the cosmos.[7] Linking music with cosmology, he states that "[m]usic is…the science of the effects of Love on rhythm and harmony" (187c). He states that there are two species of love (heavenly and vulgar) which are modeled by two types of music: the love that is "produced by the melodies of Urania, the Heavenly Muse" and the love that is produced by the vulgar music of

---

[6] Plato, *Philebus*, trans. Dorothea Frede, in *Plato: Complete Works*, ed. John M. Cooper (Indianapolis: Hackett Publishing Company, 1997), 58a.

[7] Plato, *Symposium*, trans. Alexander Nehamas and Paul Woodruff, in *Plato: Complete Works*, 186b.

Polyhymnia (187e). To be pious is to learn to love according to the ordered melody of the spheres. Impiety, on the other hand, is disordered love (188c).[8]

Diotima's speech (recounted by Socrates) introduces the idea of the ladder of love, as one learns to love divine things by first learning to love earthly things: "The man who has been thus far guided in matters of Love, who has beheld beautiful things in the right order and correctly, is coming now to the goal of Loving: all of a sudden he will catch sight of something wonderfully beautiful in its nature" (210e–211a). This thing is the world of Being. It is wholly beautiful and it is "itself by itself, with itself, it is always one in form; and all the other beautiful things share in that" (211b). She states, "This is what it is to go aright, or be led by another, into the mystery of Love: one goes always upwards for the sake of this Beauty, starting out from beautiful things and using them like rising stairs…and from these lessons he arrives in the end at this lesson, which is learning of this very Beauty" (211d). Beholding the Beautiful in its singular form then leads to "true virtue" (212a). In this way, the study of music and the cosmos (the two highest disciplines of the quadrivium) enables one to behold and love the Beautiful, leading to a virtuous life through imitation of the Good and Beautiful.

The Republic

Plato discusses in more detail the relation of the quadrivium to knowledge and love of the Good in Book VII of the *Republic*. After giving the discourse on the divided line (Book VI) and the "analogy of the cave" (Book VII), Socrates explores the means through which education helps the student ascend to knowledge and love of the Good. The Good is that which "gives truth to the things known and the power to know to the knower."[9] It is both the "cause of knowledge and truth" and also the "object of knowledge" (508e). The way that the soul comes to see the Good is through education (518d). He calls philosophy a "turning of the soul from a day that is a kind of night to the true day—the ascent to what *is*"—that is, to being as such (521c, emphasis added). Socrates maintains that the soul has the capacity to see and love the Good but must be given the ability to do so: this is the purpose of education and philosophy more directly. But in order to begin the

---

[8] Augustine was clearly influenced by this idea in *Confessions* and *The City of God*.
[9] Plato, *Republic*, trans. G. M. A. Grube, revised by C. D. C. Reeve, in *Plato: Complete Works*, 508e.

process of moving from darkness to light, from "the Cave" to the real world, the person must be equipped by the quadrivium.

The discussion turns from the need for education to the subjects that "draw the soul from the realm of becoming to the realm of what is," focusing on how the "four ways" of the mathematical arts are uniquely suited for this task (521d). Socrates says that we usually think of number in terms of its use, but that its primary power is in its ability to "draw one towards being" (523a). To explain the mechanism that number possesses to do this, he makes a keen distinction between two kinds of sense perception. There is one kind of sense perception that doesn't "summon the sense perception to look into [it]" because the sense perception can grasp the whole, while the other kind encourages the observer to look deeper into it, because these sense perceptions seem to go in two directions simultaneously, being something and its opposite (523b–524d). Oneness is like the latter kind that moves us to inquire into being, because "nothing is apparently any more one than the opposite of one" (524e–525a). In other words, things possess unity and multiplicity at the same time. Because of this paradox, the soul must inquire further into the very nature of the object, searching the contours of number in order to search out substance, being, and unity itself.

To do this, the soul must engage in the task of abstract inquiry, for when contemplating abstract number, the soul is compelled to "use understanding itself on the truth itself" (526b). The process of abstract investigation leads to the discovery of more fundamental truths about the eternal forms that always abide beyond sense perception. Geometry, for example, makes it easier to "see the form of the Good," for "it compels the soul to turn itself around towards the region in which lies the happiest of the things that are, the one that the soul must see at any cost," the form of the Good (526d–e). Pure geometry is the study of being itself, for it is "the knowledge of what always is" in the world of being, not simply the imperfect shapes in the world of becoming (526e–527b).

Like geometry, astronomy (or cosmology) does the same thing: "In every soul there is an instrument that is purified and rekindled by such subjects when it has been blinded and destroyed by other ways of life…since only with it can the truth be seen" (527e). Many in Socrates's day said astronomy "compels the soul to look upward and leads it from things here to things there" (529a) but he is less interested in looking at the actual stars as opposed to the true invisible things of which they are a model (529b–c).

Men should study astronomy like geometry, leaving the material things behind to study by means of problems (530b).

What the eyes do with astronomical motions, the ears do with harmonic motions (530d). True study of this seeks out "the numbers that are to be found in these audible consonances" and then ascends to harmonic problems to investigate "which numbers are consonant and which aren't" (531c). This endeavor is "useful in the search for the beautiful and the good" (531c). In this way, the study of music is a mediating endeavor, enabling the soul to find the source of all harmony by means of philosophy: "All these subjects are merely preludes to the song itself that must also be learned" (531d). This is the song of dialectic. The only way one can use dialectic to inquire into being is if someone is experienced in the study of the quadrivium (533a).

In a beautiful summary of Socrates's philosophy of the quadrivium's essential place in the education of philosophy, he states that "[the mathematical arts] have the power to awaken the best part of the soul and lead it upward to the study of the best among the things that are, just as, before, the clearest thing in the body was led to the brightest thing in the bodily and visible realm" (532c). Through education, the soul can ascend to the realm of true being and behold the "love that moves the sun and the other stars."[10] But without the aid of the quadrivium, this education could never accomplish its goal.

Timaeus

The most challenging of Plato's dialogues, the *Timaeus* presents the fullest picture of Plato's cosmology, explaining more clearly the link between number and being, as well as the ethical implications of the quadrivium as the study of the order of the cosmos. Early in the dialogue, Plato makes an essential distinction between the world of being—"that which always is and has no beginning"—and the world of becoming—"that which becomes but never is."[11] The world of sense perception is the world of becoming, while the world of the eternal forms is the world of being. The latter is grasped by understanding, the former by opinion and sense perception (28a).

---

[10] Dante, *Paradiso*, trans. Anthony Esolen (USA: Random House, 2014), 33.144–45.

[11] Plato, *Timaeus*, trans. Donald J. Zeyl, in *Plato: Complete Works*, 27d.

When a craftsman beholds something that always is (such as, perhaps, a geometric square) and uses the changeless thing as a model and "reproduces its form and character," then he has made something beautiful (28a–b). In the same way, the cosmos was created according to an eternal model, and thus it is beautiful: "It is a work of craft, modeled after that which is changeless and is grasped by a rational account, that is, by wisdom" (29a). This is the essential explanation for why the study of number is a bridge between the material and immaterial worlds; this reveals how number can apply to the world of becoming but also give insight into the nature of the unchanging realities that find the source in God himself; it gives insight into the transcendental characteristic of beauty, how beauty is related to order, and how the quadrivium studies the intersection of order, beauty, and being—and thus the God who is the source and ground for these eternal transcendentals.

Timaeus begins his "likely tale" by discussing why the Creator made the cosmos: "He was good, and one who is good can never become jealous of anything. And so, being free of jealousy, he wanted everything to become as much like himself as was possible" (29e). In some ways, then, the cosmos is an image of the Maker. He then gives an account of the god taking matter that was in "discordant and disorderly motion" and bringing it into a state of order and harmony, in the end "making it a symphony of proportion" (32c). The god takes the four elements and gives them order by giving them form and number (53b). This "likely story" coheres with many different creation myths that describe the act of creation as ordering matter out of disorder and chaos. The fundamental assertion is twofold: 1) the cosmos is ordered, and 2) chaos is bad. Given that the elements themselves are given order, shape, and purpose according to a transcendent ideal, the study of order in the material world is a mirror of the transcendent order of unchanging being.

From this premise, Timaeus gives a geometric and numerical account of the cosmos. In simple terms, he draws ethical implications from the intelligible cosmos, asserting that the *telos* of intelligent creatures is to master their emotions and be just and good, patterning their lives in conformity to the perfect harmony of the cosmic order until they reach a state of virtue (42d). Through our sight, we see the revolution of the cosmos. From that we derive notions of number and time, which is the "path to inquiry into the nature of the universe" culminating in philosophy, the "gift from the gods" (47a–b). Thus, the study of number and cosmology has ethical implications:

> The god invented sight and gave it to us so that we might observe the orbits of intelligence in the universe and apply them to the revolutions of our own understanding....So once we have come to know them and to share in the ability to make correct calculations according to nature, we should stabilize the straying revolutions within ourselves by imitating the completely unstraying revolutions of the god (47c).

The study of number leads to knowledge of the fundamental order of the cosmos, which leads to our ability to not merely behold the Beautiful and the Good, but to put in right order our very souls.

COSMOLOGY AND ETHICS

Cosmology—or astronomy—has often been regarded as the pinnacle of quadrivium studies because it is the culmination of the other three numerical arts: number and extension in space and time. Thus, it is often associated with "the music of the spheres" and is the immediate precursor to philosophy or theology and the study of the sublime. It has also been understood as a natural handmaiden to ethics, for the idea of virtue and order finds a significant justification and imitation in the order of the cosmos—a word which means "ordered whole."

Biblical Cosmology

Even though they didn't have a word for an ordered whole, most ancient cultures had a concept of an order that runs through the universe. For the Egyptians, this was *ma'at*. For the Greeks, it was *themis* or *logos*. For the Hebrews it was wisdom. Remi Brague explains that "this concept would express the way the universe forms a harmonious whole in which man must find his rightful place—the word 'rightful' implying both the idea of right, of harmony, as well as that of justice."[12] For the Greeks it was the wise and just ordering of the universe that provides a model for society to imitate.[13]

On the one hand, Hebrew ethics and religion seem to be understood as a means of maintaining the order of the natural world. As Deuteronomy 28 outlines, proper liturgical and social order leads to blessing and improper order leads to curse. These blessings and curses are understood primarily in natural and cosmological terms and the prophets often take these cosmological images to represent covenant blessing and curses. Falling stars and cosmological disaster, for example, became primary symbols for the consequences of sin. But there is no sense in which the Hebrews thought they had power or influence over the elements of the cosmos; clearly Yahweh is the one who controls these things.

The source of the cosmological link between Hebrew ethics and the natural order is found not in the city or the temple, but in the covenant relationship Yahweh establishes with the Hebrews and the bonds created by covenant obligations. The link between the cosmos and mankind is based on law and covenant, and Yahweh as Creator and sustainer is the one who maintains the cosmological order. Thus, even the seeming chaos of drought and plague and invasion is actually functioning according to a cosmological order guided by the wise providences of Yahweh-Elohim.

Because of the link between cosmology and covenant, the Hebrew cosmology also shares features with Greek philosophy, for the covenant God is also the Creator God, and the wisdom that ordered creation is the same wisdom that leads the Hebrews in covenant faithfulness. This can be seen with a cursory reading of Genesis 1 and Proverbs 8, which is brought together explicitly in Isaiah 45 to reveal the cosmological ethics of the Old Testament.

Genesis 1

One of the primary ways the Genesis narrative speaks of the creation is the act of ordering what is disordered. As Dennis J. McCarthy contends, "Creation cannot be divorced from the concept of chaos," and thus creation is often understood as "ordering," for there always exists within the Hebrew

---

[12] Remi Brague, *The Wisdom of the World*, trans. Teresa Lavender Fagan (Chicago: University of Chicago Press, 2003), 15.
[13] Brague, *Wisdom of the World*, 14–15.

worldview a tension between creation and chaos.[14] Elohim doesn't merely speak the cosmos into existence; he does it in such a way that he forms the formlessness and fills the void, putting number, weight, and measure to *tohu* (formlessness) and *bohu* (void). Through the act of ordering that which was without order, Elohim puts everything in its proper place, harmonious and proportional. The way the opening chapter of Genesis describes the creation process establishes some of the fundamental ethical and covenantal categories that run throughout the rest of Scripture.

Tohu has a variety of meanings ranging from "chaos" to "wilderness" to "formlessness" to "confusion." The word is used twenty times in Scripture, and it is used negatively in every instance. While Elohim is a God of order, *tohu* produces chaos. While Elohim creates verdant growth, *tohu* is a wilderness. While Elohim creates wisdom and understanding (Prov. 8:22–31), *tohu* brings confusion. The presence of *tohu* at the creation of the world indicates that Elohim must in some way re-form the formlessness, creating order from chaos.

Bohu is never positive—it is only used a handful of times in Scripture, each time in reference to the creation event or a reference to a desolate wasteland (Isa. 34:11, Jer. 4:23). Emptiness and void are at the very least a state of being unfinished or uncreated. And it might indicate a type of wild emptiness—something without a name or identity, something without the presence of anything that can be known or named. So for Elohim to create the world, he must in some way fill this emptiness, giving it a name and the

---

[14] James L. Crenshaw, *Urgent Advice and Probing Questions: Collected Writings on Old Testament Wisdom* (Macon: Mercer, 1995), 119. There is a lot of debate among Hebrew scholars about how to understand what the Genesis text is communicating when speaking of *tohu* and *bohu*. John Currid and C. John Collins are correct to argue that Genesis 1 is not presenting a creation narrative akin to the ANE creation narrative of the gods forming order out of eternal, uncreated chaos and matter. Nevertheless, for polemical and redemptive-historical reasons, the Genesis narrative is communicated in a way that closely resembles this familiar creation narrative as a way to represent what Elohim is doing when He creates the cosmos out of nothing. Too often scholars miss the polyvalent meaning embedded in the literary way Scripture describes the indescribable. While maintaining creation *ex nihilo*, the thoughtful reader is challenged to understand the theological implications of Genesis 1 framing the creation in specifically this way. See John Currid, *Against the Gods: The Polemical Theology of the Old Testament* (Wheaton: Crossway, 2013); and C. John Collins, *Genesis 1–4: A Linguistic, Literary, and Theological Commentary* (Phillipsburg: P&R Publishing, 2006).

presence of something to abide within it. He must not only give it shape, but give it meaning and content.

The creation account presents a scene between two enemies competing over the unformed and unfilled earth. On the one hand darkness looms over the deep (presumably in reference to *tohu* and *bohu*). On the other hand, the Spirit of Elohim hovers over the waters (also a reference to *tohu* and *bohu*). These two figures—darkness and Elohim—seem to be pitted against each other, but with decidedly different purposes. Darkness is most often used in Scripture to refer to a state of evil, sin, idolatry, or ignorance. It is Scripture's chief symbol for everything that is wrong with the world and the people who fill it. But while the darkness looms over the unformed and unfilled earth, the Spirit of God "hovers" over the waters as a mother bird hovers over her nest to protect and nurture it (cf. Deut. 32:11).

The stage is set for Elohim to begin the act of fashioning his kingdom and conquering his enemies, which is precisely what he begins doing in verse 3 when he speaks the words "let there be light." And light becomes the first thing Elohim calls "good," establishing the metaphysical and ethical association of goodness and proper order with the Word.

It is significant that these are Elohim's first words of creation because they are in direct opposition to the darkness that is looming over the earth. For Elohim to begin the process of forming the formlessness and filling the void, he must first conquer the darkness that is looming over it. The light pierces the darkness and conquers it. In fact, the darkness could have been vanquished forever if Elohim had not quickly separated the darkness from the light (for we know that light always triumphs over darkness).

After subduing the darkness, he creates the rhythm and order of evening and morning that will forever reflect Elohim's initial act of creation. In this, Elohim forever relegates darkness to the status of a defeated foe, one who daily must review and relive his defeat as morning daily overcomes evening's shadow, embodying in the order of the cosmos a deep ethical and redemptive symbol. This is why Elohim describes the day as "evening and morning" rather than "morning and evening." A day that begins in the evening reflects the beginning of creation, a time of darkness. And the movement from darkness to dawn reflects the victory of light over darkness and day overnight. Daily the conquering King declares his first victory over the darkness that loomed over the uncreated earth. The cosmos itself declares the glory of God (Psalm 19).

Having dealt with the darkness, Elohim then goes about forming the formlessness and filling the void. Many scholars have noted the pattern and structure of Elohim's creative process—a structure that runs counter to the chaos of *tohu* and *bohu*. According to his wisdom, in the first three days of creation Elohim forms kingdoms out of *tohu*: the kingdoms of heaven (day 1), sky and water (day 2), and earth (day 3). In the second three days of creation Elohim fills his kingdoms: the heavens are filled with stars, and the sun and moon are established as "rulers" over this kingdom (day 4); the sky is filled with birds and the seas with fish (day 5); the earth is filled with animals and mankind is established as ruler over the seas and earth (day 6). Having finished his work of conquering his enemies and building his kingdom, Elohim rests on the seventh day as a king would, a declaration that "it is finished." In this whole creation process, Elohim establishes a proper ordering of the cosmos that imbues the creation itself with ethical and redemptive symbolism—one that can be understood and imitated.

Proverbs 8

Proverbs revisits the above theme explicitly, showing how the creation narrative and the cosmological order bear relation to the ethical realm. The precise nature of Lady Wisdom in Proverbs 8 is a hotly debated topic, but a broad understanding of her claims reveals that, at some level, wisdom is the means by which Yahweh established the order of the cosmos. She claims that she was present when Yahweh established the heavens and put boundaries on the sky and the seas and marked out the foundations of the earth. Using this as the basis for her argument, Lady Wisdom calls out to the reader to imitate her: "Hear instruction and be wise… For whoever finds me, finds life" (Prov. 8:33–35). In doing so, Lady Wisdom claims that there is a direct link between the wisdom present in the ordering of the cosmos and the life of wisdom.

In Proverbs 8, Lady Wisdom makes many linguistic connections and allusions to the creation account in Genesis 1—particularly "beginning," "oceans," and establishing the boundaries of the oceans.[15] Because creation and wisdom are closely tied, it is important to recognize the close association creation has with the religious ideas of chaos and worship. Because ordering

---

[15] Tremper Longman III, *How to Read Proverbs* (Downer's Grove: InterVarsity, 2002), 105.

was such an important part of the creation, Yahweh must make great use of Lady Wisdom in is act of ordering the cosmos and subduing chaos. This has both practical and religious implications, for the idea of chaos is distinctly religious in nature. This underscores the theme of worship ubiquitous in Proverbs 1–9, for the choice between the two women in Proverbs 1–9 is specifically the choice between worshiping Yahweh and worshiping idols.[16] Wisdom herself, as an agent against chaos, asserts her dominance over the forces of evil and thus emphasizes her close association with the "way of Yahweh" and the way of covenant worship.

By expressly contending that she existed before creation (8:22–26) and was present at creation (8:27–29), Lady Wisdom lays claim to existing before the world was made crooked by the Fall; she was present when chaos submitted to the rule of God and mankind found delight in his eyes. She observed the "way" of God, and God laid hold of Lady Wisdom and used her to establish his "way." By highlighting her primordial relationship with God, "she is uniquely privileged to have seen God's will for the world from the outset. By implication, therefore, she offers the best way of discerning that will, and of obtaining divine favor."[17]

In short, Wisdom presents herself as the one with the greatest knowledge of God and of the way of covenant faithfulness, so much so that later Jewish writers understood Wisdom as an embodiment of the Torah itself.[18] She associates herself with the creative word and the covenant word of Yahweh, and like a prophet she calls Israel to listen, obey, and love.[19] She delights in the children of man (8:31) and longs that they might love her back so that they can find the way of Yahweh and delight in him as she does (8:20–21; 36–37). In her is life, for she knows the way of Yahweh and walks in the way faithfully, and thus those who find her find life and the covenant blessings of Yahweh (8:35–36). In short, Wisdom was present at the ordering of creation and is an intrinsic link between the order of the cosmos and the

---

[16] Longman, *How to Read Proverbs*, 110.

[17] Stuart Weeks, "The Context and Meaning of Proverbs 8:30a.," *Journal of Biblical Literature* 125, no. 3 (2006): 436–37.

[18] Shimon Bakon, "Two Hymns to Wisdom: Proverbs 8 and Job 28," *Jewish Bible Quarterly* 36, no. 4 (2008): 226. The Midrash states, "The Torah says, 'I was the architectural instrument of the Holy One.'"

[19] Alan Lenzi, "Proverbs 8:22–31: Three Perspectives on Its Composition," *Journal of Biblical Literature* 125, no. 4 (2006): 687–88.

order of the law, such that as one imitates wisdom, one learns how to walk according to covenant faithfulness.

Isaiah 45

Isaiah 45 vividly brings the idea of Genesis 1 and Proverbs 8 together to give a cosmological-ethical call for Israel to return to covenant faithfulness. Yahweh calls on the heavens to rain down righteousness and the earth to sprout salvation (Isa. 45:8), calling on mankind to attend to the ways of Yahweh, for he as Creator has formed them as he formed the ordered cosmos (45:9); he emphasizes that just as he formed the heavens, so he stirs up righteousness and forms a city for himself (45:13–14). His call to covenant faithfulness is rooted in the link between his operation as Creator and covenant maker:

> For thus says the Lord,
> who created the heavens
>   (he is God!),
> who formed the earth and made it
>   (he established it;
> he did not create it empty [*tohu*],
>   he formed it to be inhabited!):
> "I am the Lord, and there is no other.
> I did not speak in secret,
>   in a land of darkness;
> I did not say to the offspring of Jacob,
>   'Seek me in vain [*tohu*].'
> I the Lord speak the truth;
>   I declare what is right (45:18–19 ESV).

Here, referring to *tohu* and darkness at the beginning of creation and his act of ordering the creation, Yahweh calls his people to covenant faithfulness and attendance to wisdom and the way. As Remi Brague notes, "It is not in the chaos preceding creation that [God] must be sought, precisely because that chaos was overcome by the order of creation. One must seek him in the order of the created world, in what is intelligible in that world."[20]

---

[20] Brague, *Wisdom of the World*, 46.

The Hebrew concept of creation and cosmology reveals why attending to the wisdom of the cosmos along with the revealed law of God can lead to covenant faithfulness, for creation and covenant are inextricably linked. Hebrew cosmology welcomes the study of the natural world, for it not only declares the glory of the Ccreator and reflects his handiwork, but it provides the pattern for covenant faithfulness and the way of wisdom that leads to life.

The New Testament

Paul revisits this theme in the New Testament, discussing how Christ delivered man from "the elements of the world," (Gal.4:3, Col. 2:8, 20) providing a new cosmology rooted in Christ as the "heart of creation." The overall implication for Pauline cosmology is that God can in a general sense be known "through the things that are made" (Rom. 1:19) enough to exert a moral influence and provide a basis for natural law (Rom. 1–2), but that God's full revelation of Himself and his "Way" comes through the incarnate Christ, introducing new elements that constitute the ordered life of the believer. Thus, natural and special revelation, being and becoming, creation and new creation, beginning and end are brought together in the person of Christ (Col. 1:15–20). Christ the heart of creation "plays in ten thousand places" and reveals himself by Word and sacrament, through the wisdom of the world and by divine illumination.

MEDIEVAL COSMOLOGICAL ETHICS

The medieval model was a kind of synthesis of Old Testament and New Testament understandings of the cosmos—which emphasized that wisdom and imitation are finally rooted in the Creator and within a covenant—with the Platonic model, which emphasized the orderliness of the cosmos as the root of ethics. The cosmographic constructions of the universe were rooted in the ethical and existential question of "being-in-the-world," not primarily in describing the literal composition and arrangement of the heavenly bodies. Cosmology became axiology.

The cosmological model separated the sublunary from the lunary spheres, which are made of different elements. The stars are associated with angelic beings, and while humans are situated as the highest form of animal in the sublunary realm, the cosmological model creates a moral yearning in them to ascend to the higher realm of the heavenly beings.[21] In this sense, "man's place among all beings is not assigned to him at the outset, but is the result of his freedom to assimilate either into what exists above him, or into that which he ought to overcome."[22] Although this is strange to our sensibilities, "physical realities (stars/earth) are placed alongside living things that are seen as various modes of life or forms of soul ('angels'/plants and animals).”[23]

Man is situated in the world and is himself a microcosm that is ordered according to the same wisdom as the macrocosm. Present within both is the same wisdom from the same Creator, a wisdom and intelligence that leads to imitation of God and communion with him.[24] To summarize the medieval model, man lives in an "ethical cosmos" which leads to developing a "cosmological ethics."

In his commentary on Aristotle, Simplicius (c. 480–560 AD) states that physics is useful because, among other things, it "contributes to leading the superior part of the soul, which is the intellect, toward its perfection—for which a study of theology is particularly valuable; it is an auxiliary for moral virtues; a ladder that leads toward knowledge of God and ideas; and, finally, it incites us to piety and to acts of thanksgiving toward God."[25] In other words, knowledge of God and the ability to act wisely is mediated through a knowledge of the things that God has made: "It is through the mediation of the world that man becomes what he must be, and consequently, what he is. Wisdom thus defined is indeed a 'wisdom of the world.'"[26] Thus, contemplation of the world is a precursor to ethical action.[27] At its most basic, this is because ethical action is carried out in the *polis*, which is structured on the order of the cosmos and is "cosmopolitan" in its literal sense.[28]

---

[21] Brague, *Wisdom of the World*, 91–93.

[22] Brague, *Wisdom of the World*, 92.

[23] Brague, *Wisdom of the World*, 92.

[24] Brague, *Wisdom of the World*, 93–94.

[25] Simplicius, quoted in Brague, *Wisdom of the World*, 116.

[26] Brague, *Wisdom of the World*, 121.

[27] Brague, *Wisdom of the World*, 121.

[28] Brague, *Wisdom of the World*, 124.

We can see this worked out in the way Ptolemy (c. 100–170 AD) and other astronomers discussed the significance of their science. Ptolemy wrote the *Almagest* not merely to discuss the scientific understanding of how planets orbited each other. His main goal was the contemplation of beauty, leading to worship and virtue:

> We accordingly thought it up to us so to train our actions even in the application of the imagination as not to forget in whatever things we happen upon the consideration of their beautiful and well-ordered disposition, and to indulge in meditation mostly for the exposition of many beautiful theorems and especially of those specifically called mathematical.[29]

In other words, the mathematical arts are fundamentally the exploration of beauty and order, mirrored in the world, leading to a greater understanding of the Love that moves the stars.

Ptolemy sides with Aristotle in delineating three kinds of sciences: physical, mathematical, and theological. Theological science studies immaterial being and first causes, moving to the indivisible and unchanging God. The physical sciences study the material universe, the world of the senses. The mathematical sciences investigate "forms and local motions, seeking figure, number, and magnitude, and also place, time, and similar things" (1.1). This science is a mediating science between the other two, "not only because it can be conceived both through the senses and without the senses, but also because it is an accident in absolutely all beings both mortal and immortal, changing with those things that ever change, according to their inseparable form, and preserving unchangeable the changelessness of form in things eternal and of ethereal nature" (1.1). Here, Ptolemy expresses more clearly Nichomachus's claim that the mathematical arts are a bridge between the material and spiritual worlds, the methods by which nature can proclaim the reality which is found "deep down things."[30]

Ptolemy looks to arithmetic and geometry as leading the way to astronomy, which is focused on studying "divine and heavenly things; it is

---

[29] Ptolemy, *Almagest*, trans. R. Catesby Taliaferro, in *The Great Books of the Western World*, ed. Mortimer Adler, 2nd ed., vol. 15 (USA: Encyclopedia Britannica, 1993), 1.1.

[30] This phrase is from Gerard Manley Hopkins's poem "God's Grandeur."

the only [discipline] concerned with the study of things which are always what they are, and therefore able itself to be always what it is....For that special mathematical theory would most readily prepare the way to the theological" (1.1). Thus, in studying the order and beauty of the stars, one is equipped to contemplate the divine. Not only this, but such study moves the soul toward virtue (1.1). Understanding the *ethos* of the cosmos leads to love of that order and from love to imitation.

Even though he introduced a rival cosmology that upended the Ptolemaic cosmological map, Copernicus (1473–1543) agreed that study of cosmology as "the head of all the liberal arts and the one most worthy of a free man" would lead to virtue and right ordering of the soul.[31] In a beautiful passage worth quoting at length, Copernicus maintains the ethical and theological implications of diligently studying the order and beauty of the stars.[32] Through the things God has made, he draws men to himself, preparing them for deeper understanding and contemplation of the Creator by kindling the love and wonder and image necessary for deeper knowledge revealed through God's Word.

Because of these ideas, the medieval model of education greatly emphasized the study of the quadrivium, culminating in cosmology for the sake of theology and ethics. But at the same time, Christianity has always felt a tension with this idea because it can slip into idolatry—worship and imitation of the creation rather than the Creator—and a lack of emphasis on the revealed will of God through the law and Scriptures and ultimately Christ. This is why the quadrivium should always be joined with the trivium, just as the sacraments are joined with the preached Word. God is known through his creation and his covenant Word; God is seen "in the mirror of the world" and the face of Christ; we learn to see the Good as it presents itself before us in image and idea, number and word; the ordered cosmos is a kind of "cosmonomy," reinforced by our conscience, while the law is a kind of "logonomy," reinforced by the spoken word.

Another significant reason for the ancient and medieval emphasis on the quadrivium is the reality that we need to be trained in our affections and our thinking. To know or love things like God or the Good, we need to start

---

[31] Copernicus, *The Revolutions of the Heavenly Spheres*, trans. Charles Glenn Wallis, in *The Great Books of the Western World*, ed. Mortimer Adler, 2nd ed., vol. 15 (USA: Encyclopedia Britannica, 1993), 150.
[32] Copernicus, *Revolutions*, 150.

with learning to know or love small things. We are not born with the knowledge of God or the natural ability to love and imitate him. The quadrivium is thus a tool in two different senses: it trains the mind to be equipped to know the more fundamental and deep things of reality. It also trains the affections to love these things. The Platonic Ladder of love and the relationship of the quadrivium to beauty is a prime example of this. This provides the reason for the emphasis on quadrivium studies among Christian theologians in the early centuries of the Church.

QUADRIVIUM STUDIES IN EARLY CHRISTIANITY

Many Christian theologians have seen how the quadrivium should be embraced as a means of knowing, loving, and imitating God. Even by the second century, Christians were already exploring the uses of the quadrivium in Christian education.

Clement of Alexandria

From all accounts, Clement of Alexandria (c. 150–c. 215 AD) was the earliest proponent of applying Greek philosophy to Christian education. In his *Stromateis*, he lays out the shape of Christian education and explains how philosophy and the liberal arts can be a "preparatory science" for Christianity. What is central for Clement is that the liberal arts and philosophy train the mind so that it has the ability to comprehend divine truths. He says that we become "ready" to receive revelation due largely to this "preliminary training"; and "this training must be in perceiving the intelligible objects with the mind."[33] He delineates their nature into three kinds: number, size, and definition. Thus, through the study of number, the mind is tutored and equipped to contemplate the divine—to know God.

Rhabanus Maurus (Eighth and Ninth Centuries)

Rhabanus Maurus (c. 780–856 AD) was a student of Alcuin and helped lead the Carolingian Renaissance in the eighth and ninth centuries. It is from these

---

[33] Clement of Alexandria, *Stromateis*, trans. John Ferguson, in *The Great Tradition: Classic Readings on What It Means to Be an Educated Human Being*, ed. Richard M. Gamble (Wilmington: ISI, 2012), 161.

two that the medieval university developed its liberal arts curriculum. What is intriguing, however, is how Maurus discusses the usefulness of the quadrivium for training the clergy. In his work *The Education of the Clergy*, he begins by showing how a knowledge of Scripture and the faith enables one to discover more knowledge: "Every truth, which is discovered by any one, is recognized as true by the truth itself through the mediation of the truth."[34] Here, Maurus emphasizes that liberal education begins and ends with theology; it is "faith seeking understanding." In this sense, the liberal arts are not the beginning nor the end of proper study, but they are the bridge from faith to faith. He then elucidates how the quadrivium can aid in the service of the Christian and particularly the minister.

In discussing arithmetic, he says that it does two things: 1) it enables the mind to turn away from the fleshly and material to higher, spiritual, formal realities; 2) it also kindles the affections, giving the desire to search out the mysteries and beauties of divine truths. He states, "The holy Fathers were right in advising those eager for knowledge to cultivate arithmetic, because in large measure it turns the mind from fleshly desires, and furthermore awakens the wish to comprehend what with God's help we can merely receive with the heart."[35] The reason for these two things is that number is the means by which God made the world. Quoting the Book of Wisdom 11:21, he reminds his readers, "Thou hast ordained all things by measure, number, and weight."[36] Because of this, the cosmos is a means of loving God and ordering oneself properly. The cosmos as organized into a harmonious whole embodies eternal truths that kindle our hearts and prepare our minds to desire to know and love God. Similarly, Maurus claims that geometry studies the underlying forms of God's created things; music shapes and fashions a beautiful and well-ordered life; and astronomy is the contemplation of the "sublime structure" and mystery of the cosmos. Music can lead to greater knowledge of God and to a beautiful and well-ordered life.[37]

---

[34] Rhabanus Maurus, *The Education of the Clergy*, in *The Great Tradition*, 250.
[35] Maurus, *Education of the Clergy*, 252.
[36] Maurus, *Education of the Clergy*, 253.
[37] Maurus, *Education of the Clergy*, 253.

Hugh of St. Victor

In his *Didascalicon* and *De Sacramentis*, Hugh of St. Victor (c. 1096–1141) also contends that the liberal arts, and the quadrivium in particular, are essential for Christian formation and theological knowledge. Speaking of knowledge, there are two kinds: knowledge of words (trivium) and knowledge of things (quadrivium).[38] Knowledge of the quadrivium leads to an understanding of the sacramental nature of reality as well as the Christian sacraments specifically. It also helps the mind grasp the meaning of Scripture:

> It is clear that all the arts of the natural world serve divine science, and that the lower wisdom—rightly ordered—leads to the higher. [The trivium serves the literal meaning of Scripture; the quadrivium serves the allegorical and tropological meaning.] Allegory teaches right faith…tropology teaches good work. In these consist knowledge of truth and love of virtue; and this is the true restoration of man.[39]

Thus, the mind is equipped by the quadrivium to understand spiritual meanings of Scripture, for number is like the spiritual meaning embedded within physical reality. As the mind is trained to engage with abstract number to see the underlying substance of material things, so the mind can see the underlying spiritual significance of the literal words of Scripture.[40]

---

[38] Hugh of St. Victor, *De Sacramentis*, trans. Roy J. Deferrari (Ex Fontibus, 2016), 5.

[39] Hugh of St. Victor, *De Sacramentis*, 5.

[40] For further exploration into the medieval understanding of the quadrivium, Boethius is a wonderful resource. As he was one of the fathers of quadrivium studies in the early Middle Ages, much scholarship has devoted itself to his work and its relationship to the quadrivium. See: Henry Chadwick, *Boethius: The Consolations of Music, Logic, Theology, and Philosophy* (Oxford: Clarendon Press, 1981); and Michael Fournier, "Boethius and the Consolation of the Quadrivium," *Medievalia et Humanistica* 34, ed. Paul Maurice Clogan (2008): 1–21.

CONCLUSION

At its heart, the quadrivium is an investigative study that serves those who wish to know God, love God, and imitate God by means of the things that he has made. As philosophers and theologians of the past wrestled with the means by which we can know things and be virtuous, they constantly returned to the quadrivium as one essential means of doing this. This conviction flows from a tacit recognition of the fact that the universe is an ordered whole, patterned after the Goodness and Beauty of the Creator; that the cosmos speaks through the language of number, revealing some of the most profound truths that abide at the heart of being; that mankind must be equipped with tools in order for him to learn wisdom and practice virtue; and that the quadrivium is a means of knowing the truth, kindling a desire for the love and beauty at the heart of Creation, and equipping the soul to ascend. It is not the end nor is it the beginning, but it is a mediating way that man does well to walk in order to reach his ultimate end in the knowledge and love of God. Classical educators looking to revive the study of the seven liberal arts would do well to consider returning the quadrivium to its rightful place.

BIBLIOGRAPHY

Adler, Mortimer. "Quantity." In *The Syntopicon of the Great Books of the Western World*, edited by Mortimer Adler, 2nd ed., vol. 2. USA: Encyclopedia Britannica, 1993.

Aquinas, Thomas. *Summa Theologica*. NewAdvent.org.

Bakon, Shimon. "Two Hymns to Wisdom: Proverbs 8 and Job 28." *Jewish Bible Quarterly* 36, no. 4 (2008): 222–30.

Brague, Remi. *The Wisdom of the World*. Translated by Teresa Lavender Fagan. Chicago: University of Chicago Press, 2003.

Chadwick, Henry. *Boethius: The Consolations of Music, Logic, Theology, and Philosophy*. Oxford: Clarendon Press, 1981.

Clement. *Stromateis*. Translated by John Ferguson. In *The Great Tradition: Classic Readings on What It Means to Be an Educated Human Being*, edited by Richard M. Gamble, 169–75. Wilmington: ISI, 2012.

Collins, C. John. *Genesis 1–4: A Linguistic, Literary, and Theological Commentary*. Phillipsburg: P&R Publishing, 2006.

Copernicus. *The Revolutions of the Heavenly Spheres*. Translated by Charles Glenn Wallis. In *The Great Books of the Western World*, edited by Mortimer Adler, 2nd ed., vol. 15, 505–844. USA: Encyclopedia Britannica, 1993.

Currid, John. *Against the Gods: The Polemical Theology of the Old Testament*. Wheaton: Crossway, 2013.

Crenshaw, James L. *Urgent Advice and Probing Questions: Collected Writings on Old Testament Wisdom*. Macon: Mercer, 1995.

Dante. *Paradiso*. Translated by Anthony Esolen. USA: Random House, 2014.

Fournier, Michael. "Boethius and the Consolation of the Quadrivium." *Medievalia et Humanistica* 34 (2008): 1–21.

Hugh of St. Victor. *De Sacramentis*. Translated by Roy J. Deferrari. Ex Fontibus, 2016.

Lenzi, Alan. "Proverbs 8:22–31: Three Perspectives on Its Composition." *Journal of Biblical Literature* 125, no. 4 (2006): 687–714.

Longman III, Tremper. *How to Read Proverbs*. Downer's Grove: InterVarsity, 2002.

Maurus, Rhabanus. "The Education of the Clergy." In *The Great Tradition:*

Classic Readings on What It Means to Be an Educated Human Being, ed. Richard M. Gamble, 250–55. Wilmington: ISI, 2012.

Murphy, Roland E. "The Personification of Wisdom." In *Wisdom in Ancient Israel*, edited by John Day, Robert P. Gordon, and H. G. M. Williamson, 222–33. Cambridge: Cambridge University Press, 1995.

Nichomachus. *Introduction to Arithmetic*. Translated by Martin L. D'ooge. In *The Great Books of the Western World*, ed. Mortimer Adler, 2nd ed., vol. 10, 599–636. USA: Encyclopedia Britannica, 1993.

Plato. *Philebus*. Translated by Dorothea Frede. In *Plato: Complete Works*, edited by John M. Cooper. Indianapolis: Hackett Publishing Company, 1997.

———. *Republic*. Translated by G. M. A. Grube, revised by C. D. C. Reeve. In *Plato: Complete Works*, edited by John M. Cooper. Indianapolis: Hackett Publishing Company, 1997.

———. *Symposium*. Translated by Alexander Nehamas and Paul Woodruff. In *Plato: Complete Works*, edited by John M. Cooper. Indianapolis: Hackett Publishing Company, 1997.

———. *Timaeus*. Translated by Donald J. Zeyl. In *Plato: Complete Works*, edited by John M. Cooper. Indianapolis: Hackett Publishing Company, 1997.

Ptolemy. *Almagest*. Translated by R. Catesby Taliaferro. In *The Great Books of the Western World*, ed. Mortimer Adler, 2nd ed., vol. 15, 1–480. USA: Encyclopedia Britannica, 1993.

Weeks, Stuart. "The Context and Meaning of Proverbs 8:30a." *Journal of Biblical Literature* 125, no. 3 (2006): 433–42.

VI:
FORM, CONTENT, AND PURPOSE: REFLECTIONS ON EARLY MODERN EDUCATION FOR TODAY

Michael J. Lynch, Delaware Valley Classical School

INTRODUCTION

IN MAY 2021, Princeton University announced it was no longer going to require Latin or Greek for its Classics undergraduate program.[1] The stated reason—as with many of the recent decisions higher education has been making regarding the lowering of their standards—is diversity. Obviously, these changes to the landscape of higher education don't occur in a vacuum. Many of them are, no doubt, symptoms of what Anthony Kronman and others have deemed to be the egalitarianization (or democratization) of higher education, valuing diversity over and against excellence.[2] This paper, however, will not examine modern education. Experienced educators are already well-aware of its problems. In this essay, we will rather sketch out a world in which every university student was required not just to have a working knowledge of Latin and Greek to get into a classics program, but a level of fluency in those languages which almost certainly would exceed the great majority of modern-day classics professors' fluency by the time said student entered into university at the age of fifteen.

---

[1] Carlett Spike, "Curriculum Changed to Add Flexibility, Race and Identity Track," *Princeton Alumni Weekly*, May 2021, accessed March 29, 2022, https://paw.princeton.edu/article/curriculum-changed-add-flexibility-race-and-identity-track.

[2] Anthony T. Kronman, *The Assault on American Excellence* (New York: Free Press, 2019).

The goal is modest. We will sketch a fairly detailed picture of early modern education in the hopes that we might be able to examine why it is that they did what they did, which ought to better highlight ways in which our education system has changed in 300 or so years since, for better or worse. At the end of this essay, we will try to highlight a few significant areas of disharmony between modern education and early modern education.

EARLY MODERN EDUCATION

At the outset, we must make some prefatory comments from the vantage point of a historian about discussing early modern education. First, generalizations are a must here—not only because education in any given locale such as Germany, France, England, and Italy would have looked different, but because educational pedagogies, especially in the lower schools, were constantly modified and adapted to the changing landscape of university education, seeing that the former were largely tied to the necessities of the latter. Because of this diversity, our sketch will be largely limited to early modern *English* education, generally between 1550 and 1700, with reference to some broader European sources at time.[3] Second, we must be aware of the limits of studying such educational systems given that the most accessible documents—at least for lower school education—are the official documents related to the grammar schools. As we know, *theory*, which we glean, for example, from the writings of headmasters and school charters, can often differ quite substantially from the *practice* of schools and teachers. This normal dissonance is often only recognized through reading firsthand accounts from the period. We might read, for instance, that a certain grammar school in London required that boys speak Latin on their way to and from school. Does that mean they actually did? Of course, it doesn't. And we do, in fact, read that because such a rule was not so easily enforced, certain students may have been actually employed by some schools to spy on their peers and tattle on them! Theory and practice do not always coincide.

---

[3] Much of my sketch of early modern English grammar school education, as well as the mention of various primary sources cited in this essay, is based on Francis Watson's magisterial *The English Grammar Schools to 1660: Their Curriculum and Practice* (Cambridge: Cambridge University Press, 1908).

PETTY SCHOOL AND GRAMMAR SCHOOLS

Speaking generally for England at least, there were two schools one might have attended before a student went off to university. First, he could have attended a petty or elementary school (*schola trivialis*), which had one simple task: to teach a child to read. This job, which was in the medieval and early part of the early modern period the job of a grammar school, was deemed too tedious and time-consuming for grammar school headmasters. Thus, local towns formed schools where children were taught to read in English. Children usually attended the petty school at the age of five or so.

After the elementary or petty school, one would attend a grammar school, at the age of seven or eight. Given that the child needed to practice his reading, little easy readers were written to teach manners and basic virtue. Note this extract from one such easy reader discouraging walking about in church; it's written in verse:

> IN seat sit thou quiet, and walke not about,
> For tis most vnséemely, without any doubt,
> Tis fit in a faire, or in some market towne,
> And not in Gods house for to walke vp and downe.
> The Church is ordained for sermons, orations,
> And prayers diuine for the soules recreations.
> And not like a play house, vnhallowed to be,
> Despising the reuerence to Gods Maiestie.
> Giue eare most attentiue to what thou shalt finde,
> For Gods word is light to the godly in minde,
> Great ease commeth (out of the reuerent text)
> For troubled in heart and in conscience perplex.[4]

Of course, perhaps no writer on education was more influential in the sixteenth and seventeenth centuries across Europe than Desiderius Erasmus along with his famous work *De civilitate morum puerilium* (*About the Cultivation of the Manners of Boys*), which was translated into half a dozen languages, including twice into English in the sixteenth century.[5] Even the famous

---

[4] Richard West, *The schoole of vertue, the second part: or, The young schollers paradice Contayning verie good precepts, wholesom[e] instructions, the high-way to good manners, dieting of children, and brideling their appetites. Godly graces, and prayers. Verse fit for all children to learne, and the elder sort to obserue* (London: Edward Griffin, 1619), fol. B4ʳ.

[5] Desiderius Erasmus, *De Civilitate Morum Puerilium* (Leipzig: Nickel Schmidt, 1535).

educator Charles Hoole, still in 1660, recommended the reading of this little work by Erasmus.[6] Erasmus argues in the preface to this aforementioned work four distinct ends in the education of youth.[7] First, it ought to instill the seeds of piety. Second, it ought to impart a knowledge and love for the liberal studies (*liberales disciplinae*). Third, a child should be instructed in his duties of life. Finally, he ought to be taught the customs and manners of civility. Both the petty schools and grammar school educators undoubtedly would have agreed.

THE AIMS OF GRAMMAR SCHOOLS

Piety

We can identify a few ends besides the Erasmian ones mentioned above for these grammar schools. First and foremost, these schools had a practical aim: to prepare a student for university by the age of around fifteen. This preparation would include a couple subordinate ends. First, the continuation of virtue formation and piety were essential. Almost every text which would have been read was read in such a way as to inculcate the cardinal and theological virtues. Accordingly, young students, beginning their practice with Latin, would learn the Lord's Prayer, the Apostle's Creed, or the Decalogue in Latin. These books often began with the simple Latin of creeds and prayers and would eventually move to more complicated verse. The great Lutheran pedagogue and scholar Phillip Melanchthon, e.g., in his *Enchiridion Elementorum Puerilium* or *A Handbook of Basics for Youths*, begins with the *Pater Noster*, works its way through various biblical material, including an extended reading of the Sermon on the Mount and Romans 12, then to a few Psalms in verse, and finally introduces some of the classic authors, like Plautus, Ausonius, and Ovid.[8] All the chosen texts have in view virtuous living, whether they be Christian or classical.

An early modern boy could not escape the emphasis on piety and good manners even in his Latin grammar book—the official Latin grammar of

---

[6] Erasmus, *De Civilitate*, fols. A2^r–A2^v.

[7] Charles Hoole, *The Petty-Schoole*, in *A New Discovery of the Old Art of Teaching Schoole* (London: J. T., 1660), 33.

[8] Philip Melanchthon, *Enchiridion Elementorum Puerilium* (1534).

early modern England was William Lily's *Latin Grammar*.[9] The beginning 86-line poem entitled *Carmen de Moribus* [A Song About Manners], which every little boy would translate and memorize in Latin near the beginning of his journey through Lily's Grammar, commands the would be "student of mine [i.e., Lily]" to "go to church and worship God."[10] When the student is sent off to school, he is commanded to "put aside [his] idleness" and not sluggishly delay his arrival. He is to greet his teacher and fellow peers and sit down unless told otherwise. Among such practical advice are many maxims which, no doubt, a teacher would turn to quite regularly. For example: *Nil tam difficile est, quod non solertia vincat.* ("Nothing is so difficult, which skill [or cleverness] cannot overcome.") Or, take this James-like maxim, *Est vitae, ac pariter ianua lingua necis.* (Language is equally a door of life as it is a door of death). In other words, a student needs to take great care of the language he uses, lest he curse his peers, etc.

Arithmetic

Another subordinate aim for these grammar schools was the practical goal of teaching children the basics of arithmetic so they could compute numbers in their commercial endeavors. Indeed, even today we want to make sure that the innkeeper or bartender isn't ripping us off. While grammar schools did not seem to go far beyond basic arithmetic, they or the petty school often did teach mathematics at a basic level.

Latin

Yet, the most important goal of grammar school education in the service of university preparation was mastering Latin. The grammar school was centered on this goal. The *sine qua non* of university studies was Latin and the grammar school was the means of acquiring it. After memorizing some basic catechetical pieces, such as the Creed, the Decalogue, etc. in Latin and English, the student would begin his first school form (out of six), wherein

---

[9] There are many editions. William Lily, *A Short Introduction of Grammar: Generally to be Used: Compiled and Set Forth for the Bringing Up of All Those that Intend to Attain to the Knowledge of the Latine Tongue* (John Norton, Printer to the Kings Maiesty in Latine, Greeke and Hebrew, 1608).

[10] Lily, *A Short Introduction of Grammar*, [*ad finem* of the Accidence].

he was required to master his accidence. The accidence, which was the very first formal part of grammar education, explained in English (and remember, students had only been reading English for a couple years) the parts of speech applied to Latin. In the accidence, one is introduced to the noun declensions, the basic terminology necessary to learn Latin (and I might add, English) grammar, such as what an infinitive is, the various verbal moods, tenses, and conjugations, the nature of participles, etc. Finally, the accidence covers prosody, or how to properly pronounce words. Accordingly, they were taught vowel quantity, length, etc. The grammarians (that is, the grammar school teachers) consistently emphasized the necessity to learn the accidence *ad unguem* (precisely).[11] As one historian put it, the method was to "learn but little at a time, and that little perfectly."[12] It should be borne in mind that this accidence served a dual purpose—it also indirectly taught the children the grammar of their own language, albeit by means of learning Latin grammar.

Many teachers supplemented this accidence with the memorization of *sententiae pueriles* or other basic Latin maxims. Moreover, it was a widespread practice to test the students regularly on the accidence (and indeed on all the other grammar they would learn) via a question-and-answer format. So, for example, in one of the many supplements published for Lily's accidence and grammar, the first question begins with some form of "what are the 8 parts of speech?"[13] It then moves on through what is a noun, how many cases are there, etc. Charles Hoole's 1651 *An Easie Entrance to the Latine Tongue* summarizes well the types of things a first year Grammar student would learn: 1) The Grounds of Grammar; 2) Common Vocab (which was best found in Comenius's *Orbis Pictus*)[14]; 3) Some basic proverbs or maxims which illustrated the grammar rules (such as noun-verb number agreement and adjectival agreement in case, number, and gender), which Lily calls the Concordes (i.e., the final part of the accidence, also in English), etc.[15]

---

[11] E.g., John Brinsley the Elder, *Ludus Literarius: Or The Grammar Schoole* (London: Thomas Man, 1622), 86.

[12] Watson, *The English Grammar Schools to 1660*, 293.

[13] E.g., John Stockwood, *Disputatiuncularum Grammaticalium Libellus, ad Puerorum in Scholis* (London: Johannes Battersbie, 1619), fol. B2^r.

[14] Johann Amos Comenius, *Orbis Sensualium Pictus Quadrilinguis...* (Nuremberg: Michael and Johannes Friderich Endter, 1666).

[15] Charles Hoole, *An Easie Entrance to the Latine Tongue* (London: William Du-gard, 1649).

The second form of grammar school instruction began to draw from the exclusively Latin part of Lily's grammar (that is, the Latin instruction was itself in Latin).[16] In this form especially, grammarians worked very hard at the goal of speaking Latin. To that end, they studied various *colloquia* which would often be in both English and Latin, to help introduce various common sayings for spoken Latin. One of the ways for learning vocabulary is found in the Rivington Grammar School Statues of 1566:

> As the young scholar is thus learning to decline a noun and a verb, the Usher [or schoolmaster] shall daily exercise him with diversity of words in every comparison, declension, gender, tense, and conjugation, teaching him the English of every such Latin word; and examine him oft what is Latin for every such thing, that by this means he and others that hear may learn what everything is called in Latin , and so be more ready to understand every word, what it signifieth in English, when they shall come to construction. As first to begin with Latin words for every part of a man and his apparel; of a house and household stuff, as bedding, kitching, buttery, meats, beasts, herbs, trees, flowers, birds, fishes, with all parts of them; virtues, vices, merchandise, and all occupations; as weavers, tanners, carpenters, ploughers, wheelwrights, tailors, tilers, and shoemakers; and cause them to write every word that belongs to one thing, together in order. And if this be done often and loud, that every one may hear and give ear, they will strive who shall learn and remember most Latin words, and will rejoice in it, one opposing another who can do the best.[17]

Note the express desire to breed competition near the end. I'll have more to say about that at the end of my essay.

The third form—usually nine- and ten-year-olds—was focused especially on reading proficiency and speed. Since schools were supposed to inculcate piety, prayers were always an essential element of grammar instruction. Notably, one of the key texts for seventeenth-century grammar school boys in England (and, no doubt, elsewhere) was the Lutheran Johann Gerhard's *Prayers and Meditations*, which was published in England numerous

---

[16] Lily, "Brevissima Institutio," in *A Short Introduction of Grammar*.

[17] As cited in Watson, *The English Grammar Schools to 1660*, 384–85.

times in both English and Latin.[18] Along with the reading of many other books like this, they were also often required to translate from English into Latin something like William Perkins's *The Foundation of Christian Religion*, which was a forty-page summary of the Christian faith in question-and-answer form.[19]

It might be worth pausing for a moment to observe that spoken Latin was one of the primary vehicles for the learning of Latin. In fact, grammar schools all across England (again, not to mention, Europe) forbid grammar educators, and even the latter form students, from speaking anything but Latin (or Greek and Hebrew, where schools also taught those). Indeed, at some grammar schools, they would put on Latin plays each winter to the end of furthering the student's proficiency. Melanchthon, whom I've already mentioned, wrote of the Latin playwright Terence:

> Hardly any book is more worthy to be in the hands of all mankind. In exact adjustment of the expression to the thought, he has surpassed them all. If St. Chrysostom delighted in Aristophanes (doubtless as a model of eloquence), how much more is Terence to be prized, whose pieces are free from the disgusting grossness of the Greek poet, and whose style is even more perfect. Therefore, I exhort schoolmasters to recommend this author in the most pressing way to young students. For he seems to me to form the judgment on affairs of the world better than most of the books of philosophers. And no other author will teach the boys to speak Latin with equal purity, or train them to a style which will stand them in better stead.[20]

Apparently, the humanist Johann Sturm, who founded a famous grammar school in Strasburg, took Melanchthon's advice quite seriously as he is said

---

[18] Johann Gerhard, *Meditationes Sacrae* (Leiden: The Elseviers' Printing House, 1629).

[19] William Perkins, *The Foundation of Christian Religion Gathered into Sixe Principles* (London: Thomas Orwin, 1591).

[20] Quoted in Charles Stuart Parker, "On the History of Classical Education," in *Essays on a Liberal Education*, ed. F. W. Farrar (London: Macmillan and Co., 1867), 33. If anyone finds the original Latin, let me know!

to have put on the production of all the plays of Terence and Plautus, with the older children performing and the younger watching.[21]

Another avenue a grammar educator used to teach spoken Latin was the very popular *colloquia*, which typically took the form of either a teacher and the pupil or two pupils discussing every part of daily life (and I suspect that modern historians often overlook these valuable *colloquia* as vivid descriptions of daily life in various parts of Europe because they are in Latin). One such popular German grammar school *colloquium* comes from the 1525 *Confabulationes tironum litterariorum* (*Conversations of Young Schoolboys*).[22] Containing 123 short dialogues on the life of German schoolboys, they cover the full range of life as a grammar student. The very first dialogue discusses why Latin is difficult, and why the language is called Latin. I'd be remiss not to make mention of the comment that one boy makes, "Nisi quis semper loquatur Latine, aegre addiscet" ("Unless a person always speaks in Latin, he or she will scarcely learn Latin").[23] Most are clearly educational, with an emphasis on vocabulary acquisition (e.g., the dialogues on morning, afternoon, and evening greetings or conversations about the various seasons), but almost all of them incorporate humorous elements, usually added near the end of the dialogue.

In the preface to the book, the author, Hermannus Schottenius Hessus notes that this was intended for his own students and "those who are intellectually infants, and who have not yet started upon the Latin language nor attempted it with their first words."[24] A great amount of these sort of *colloquia* were published in early modern Europe. They were universally popular in grammar education.

Once students moved into the higher forms—their fifth and sixth forms—they begin to read more difficult Latin, or what were called the higher authors, which included Virgil, Ovid, Livy, Cicero, Horace, Persius, Juvenal, et al. Interestingly, they were also regularly employed to help the younger students with their own Latin, asking them various questions related to Latin grammar and the accompanying grammatical and syntactical rules. They also practiced reading Latin with the younger students, making them

---

[21] Johann Sturm, "Book I," *Classicarum Epistolarum Libri Tres* (Strassburg, Germany: Josias Rihelius, 1565).

[22] Hermannus Schottennius, *Confabulationes Tironum Litterariorum* (1544).

[23] Schottennius, *Confabulationes*, A2ᵛ.

[24] Schottennius, *Confabulationes*, A1ᵛ.

translate the Latin (according to very strict rules) and then, practicing what is called double translation, demanding that students translate the carefully formed English back into Latin.[25] One rule instilled in the older students for the reading of difficult texts was to ask "Quis, cui, causa, locus, quo tempore, prima sequela."[26] Finally, these older students would be required to give Latin orations on various questions or topics chosen at the discretion of the teacher. A student might have to discuss the morality of Lucretia's suicide while another discussed whether or not the pithos of Diogones (the large jar that Diogones had apparently slept in)—a sign of poverty—was preferable to Alexander's throne.[27]

The older students not only helped the younger students and continued to work on Latin, but they also often began to learn Greek and Hebrew at these higher forms. At the grammar school, Greek would include Homer, Pindar, Xenophon, Euripides, Sophocles, Aristophanes, et al. In this way, they were truly fulfilling the chief aim of early modern grammar education—to give them the linguistic tools to do any university work.

UNIVERSITY EDUCATION

Much more could be said, but it is necessary to say something about university education. As noted earlier, a young man would often enter university at around the age of fifteen—though there are many instances of those attending university both later and earlier. John Owen, for example, matriculated at the age of twelve or thirteen. The curriculum was largely left up to the college tutor—playing a paternal role—who was assigned to the young man. The day would begin between 5:00 and 7:00 a.m. with a brief chapel service; then after breakfast until around 11:00, students would attend lectures or study on their own. After an hour lunch, they would spend an hour for recreation; and then at around 1:00 PM, afternoon studies would commence for two or three hours. Students would spend the rest of the day

---

[25] Cf. William E. Miller, "Double Translation in English Humanistic Education," *Studies in the Renaissance* (Cambridge: Cambridge University Press, 1963), 10:163–74.

[26] W. T. Master, *Lily, Improved, Corrected, and Explained* (London: R. Bentley, 1696), 139.

[27] John Clarke, *Formulae Oratoriae, in Usum Scholarum Concinnatae* (London: Robert Milbourn, 1637), 248–50.

in either entertainment or rest before the tutor would engage his five or so students in conversation and prayers before bed.

Because of the diversity and fluidity of university curriculum in the early modern period, we will focus on one very famous course of study laid out by Richard Holdsworth, who was Master of Emmanuel College at Cambridge and also a member of the Westminster Assembly.[28] Holdsworth envisioned the four-year college student studying according to a quarterly schedule of morning and afternoon study. Thus, for year one, the student would spend the mornings studying what amounts to be the medieval curriculum beginning with logic and the afternoons on the classical authors and classical literature—of course, in their original Latin and Greek respectively. During the mornings of the first quarter (January, February, and March), Holdsworth recommends the student to read one minor logic text and then a major one; in other words, an introductory text and a more advanced one. Giving detailed instructions for every part of the curriculum, Holdsworth begins: "This [that is, reading the logic texts] will give you the grounds of Logick, and therefore as a groundworke must be gott very perfectly, and exactly."[29] Holdsworth compares this beginning with a grammar student's introduction to Latin and the necessity to learn one's Latin grammar perfectly. Holdsworth demands that the student read through the introductory or smaller logic text twice through before moving on to the larger, more advanced one. After spending two months on the first logic text, the student is to read the second logic text while noting in a notebook how the larger logic text answers such questions as where do we get the term 'logic,' what are its ends and uses, why is logic an art rather than a *scientia*, etc. In the second quarter, the student is to continue studying logic in the morning, comparing other logic texts he can get his hands on with the major one he read the previous quarter; in the last month of the second quarter a third logic text is to be fully read. The third quarter morning is to be dedicated to controversies in logic, and finally, in the fourth quarter, the student should begin to study ethics after a similar manner. In the following three years, the morning quarters cover: physics, metaphysics, natural history, and Aristotle's

---

[28] Richard Holdsworth, "Directions for a Student in the Universitie," *The Intellectual Development of John Milton*, ed. Harris Francis Fletcher (Urbana: University of Illinois Press, 1961), 2:623–55.

[29] Holdsworth, "Directions for a Student," 634.

major works (the *Organon, Physics, Ethics, On the Soul, On the Heavens, Meteorology*), concluding with a final quarter devoted to theology.

In the afternoons the student was to dedicate himself to reading Latin and Greek history, oratory, and poetry. The first quarter begins with one of the only English books on the list, Thomas Godwyn's *Roman Antiquities*.[30] This book summarized in 270 pages the history, customs, etc. of the Roman people. Holdsworth clearly realized (as he himself says) that reading the various Latin and Greek classics with some background in Greco-Roman history, customs, and mythology was an absolute must. Therefore, the next work to be read was Justin's *Historia*. After the young man had read a dictionary of mythology, he would be ready to read Ovid's *Metamorphoses*. He is also required in this first year to read the Greek New Testament. The first year was rounded out with Cicero, Terence, and Erasmus. The rest of the three years includes the study of lots of Cicero, Quintilian, Aesop's Fables in Greek, Virgil, more Ovid, Martial, Hesiod, Homer's *Iliad* and *Odyssey* (in Greek), Demosthenes, Plautus, Aulus Gellius, Seneca, et al. This was a university education.

REFLECTIONS ON EARLY MODERN EDUCATION FOR TODAY

At this point, we are able to make some observations not only about early modern education, but how it compares to our modern educational system. In doing so, we can make a few suggestive comments about how we might modify Christian education.

First, early modern education, at both the grammar and university level, was focused on spiritual and social maturity. The byproduct of such a focus inevitably undermined egalitarianism. By their education, some people unavoidably become more spiritually mature and socially adept than others. Education, it seems, has always done this. To the degree that our educational institutions no longer provide pathways to inculcate the various political, social, and spiritual virtues which mark a well-educated person, to that same degree our society has wandered away from traditional educational aspirations. Indeed, while this author used to be of the opinion that education need not (and perhaps ought not) involve the religious aspect of our

---

[30] Thomas Godwyn, *Romanae Historiae Anthologia Recognita et Aucta; An English Exposition of the Roman Antiquities* (London: R. W., 1661).

humanity, this is no longer the case, nor would this have been conceivable in the early modern period. Melanchthon, for example, continually describes education as a way of protecting and promoting the mission of the Church. In fact, even a cursory read through his various orations on the academic disciplines reinforces the inseparability between religion and the academy in Melanchthon's thinking. It is more than mere happenstance that medieval education was usually held in churches and the schoolmasters were monks or priests.

Second, note the simplicity of the education model. In the first eight to ten years of education, the sole focus was on language acquisition. Day after day was spent on learning Latin (and near the end, Greek/Hebrew). Even at university, only two subjects were studied at any given time and half the day was dedicated to each of those subjects. If you attended grammar school and then university in early modern England, it was possible, even likely, that you would never have to study more than two disciplines at a time to graduate from each. Nowadays, the average primary and secondary school student divides his or her time on six or seven different disciplines simultaneously, not to mention all the extracurricular subjects (music, sports, church youth group, Boy Scouts, etc.). In this author's own time at university, there was never a time where at least four or five different courses of study couldn't be taken at the same time. Could it be possible to get more out of students with less? The human mind is generally not adept at giving sustained focus to something in short periods. Many of the later pedagogues, such as Comenius, argued for a diversity of disciplines to be taught simultaneously in order to avoid student boredom; but have we actually undermined the ability to give sustained thought to a given topic? And this is to say nothing about havoc wrought by modern media on our ability to concentrate.

Third—and this is somewhat connected to the second—everything which was done had a strong practical motive behind it. Why did small children learn the basics of arithmetic? Because every person had to do basic math in real life, tallying and paying a bill, buying or selling goods, etc. Why did grammar students spend so much time on Latin? Because of the demands of university education. What was the aim of university studies? To train men in the foundational texts for law, theology, medicine, or other such professions in early modern Europe. We are prone to think that, in a bygone age, education was done for the mere, or at least, mainly for personal humanistic well-being purposes. It makes us better people to read the *Iliad* and learn Latin. While some of that is no doubt felt in the background of early modern pedagogy, we often downplay how practical everything the child learned was. If you went to grammar school after the petty school, it was to go to university. If you went to university, it was usually to get a job which demanded a university education. When a parent today asks me why their child has to learn Latin, a teacher should have a strong practical reason to give them. Sometimes they do—some children ought to be going into professions in which they would strongly benefit from being able to read the older writers. But, for most, this is simply not true. And we are lying to ourselves if we think otherwise. Much the same could be said of much higher mathematics. Perhaps we should think more critically, then, about the actual aims of our schools. What do we want the students to become? Of course, per the first point, we ought to want them to become socially and religiously mature; but no one needs to learn Latin to do that today.

Fourth, it is noteworthy that education was male-oriented. It may not have been evident in what has been discussed, but the primary literature assumes a fair amount of competition going on in the classroom. Students are put against other students to see who can name the most amount of new vocabulary words from a newly assigned section. Seating arrangement in the classroom was oftentimes indicative of proficiency. Tallies were taken for how many times a certain lower form student was able to answer a question which a higher form student was unable to answer. Competition wasn't the only masculine-oriented pedagogical trait. The various questions and classical proverbs learned are clearly masculine-leaning, if not downright chauvinistic (by modern standards). Take, for example, these three Latin proverbs to be memorized by first and second form students.[31] The first, from the Aeneid: *Varia et mutabilis semper foemina* ("A woman is always changeable and fickle). *Uxorum vitia post nuptias discimus* ("We learn the faults of our wives after marriage"); and *Uxor, quae pudicitiam amisit, omnia perdidit* ("A woman who loses her chastity loses everything"). One of the themes for declamation for the higher forms of grammar students was, *An qui ducit uxorem, libertati valedicit?* ("Whether the one who takes a wife says goodbye to freedom?"). Such discussions (leaving aside for a moment whether they are edifying) would have undoubtedly created a certain atmosphere which can't be had as easily with mixed-sex company. Indeed, to press the broader point a bit

---

[31] Hoole, *Latine Tongue*, 331–62.

further, let us focus our attention one last time on the first point, regarding the aim of education. John Milton describes this aim:

> But here [at grammar school and university] the main skill and groundwork will be, to temper them such lectures and explanations upon every opportunity as may lead and draw them in willing obedience, inflamed with the study of learning, and the admiration of virtue; stirred up with high hopes of living to be brave men, and worthy patriots, dear to God, and famous to all ages. That they may despise and scorn all their childish, and ill-taught qualities, to delight in manly, and liberal exercises: which he who hath the art, and proper eloquence to catch them with, what with mild and effectual persuasions, and what with the intimation of some fear, if need be, but chiefly by his own example, might in a short space gain them to an incredible diligence and courage: infusing into their young breasts such an ingenuous and noble ardor, as would not fail to make many of them renowned and matchless men.[32]

Notice the repeated emphasis on greatness. Milton envisions education to make those "stirred up with high hopes of living to be brave men and worthy patriots, famous to all ages." He desires them to "delight in manly, and liberal exercises"; that is, exercises which teach one how to be a gentleman. In short, Milton thinks the ideal student will be one of "incredible diligence and courage," having an "ingenuous and noble order," which would unquestionably make them "renowned and matchless men." How is this even possible when we mix girls and boys together? Was there ever a conscious societal decision that our educational aims are no longer those of Milton's or did it simply fall out of our view?

To be sure, there were many pedagogues in the early modern period who argued that girls should be taught to read, and, hence, should be allowed to attend the grammar school; but most of them would still have, no doubt, acquiesced to the famous humanist Juan Luis Vives's advice on the education of a Christian woman.[33] Vives is interesting because he does, in fact, encourage parents to have their young daughters taught to read. He wants

---

[32] John Milton, "Of Education," *The John Milton Reading Room*, accessed February 1, 2021, https://milton.host.dartmouth.edu/reading_room/of_education/text.shtml.

[33] Juan Luis Vives, *De Institutione Foeminae Christianae*, in *Opera*, vol. 2 (Basel: 1555).

them to be able to learn, through books, how a woman ought to live a chaste and sober life. But he still places the emphasis on domestic duties, believing that the aim of educating a woman is domestic life. How has the loss of such aims in education impacted the way our modern world is structured? Is it any wonder that women eschew family life in an ever-increasing way, when we've educated them for other aims?

These four reflections upon early modern education should give both encouragement and warning to those interested in the furthering of Christian classical education. In seeking a properly *Christian* classical education, we stand in a venerable tradition, seen throughout the early modern period, which assumes that moral and spiritual formation are properly part of an education. Likewise, against the contemporary urge to direct students into ever more atomized areas of specialism, those of us who suspect that an education which does a few things well are in good company with the educators of the Reformation era. Yet we would also perhaps do well not to seek to revive early modern education wholesale, without reflecting prudently upon our own circumstances. It is very easy to feel as if one is providing a "classical education" by forcing children to learn Latin, but our educational and professional worlds are simply not those of seventeenth-century England. Similarly, given that boys and girls now receive equal amounts of education in childhood, we should think more carefully about how egalitarian pedagogies have replaced the male-oriented early modern pedagogy in our homes and classrooms.

BIBLIOGRAPHY

Brinsley the Elder, John. *Ludus Literarius: Or The Grammar Schoole*. London: Thomas Man, 1622.

Clarke, John. *Formulae Oratoriae, in Usum Scholarum Concinnatae*. London: Robert Milbourn, 1637.

Comenius, Johann Amos. *Orbis Sensualium Pictus Quadrilinguis*. Nuremberg: Michael and Johannes Friderich Endter, 1666.

Erasmus, Desiderus. *De Civilitate Morum Puerilium*. Leipzig: Nickel Schmidt, 1535.

Gerhard, Johann. *Meditationes Sacrae*. Leiden: The Elseviers' Printing House, 1629.

Godwyn, Thomas. *Romanae Historiae Anthologia Recognita et Aucta; An English Exposition of the Roman Antiquities*. London: R. W., 1661.

Holdsworth, Richard. "Directions for a Student in the Universitie." In *The Intellectual Development of John Milton*, edited by Harris Francis Fletcher, vol. 2. Urbana: University of Illinois Press, 1961.

Hoole, Charles. *An Easie Entrance to the Latine Tongue*. London: William Dugard, 1649.

———. *The Petty-Schoole*. In *A New Discovery of the Old Art of Teaching Schoole*. London: J. T., 1660.

Kronman, Anthony T. *The Assault on American Excellence*. New York: Free Press, 2019.

Lily, William. *A Short Introduction of Grammar: Generally to be Used: Compiled and Set Forth for the Bringing Up of All Those that Intend to Attain to the Knowledge of the Latine Tongue*. John Norton, Printer to the Kings Majesty in Latine, Greeke and Hebrew, 1608.

Master, W. T. *Lily, Improved, Corrected, and Explained*. London: R. Bentley, 1696.

Melanchthon, Philip. *Enchiridion Elementorum Puerilium*. 1534.

Miller, William E. "Double Translation in English Humanistic Education." In *Studies in the Renaissance*, vol. 10. Cambridge: Cambridge University Press, 1963.

Milton, John. "Of Education." *The John Milton Reading Room*. Accessed February 1, 2021. https://milton.host.dartmouth.edu/reading_room/of_education/text.shtml.

Parker, Charles Stuart. "On the History of Classical Education." In *Essays on a Liberal Education*, edited by F. W. Farrar. London: Macmillan and Co., 1867.

Perkins, William. *The Foundation of Christian Religion Gathered into Sixe Principles*. London: Thomas Orwin, 1591.

Schottennius, Hermannus. *Confabulationes Tironum Litterariorum*, 1544.

Stockwood, John. *Disputatiuncularum Grammaticalium Libellus, ad Puerorum in Scholis*. London: Johannes Battersbie, 1619.

Sturm, Johann. *Classicarum Epistolarum Libri Tres*. Strassburg, Germany: Josias Rihelius, 1565.

Spike, Carlett. "Curriculum Changed to Add Flexibility, Race and Identity Track." *Princeton Alumni Weekly*. May 2021. Accessed March 29, 2022. https://paw.princeton.edu/article/curriculum-changed-add-flexibility-race-and-identity-track.

Vives, Juan Luis. *De Institutione Foeminae Christianae*. In vol. 2 of *Opera*. Basel, 1555.

Watson, Francis. *The English Grammar Schools to 1660: Their Curriculum and Practice*. Cambridge: Cambridge University Press, 1908.

West, Richard. *The schoole of vertue, the second part: or, The young schollers paradice Contayning verie good precepts, wholesom[e] instructions, the high-way to good manners, dieting of children, and brideling their appetites. Godly graces, and prayers. Verse fit for all children to learne, and the elder sort to obserue*. London: Edward Griffin, 1619.

VII:
A CONFESSIONAL EDUCATION: ABRAHAM KUYPER, J. GRESHAM MACHEN, AND THE CHRISTIAN ACADEMY

Eli West, Covenant High School

INTRODUCTION

IN 1932, J. Gresham Machen wrote an essay for the *Contemporary American* explaining how it was that a decorated professor such as himself was still a Christian despite the aggressive, opposing "current of the age."[1] "The answer," he wrote, was multifaceted but could be found primarily "in the home in Baltimore" in which he grew up. The classical orientation of his parents' interests had taught him "that Christian conviction" was not opposed to the "pursuit of learning."[2] It was in thanks to upbringing, and in contrast to many of his adult peers, that Machen saw no conflict between intellect and faith. From his father he saw that "true learning and true piety went hand in hand," and from his mother he witnessed a "reverence for the author of all beauty and truth."[3] The rich aesthetic tastes and deep piety of Machen's parents had a profound influence on his understanding of faith and culture.

Even more significant for young John, however, was the confessional aspect of his parents' religion. From Arthur and Mary Machen, he learned

---

[1] J. Gresham Machen, "Christianity in Conflict," in *Selected Shorter Writings*, ed. D. G. Hart (Phillipsburg, NJ: P&R Publishing, 2004), 547.
[2] Machen, "Christianity in Conflict," 548.
[3] Machen, "Christianity in Conflict," 550.

"what Christianity is and how it differ[ed] from certain modern substitutes."[4] His mother had taught him from home until age twelve. By that time, Machen ventured that he "had acquired a better knowledge of the contents of the Bible…than is possessed by many theological students of the present day."[5] Moreover, Machen memorized the questions and answers of the Westminster Shorter Catechism. He spoke gratefully that this was the theological curriculum of his youth as opposed to a contemporary, ecumenical one:

> When a man has once come into sympathetic contact with that noble tradition of the Reformed faith, he will never readily be satisfied with a mere 'Fundamentalism' that seeks in some hasty modern statement a greatest common measure between men of different creeds. Rather will he strive always to stand in the great central current of the church's life that has come down to us through Augustine and Calvin to the Standards of the Reformed faith.[6]

It was this facet of Machen's faith—allegiance to a written confession—that distinctly set him apart from his fundamentalist friends and modernist foes. To Machen, *true* Christianity was *confessional* Christianity. At its foundation, the Christian religion was one of systematic doctrine. Anything less was deficient at best and counterfeit at worst. As a college student, Machen had considered the idea of "a minimizing apologetic [in order to] serve the needs of the church." But he concluded, through the influence of Princeton professors like B. B. Warfield, that such a notion was "youthful folly." The attempt to uphold Christianity by abandoning "supposed rigidities of the Reformed system" was self-defeating. To him, "consistent Christianity is the easiest Christianity to defend, and that consistent Christianity—the only thoroughly biblical Christianity—is found in the Reformed faith."[7]

This conviction proved true for Machen and Abraham Kuyper alike. Consequently, when these men advocated for Christian education, what they

---

[4] Machen, "Christianity in Conflict," 548.
[5] Machen, "Christianity in Conflict," 550.
[6] Machen, "Christianity in Conflict," 551.
[7] Machen, "Christianity in Conflict," 554.

principally had in mind was a confessional education. They had personally seen the detrimental effects of non-confessional, Christian schooling.

THE NEED FOR CONFESSIONALISM

In Kuyper's situation, politicians before him had attempted to solve the Dutch School Struggle by appealing to a "Christianity above sectarian differences." This would be an education in "Christian virtues" but without reference to divisive topics like sin or redemption. What was categorized as congenial for all Christians was virulent for confessional faith. With all good intent, the Dutch had agreed to a nonsectarian education, but that soon evolved into something belligerently secular because what remained of true Christianity was hardly anything but a hollow shell. As Kuyper put it, forbidding confessionalism had "deftly shut the door to all revealed religion, to Scripture, to the name of Jesus Christ as the Redeemer—but it left the door ajar for the self-willed religion of modernism, for the catechism of the Society for the Common Good, and for presenting Jesus as a religious genius."[8] The outcome of all this was not unity between the faithful, but rather hostility toward traditional believers. "The demand to respect all convictions," he wrote, "prevented teachers as well as students from protesting against the atheist, but it did not go so far as to spare the sectarian hatred of believing Christians."[9]

The saddest part for Kuyper was how many Christians had grown comfortable with this system. Since the earliest debates on the Constitution's articles on education they had been warned that the phrase "training in Christian virtues" meant that state schools would ultimately lose "every dogmatic element, in a word everything that belong to the definition of Christianity, its truths, its facts, its history."[10] The Dutch people had been duped to think that the "minimum of Christianity [was] really the Christianity of our forefathers."[11] But now that the "mask [was] finally off," they had become complacent. The public school—despite its secular, anti-Christian bent—had become part of the Dutch national society and many Dutchmen

---

[8] Abraham Kuyper, "The Secret Betrayed: A Miscalculation," in *On Education*, ed. Melvin Flikkema (Bellingham, WA: Lexham Press, 2019), 183.

[9] Kuyper, "Secret Betrayed," 183.

[10] Quoted in "The Competitive Model for Education," in *On Education*, 171.

[11] Abraham Kuyper, "An Appeal to the Nation's Conscience," in *On Education*, 318.

had given up on the idea that they could change the system. Christians were advocating on behalf of these schools, which were now openly hostile to fundamental Christian beliefs. In Kuyper's words, the people were defending the state by essentially saying, "You will entrust to me your baptized sons and daughters, although the name of Christ may not be heard within our walls and no talk about God and immortality will be permitted."[12]

Machen was witnessing the same problems in the United States. Power holders were touting the idea of a generic "religious" or "character education" as opposed to a confessional, Christian one. Machen was alarmed by how many Christians readily accepted such a program. To him, the idea may have been "pro-religious" in word, but it was categorically anti-Christian in reality. Students were given religious training, but that training was opposed to the concept of religious doctrine. "The fundamental notion," he stated, "underlying the ordinary use of the term 'religious education' is that the business of the teacher in the Church is not to impart knowledge of a fixed body of truth which God has revealed, but to train the 'religious faculty' of the child."[13] Ultimately, the attempt to avoid sectarian differences and to unite all denominations and faiths under a common morality did not pacify religious tension. Instead, Machen argued, it undermined the "search for objective and permanent truth."[14] When the deepest truths of the universe—namely, those concerning God and the afterlife—became relative, students no longer considered truth absolute in any sense. It was for this reason that there was a necessity for confessional schools, argued Machen. Christianity, he said, is more than a "way of life"; it is, rather, a "system of truth." That system was "of the most comprehensive kind...clash[ing] with opposing systems at a thousand points." Christianity is a way of life, but one that "cannot be lived on the basis of anti-Christian thought." Said differently, there is no true Christianity apart from true doctrine.[15]

---

[12] Abraham Kuyper, "Teaching Immorality in the Public School," in *On Education*, 28.

[13] J. Gresham Machen, "The Importance of Christian Scholarship," in *Education, Christianity, and the State*, ed. John W. Robbins (Jefferson, MA: The Trinity Foundation, 1987), 15–16.

[14] Machen, "Importance of Christian Scholarship," 16.

[15] J. Gresham Machen, "The Christian School: The Hope of America," in *Education, Christianity, and the State*, 143.

Particularly repugnant to Machen was the adoption of "character codes" in public schools and their appeal to biblical ethics on a non-religious basis. State officials had attempted to pull moral teachings from a variety of faiths and combine them into a common system on which all could agree. Not only was this a form of inconsistent moral relativism, to Machen, it was completely useless. Teachers could try espousing a supposed "morality of mankind," but "the raging tides of passion," he said, "cannot successfully be kept back by the flimsy mud-embankments of an appeal to human experience."[16] Machen applied a similar logic for opposing Bible-reading in public schools. Secular schoolteachers should not read Scripture to students, he said, for when its ethical contents were taught "apart from its great redemptive core" it would lead children to think they could be good without God's grace. What the public schools (and many Christian schools too) had created was a garbled collection of religious and moral ideas. What Machen called for was a cohesive system of Christian doctrine—one that logically connected foundational truths such as man's utter depravity and God's absolute holiness.

CONFESSIONALISM AND EVANGELISM

In touting a confessional education, Machen and Kuyper were not just seeking denominational followers. At stake for them were the most precious things—the propagation of the Gospel and the salvation of souls. The key issue, Machen believed, in present-day evangelism was an intellectual one. Non-believers were closed off to the Christian faith not because Christianity was truly anti-intellectual, but because the Christianity many of them were exposed to was not logically consistent. The popular idea in the modern church was that Christians could evangelize by their character and avoid offensive confrontation by refraining from issues of doctrine. To Machen, this was not Christian evangelism, it was "an anti-intellectual, non-doctrinal Modernism."[17] Men are saved, he argued, not by the witness of Christian virtue or experience, but by faith in response to the preaching of the Word.[18] That preaching needed to be biblical and intellectually sound for it to be

---

[16] J. Gresham Machen, "The Necessity of the Christian School," in *Education, Christianity, and the State*, 77.

[17] Machen, "Importance of Christian Scholarship," 23.

[18] Machen, "Importance of Christian Scholarship," 21.

rightly winsome. To be sure, Machen acknowledged that argumentation was not sufficient in evangelism. Without "the mysterious, creative power of the Holy Spirit in the new birth" there would be no salvation. Nevertheless, while argumentation was not sufficient, neither was it unnecessary. Often it was the very means the Spirit used to draw lost sinners.[19] At present, however, Christianity was not even receiving a hearing from most Westerners because mainstream thought was so rationally opposed to the Gospel. But with rigorous scholarship and a "scholarly defense of the faith," Christian schools could meet this problem by "producing an intellectual atmosphere" where Gospel seeds could grow.[20]

The options of a "minimalist Christian" education or a "secular-morally neutral" one neither supported the religion nor cultivated the intellect of young people. Because they were logically unsound, they did damage to a child's cognitive development.[21] Because they were opposed to confessional Christianity, they were causing children to doubt the traditional faith of their ancestors. Dutchmen and Americans needed an alternative. For Kuyper and Machen, that alternative became known as *principled* (or confessional) *pluralism*.

---

[19] Machen, "Importance of Christian Scholarship," 24.

[20] Machen, "Importance of Christian Scholarship," 25–26.

[21] Machen once contrasted this deficient form of Protestant education with a parochial, Roman Catholic one:

"In a book written by two radically skeptical writers, John Herman Randall and John Herman Randall, Jr., there is an interesting passage. 'Evangelical orthodoxy,' say these skeptical writers, 'thrives on ignorance and is undermined by education; Catholic orthodoxy is based on conviction and has an imposing educational system of its own.' Is that dictum of these brilliant skeptical writers true? I am bound to say that it may seem to have certain sting of truth about it. When we contemplate a type of Protestant orthodoxy that is content to take forlorn little shreds of Christian truth and tag them here and there upon a fundamentally anti-Christian or non-Christian education, and when we contrast such a procedure with the great system of Roman Catholic schools and the serious, comprehensive effort which the Roman Catholic Church makes to inform and mould [sic] human life, we can well understand the contrast so humiliating to Protestantism, which the Randalls have so forcibly draw. Yet the dictum is not true; and in proof of the fact that it is not true I point tonight, as I would point in any company, to your Christian schools…you at least are not making the huge mistake of trying to found the gold and silver and brass and iron of Christian theological seminaries or Christian colleges upon the clay feet of non-Christian schools; you at least are not appealing to ignorance, but you believe that real Christianity should have an education system of its own." "The Christian School," 143–44.

PRINCIPLED PLURALISM

Principled pluralism is the idea that a pluralistic society can be unified when it allows all faith (and non-faith) groups to live and worship freely according to their consciences.[22] Principled pluralists believe in unity through diversity, not conformity. They do not seek to create one common cultural consensus in order to achieve peace in a pluralist world. In a society governed according to a principled pluralist philosophy, no group has establishment status; no group is forced to segregate from the rest and operate in privacy. Instead, faith groups compete for cultural influence in a free market of competition.[23] Kuyper and Machen were two such principled pluralists. It would be more accurate to call them confessional pluralists, however, because their belief system appealed to a confession, not merely to a set of principles.

Instead of uniting a pluralistic society based on its diversity, modernists in Kuyper and Machen's time attempted to unify society on a foundation of moral neutrality. In the public sphere,[24] they argued, diverse faith groups would have to put aside their irreconcilable differences and find commonality through secularism. In private areas,[25] however, these groups would be (more or less) free to operate as they pleased.

Kuyper and Machen were decisively opposed to the modernist program. In the first place, to them, the idea that Christianity could be suppressed in public but practiced in private was contradictory to the true nature of the faith. Christians could not simply worship at church and then "check" their morals at the front doors of the academy. Intellect and faith were inseparable. Culture and piety were not meant to be segmented. If forced to privatize their religion, they averred, Christians would cease to be Christians as a whole.

Second, just as impossible as the notion of a private Christianity was the idea of moral neutrality. Kuyper and Machen both argued that no person or institution is capable of being morally neutral. The Dutch public school system of Kuyper's day claimed that their secular approach made them

---

[22] Freedom, that is, insofar as those lifestyle or worship practices do not contradict the common law of a society.

[23] Again, insofar that the means of competition are nonviolent and unlawful.

[24] E.g., academy and government.

[25] E.g., home and church.

religiously impartial. Kuyper denied it. The secular public schools were not non-sectarian; they were the "sectarian schools of the Modernists."[26] Kuyper was campaigning for a diversity of confessional schools. The progressives, rather, were trying to conform everyone to their naturalistic confession. As they touted secularism in the name of fairness, they had created a monopoly that only benefited them. So-called moral neutrality, wrote Kuyper, will always end up "favoring [theological] modernism and opposing Christianity."[27] Secularism was not non-religious; it was anti-traditional religion. Going by an unnamed religion, secular schools were covertly committing moral and intellectual injury against young people. When secular schools taught on morality (because they unavoidably did), the state, said Kuyper, was effectively "teaching its own brand of religion and creat[ing] a kind of state church disguised as the public school."[28]

The liberal party in the United States and the Netherlands was claiming to be the party of tolerance, equality, and unity. Kuyper and Machen argued the opposite. A "one-size-fits-all" secular program was anything but tolerant, equal, or unifying. The Dutch prime minister winsomely contrasted the progressive idea of unity with his own using the images of a house and garden:

> There is unity and unity. As you want. Is it the unity of the house painter who covers everything with the same color, or that higher unity in the harmony of colors which the artist pursues with a rich diversity of shades and gradations? The first kind is the unity that [my opponent] wants by casting everybody in the same mold; the unity that I aim at is the unity of the flowerbed whereby each flower retains its peculiar form and color from which is born that higher harmony.[29]

In this way, Kuyper and Machen saw themselves as the real defenders of tolerance and equality. Progressives advocated their own philosophy of secularism as the archetype of tolerance. Hypocritically, however, they

---

[26] Abraham Kuyper, *Our Program*, ed. and trans. Harry Van Dyke (Bellingham, WA: Lexham Press, 2015). Quoted in "Editor's Introduction," in *On Education*, xxvii.

[27] Abraham Kuyper, "The Competitive Model for Education," in *On Education*, 170.

[28] Abraham Kuyper, "Ideas for a National Education System," in *On Education*, 163.

[29] Kuyper, "National Education System," 163.

excluded any other philosophy as a viable competitor. Similar to Kuyper, Machen once contrasted his idea of tolerance with the progressives'. "Tolerance to me," he said, "means not only tolerance for that with which I am agreed, but it means also tolerance for that to which I am most violently opposed."[30] True moral tolerance for Machen meant that he was against "any measures that involve compulsion"—whether that compulsion be in favor of Christianity, atheism, Islam, or any other faith group.[31]

THE MEANING OF TOLERANCE

Important to note is what tolerance did not mean for Kuyper and Machen. First, these men did not tout the language of tolerance because they were insecure or disloyal toward their own beliefs. Pluralism was not another form of moral relativism. Kuyper and Machen believed in objective truth. They were outwardly and proudly Calvinist in their doctrine. They held that the Reformed confession was the right one because it was truest to Scripture.[32] Confessional pluralism was for them—in fact—an outgrowth of their own confession. In advocating that all religions have equal access to public subsidies or for the free competition between state and private schools, Kuyper and Machen would appeal directly to their Calvinist faith.[33] They believed the Reformed tradition was the greatest defender of liberties of conscience.[34] No man or manmade institution had the right to burden man's conscience. Their faith taught them that God had sovereign rule in this area. The Calvinist position may have been the right one, but Kuyper and machen

---

[30] J. Gresham Machen, "Proposed Department of Education," in *Education, Christianity, and the State*, 121.

[31] Machen, "Proposed Department," 122.

[32] Wendy Naylor, "Editor's Introduction," in *On Education*, xx.

[33] James D. Bratt, ed., *Abraham Kupyer: A Centennial Reader* (Grand Rapids, MI: William B. Eerdmans Publishing Company, 1998), 69.

[34] "Kuyper argued that the rise of religious tolerance had been the fruit of the Protestant Reformation, and in particular of the Calvinist belief in the sovereignty of God regarding salvation. For if salvation was no longer considered a work of man (either as an individual or through a human institution), but entirely the work of God alone, by grace alone, then it was useless and even dangerous for the state to have as its goal the promotion of one particular religious confession. Such attempts eventually devolved into tyranny." Wendy Naylor, "Afterword: Faith, Finances, and Freedom," in *On Education*, 362.

would not allow for any temporal, state power to draw that conclusion for any individual. It was not, therefore, that these men wanted to hide their confession. Confessional pluralism, rather, was considered the rightful means of winning people to their side. When they had freedom to articulate their position in an open market of competition, Machen said, "the truth finally may prevail."[35]

Second, tolerance was not a shallow effort to ignore important differences between religions. Freedom of conscience allowed the Reformed Church—like all churches—to teach youth the dogmas of their confession without threat of persecution or entanglement with conflicting belief systems. Pluralism in education was not merely Kuyper or Machen's aim to "keep the peace" among contesting factions. It was also a means of being faithful to their church's command to catechize children in the faith of their baptism. Kuyper and Machen were aiming higher than mere coexistence with other groups. Ultimately, they wanted to be faithful to their confession and allow others to do the same.

Third, the tolerance that Machen and Kuyper articulated was not a concession given unideal circumstances. Pluralism was not an excuse for religious apathy. Given the option of fitting their religion with establishment status, they would not take it. In this way, Kuyper and Machen differed from both Christian fundamentalists and theological liberals. Those two groups were not necessarily opposed to religious establishment or laws and policies that privileged their side above another. At an earlier time in Western history, it was the confessionalists who favored uniformity. But Kuyper and Machen were confessionalists of a different kind. They were confessional pluralists who wanted equal opportunity for all faiths.[36] Although the beliefs of fundamentalists and liberals were harder to identify—because they often operated without a formal, written creed—the fervent culture wars between them demonstrated that neither was truly aiming for harmony in a pluralistic society. They wanted cultural dominance and they were willing to resort to methods that Kuyper and Machen would not.

---

[35] Machen, "Proposed Department," 123.

[36] D. G. Hart, *Defending the Faith: J. Gersham Machen and the Crisis of Conservative Protestantism in Modern America* (Phillipsburg, NJ: P&R Publishing, 1994), 168–70.

ECUMENICAL COLLABORATION

Furthermore, in contrast to the fundamentalists and liberals in their countries, Kuyper and Machen were able to ally with different faiths.[37] Due to their openness to plurality and the fact that neither was a religious nationalist, these men could sincerely work alongside other denominations to achieve their goals. Notably, both men consistently partnered with Roman Catholics in efforts to secure religious liberty. Machen's collaboration was less pronounced, but he teamed up with Catholics against liberal practices like the introduction of "character education" in public schools and the attempt to establish a federal department of education. Machen's support of the Roman Catholic Democrat candidate Al Smith in the 1928 presidential election against the Protestant Republican Hebert Hoover also shows how he was committed to cultural pluralism. Smith had worked to repeal laws in the state of New York that regulated the teachings of languages in primary public schools. In the effort to assimilate immigrants to American culture, several states had thrown out Latin and Greek from the curriculum and made English the sole mandatory language. Not only was the loss of classical languages a huge detriment to a child's education, but Machen also believed the motive was a direct challenge to civil and religious liberty.[38] Fundamentalists would never dream of supporting a Roman Catholic candidate—particularly one opposed to Prohibition. But Machen, unlike his conservative counterparts, was not trying to conform everyone to his cultural norms. He wanted liberty for all people to live and worship as they desired.

Kuyper's work with Catholics was a key factor in his victory in the Dutch School Struggle. His idea of confessional pluralism enabled an unlikely coalition between the two largest denominations in the Netherlands at the time. Although they had been bitter rivals in almost all things since the Reformation, in the war over state schools, Dutch Calvinists and Catholics had a common cause. Kuyper's political genius was to unite these groups together against the liberal elite who controlled the public-school system. At first, Kuyper had to defend his tactics before Protestants who did not want to give Catholics more cultural influence. As biographer James Bratt put it,

---

[37] Once again, while the term "fundamentalist" is an American one, I apply it to Kuyper as well given the similarities between the conservative camps that both Kuyper and Machen deviated from.

[38] Machen, "Proposed Department," 136.

"Ultra-Calvinists and those for whom Protestantism and patriotism were synonymous were mad about the idea of subsidizing Catholic schools."[39] But Kuyper eventually won them over by convincing them that collaboration was the rightfully Calvinist thing to do.

UNITY IN PLURALISM

In rebuttal to liberals, Kuyper argued that confessional pluralism would not produce disunity and religious fanaticism. This was a chief concern of critics who recalled the bitter religious wars of the Netherlands' past. It seemed to them that giving equal support to all faiths would lead to heightened cultural tensions. Kuyper's message of principled pluralism said the opposite. "Unity of the nation," he asserted before Parliament, "is not brought into danger by having children attend different kinds of schools but by wounding the right and limiting the freedom so that our citizens are offended not in their material interests but in their deepest life convictions. That sows bitterness in the hearts and divides a nation."[40] What truly created hostility was forced conformity. To Kuyper, respecting people's freedoms of conscience and association was the proper pathway to national unity.

Evidence was on his side too, because the progressive party had maintained its monopoly over the public schools for decades, but their effort to unify through secularism had "not contributed to greater tolerance; it [had] instead inflamed party passions."[41] Liberal politicians had promised that by their methods there would be an end to religious strife, yet, said Kuyper, "the battle has never as fierce as at this moment."[42] The Dutch people had been tricked to think "that the old-time religion would be harmful, but the new religion of humanity would be beneficial. [Liberals] designed an elegant system. Our school law was to be a law of liberty: it would respect the convictions of all; it would increase the benefit of general education and

---

[39] Bratt, *Abraham Kuyper*, 70.

[40] Abraham Kuyper, *Parlementaire Redevoeringen* (Amsterdam: Van Holkema & Warendorf, 1908–12), 3:174–75. Quoted in "Editor's Introduction," in *On Education*, xxxviii.

[41] Abraham Kuyper, "Speeches as a Member of Parliament, December 13, 1875," in *On Education*, 273.

[42] Kuyper, "Secret Betrayed," 184.

foster all Christian and civic virtues."[43] Clearly, however, those promises were bankrupt. Confessional pluralism would unite the nation; a state-established religion of secularism would divide it.

---

[43] Kuyper, "Secret Betrayed," 183.

BIBLIOGRAPHY

PRIMARY:

Curtis, Charles, and Daniel A. Reed. "Provisions of the Curtis-Reed Bill." *The Congressional Digest*, May 1926.

Kuyper, Abraham. *Abraham Kuyper: A Centennial Reader*. Edited by James D. Bratt. Grand Rapids, MI: William B. Eerdmans Publishing Company, 1998.

———. *On Education*. Edited by Melvin Flikkema. Bellingham, WA: Lexham Press, 2019.

Machen, J. Gersham. *Education, Christianity, and the State*. Edited by John W. Robbins. Jefferson, MA: The Trinity Foundation, 1987.

———. *J. Gersham Machen: Selected Shorter Writings*. Edited by D. G. Hart. Phillipsburg, NJ: P&R Publishing, 2004.

———. *Christianity and Liberalism*. Grand Rapids, MI: William B. Eerdmans Publishing Company, 2009.

Reed, Daniel A., and John Philip Hall. "Congressmen Discuss New Education Bill." *The Congressional Digest*, May 1926.

United States. Congress. Senate. Committee on Education and Labor. *Proposed Department of Education: Joint Hearings Before the Committee On Education And Labor, United States Senate And the Committee On Education, House of Representatives, Sixty-ninth Congress, First Session, On S. 291 And H. R. 5000*. Washington: Govt. print. off., 1926.

SECONDARY:

Bertram-Troost, Gerdien. "Christian Education in the Netherlands." In *Reaching for the Sky: Religious Education from Christian and Islamic Perspectives*, edited by Siebren Miedema, 147–62. Amsterdam, New York: Rodopi, 2012.

Bratt, James D. "Abraham Kuyper, J. Gresham Machen, and the Dynamics of Reformed Anti-Modernism." *The Journal of Presbyterian History* 75, no. 4 (Winter 1997): 247–58.

———. *Abraham Kuyper: Modern Calvinist, Christian Democrat*. Grand Rapids, MI: William B. Eerdmans Publishing Company, 2013.

Dumenil, Lynn. "'The Insatiable Maw of Bureaucracy': Antistatism and Education Reform in the 1920s." *The Journal of American History* 77, no. 2 (September 1990): 499–524.

Glenn, Charles L. "Democratic Pluralism in Education." *Journal of Markets & Morality* 21, no. 1 (Spring 2018): 117–40.

Gribble, Richard. "Countering Federalization of Education in the United States 1920–1930." *Records of the American Catholic Historical Society of Philadelphia* 108, no. 3–4 (Fall–Winter, 1997–98): 23–52.

Groenendijk, Leendert. "The Reformed Church and Education during the Golden Age of the Dutch Republic." *Nederlands Archief voor Kerkgeschiedenis* 85, no. 1 (2005): 53–70.

Harnick, George. "'Give Us an American Abraham Kuyper' Dutch Calvinist Reformed Responses to the Founding of the Westminster Theological Seminary in Philadelphia." *Calvin Theological Journal* 33 (1998): 299–319.

Hart, D. G. *Defending the Faith: J. Gersham Machen and the Crisis of Conservative Protestantism in Modern America*. Phillipsburg, NJ: P&R Publishing, 1994.

———. "Christianity and Liberalism in a Postliberal Age." *Calvin Theological Journal* 56 (1994): 329–44.

———. "Abraham Kuyper, J. Gresham Machen, and the Reformed Tradition in Twentieth-Century North America." Speech delivered in Des Moines, IA. November 4, 2013.

Marsden, George M. *Fundamentalism and American Culture, The Shaping of Twentieth-Century Evangelicalism: 1870–1925*. New York: Oxford University Press, 1980.

——— *The Soul of the American University: From Protestant Establishment to Established Nonbelief*. New York: Oxford University Press, 1994.

———. *The Twilight of the American Enlightenment: The 1950s and the Crisis of Liberal Belief*. New York: Basic Books, 2014.

———. *Understanding Fundamentalism and Evangelicalism*. Grand Rapids, MI: William B. Eerdmans Publishing Company, 1991.

McDonald, Jeffrey S. "J. Gresham Machen and the Culture of Classical Studies." *Westminster Theological Journal* 82 (2020): 95–119.

Mellink, Bram. "Having Faith: Religious Optimism in Dutch Parochial Schools during the 1960s as a Case for Secularisation." *Paedagogica Historica* 49, no. 1 (2013): 139–48.

Mitchell, William A. "Religion and Federal Aid to Education." *Law and Contemporary Problems* 14, no. 1 (Winter 1949): 113–43.

Mouw, Richard J. *Abraham Kuyper: A Short and Personal Introduction.* Grand Rapids, MI: William B. Eerdmans Publishing Company, 2011.

Oppewal, Donald. "The Roots of the Calvinistic Day School Movement (I–IV)." *Reformed Journal* 8 (September 1958): 8–14.

Price, Timothy Shaun. "Abraham Kuyper and Herman Bavinck on the Subject of Education as Seen in Two Public Addresses." *The Bavinck Review* 2 (2011): 59–70.

Ruyter, Doret J. "Christian Schools in a Pluralistic Society?" *Interchange* 30, no. 2 (1999): 213–33.

Stonehouse, Ned B. *J. Gresham Machen: A Biographical Memoir.* Willow Grove, PA: William B. Eerdmans Publishing Company, 1954.

Van Dyke, Harry. "Government Schools or Free Schools? Abraham Kuyper Addresses a Long-Standing Controversy in the Dutch Parliament." *Canadian Journal of Netherlandic Studies* 35, no. 2 (2014): 29–45.

Walford, Geoffrey. "Evangelical Christian Schools in England and the Netherlands." *Oxford Review of Education* 27, no. 4 (2001): 529–41.

VIII:
SUBALTERNATION AND THE LIBERAL ARTS: VOCATION AND FRIENDSHIP WITH GOD

Brandon Spun, New College Franklin

INTRODUCTION

THIS essay seeks to answer one question: does Christian education concern men who are free (liberal), servile (productive laborers), or servant leaders? In addressing this question, we must also address two more fundamental ones, namely: what is the aim of education, and are we justified in seeking knowledge for knowledge's sake?

The moment we ask questions about "the basic aims of education," we enter into a discussion of our entire vocation, both as human beings and Christians. A misstep here would likely affect how we understand our calling and could result in misleading those whom we, as teachers, instruct. Lest we make such a misstep, we need to clarify our subject matter a bit further. To this end, we shall first show how the questions posed above belong not to the academy as such, but to the Christian life—in fact, to all humans. Second, we shall demonstrate how Christian and classical traditions provide patterns for navigating and understanding these questions. Third, we show that answering these questions means finding wisdom in knowing God who rightly orders all things, enrapturing us in divine love and friendship.

Christian education and vocation are realized only through friendship with God. Three conclusions follow from this assertion. First, we will resolve whether (or how) we use the liberal arts (and whether or how man is free) by carefully weighing ends and means and by clarifying the sense in which man himself (and education) is *bonum utile* (a good to be used, i.e., a means) or *bonum honestum* (a good to be enjoyed, i.e., an end). Second, this work of ordering belongs principally to wisdom. Third, a recovery of wisdom is bound up with an understanding of the human person and his destiny. This is because only a free, intelligent being is capable of ordering various goods, ends, and means. In freedom alone can true Christian service be realized, service which is not merely instrumental but is itself a form of worship and love. This implies that we must attain to some sense of the unity of freedom, love, and service.

We need to discern ends and means, to negotiate various orders of value and causality. This occurs in an exemplary way through friendship with God, that is, through a conscious awareness of the radical and active benevolence of a Creator who lovingly upholds and redeems his creatures. Vocation and education can then only be sufficiently contextualized in Christ, the mystery of divine love which constitutes discernment as personal. This is because divine friendship alone permits the creature to direct himself *as a creature* to the Creator. The complex play and evaluation of various principles and ends are otherwise rendered opaque by an impersonal framework. Without wisdom, our judgments remain univocal, unilateral, and utilitarian.

Wisdom is a personal habit through which one comprehends the unity of a diverse and multifaceted order. It therefore belongs chiefly "to the wise man to order."[1] Both Christian and liberal arts traditions help us develop this habit. Christian traditions direct us to divine government, to grace, to the Gospel, to various virtues and practices, in respect of our final end. The liberal arts tradition provides an analogical framework which complements Christian tradition and praxis, directing students to comprehend the many through the one.[2] Such studies attend to multitude and complexity with the goal of attaining a unified vision of the world through its principles and causes. Insofar as wisdom is a knowledge of highest causes, its character is typified in these studies. The habits of heart and mind, encouraged by the liberal arts, correspond with those necessary to discern God's calling. While there are several ways the liberal arts foster such habits, we will chiefly attend to the principle of subalternation—the interrelation and subordination of various sciences to one another, and ultimately to theology.

---

[1] Thomas Aquinas, *Summa contra gentiles*, Book I, sec. I, trans. Anton C. Pegis, https://isidore.co/aquinas/ContraGentiles1.htm#1. See Aristotle, *Metaphysics* I.2, from which Aquinas is quoted.

[2] Peter Redpath, "The One and the Many," course notes (Holy Apostles College and Seminary, Cromwell, CT, fall 2019).

To trace out these connections, we must first ask some more basic questions: what is education? How are various human goods related? What is the relationship between the sciences? How does God utilize these various orders to realize his ends and to realize those ends in and through man?

EDUCATING WHO? EDUCATING WHAT?

Through education alone, we develop our powers to evaluate, communicate, act, and love. Education is a necessary human good, and that which distinguishes us from every other creature. Yet compared to many animals, man seems weak and ignorant. Most animals reach full maturity within the span of a few months or years. Physical maturity occurs relatively slowly for us, while emotional-intellectual maturity develops over decades and only through great effort. Man's way is not determined as other animals who each have their various modes of life marked out for them from the beginning. Some imprinting occurs through practice or training; nevertheless, their paths are determined by instinct, practice, and bodily constitution. Only minor deviations normally occur. Our food, shelter, defense, even our mode of government, are not givens, in the way that the eagle's eye, claw, and society are. Our bodies are unspecialized (excepting perhaps the hand). They express that we are governed by reason rather than instinct. Reason is open to opposites (to *is* and *is not*, being and non-being).[3] To know is to be open to contraries and therefore to contrary forms of action.[4] For instance, the doctor in his very knowledge of doctoring has knowledge of health and sickness, and so can heal or harm.[5] He acts in accord with what he knows and values. As rational animals, we must determine both how and whether to act. Put differently, of all creatures we have a capacity for free rational judgment (*liber arbitrium*). We can make choices. Man is therefore open in principle to true excellence, and to failure and sin. Human life alone can miscarry in a spiritual, moral-perfective sense. Without grace, it ultimately does.

Without education man cannot realize a truly human life. Of course, this is not at all to suggest that formal education is necessary. One's life can be good and true without ever darkening the doors of a school. Education

---

[3] Aristotle, *Metaphysics*, trans. W. D. Ross, IX.2, http://classics.mit.edu/Aristotle/metaphysics.html.

[4] Aristotle, *Metaphysics*, IX.2.

[5] Aristotle, *Metaphysics*, IX.2.

occurs fundamentally by becoming acquainted with the truths, the traditions, the manners and modes of our social and personal existence, a nexus of meaning and praxis which help us discover and realize what it means to be who we are. We are introduced to this nexus by our family, the first school of love. It is the home in which education first and fundamentally begins. This is no accident.

The family is the framework in which we learn about the world, ourselves, and what is worthy of love. It is the family through which we come into possession of our human heritage—one of history, language, practices, and values, some which extend far beyond the family, into society, into history, even transcending the natural order. For all these reasons, we are not mere instances of the human species, but unique, unrepeatable persons whose individuality is interwoven with and dependent upon the relationships and traditions in which we exist.[6] We are not merely generic humans but *sons* or *daughters*.[7] We are who we are due to parents who are themselves constituted in part by physical, social, spiritual realities.

Education can, for this reason, be characterized as dialectical. First, we are born into a society, one which we grasp existentially in our embodied existence and through language. Second, we enter into that nexus, not as specimens of humanity which must fit into place, but as persons realizing human nature for and as a self. No other being can do this for us.[8] For this reason, while it matters little if *this* or *that* ant lives, the world is decisively constituted by the individual persons who actually comprise humanity. Third, this means we not only enter into a nexus (or world) but comprise that nexus. What I mean is that a son or daughter does not merely live in a household; in part, they constitute *that* home. A parent is a parent precisely of (and because of) *that child*. The parent is *their mother* or *their father*; the child is the son or daughter of *that parent*. The character of our existence as persons is, therefore, definitively familial, interpersonal, and dialectical.

Parents are not educators in the abstract. They are educators precisely of *this child here and now*. Their mandate is not a curriculum, but a life together.

---

[6] John Paul II, "Urbi et Orbi," December 25, 1978, http://www.vatican.va/. "For God and before God, the human being is always unique and unrepeatable, somebody thought of and chosen from eternity, some called and identified by his own name."

[7] Scott Hahn uses this formulation to unpack John Paul II's *Theology of the Body*.

[8] Christ accomplishes this for us in a manner which respects and incorporates human dignity.

The home must then be informed by an inner character of love and knowledge. It is not chiefly a system-structure, like an ant hill, but a place in which love is made known by a shared life ordered to the mutual good and perfection of each member.[9] As a place of love, the home becomes a place where one can apprehend the reason and end for which he or she exists. Among the foremost things a child must learn from his or her parents is therefore that "it is good that you exist."[10] A child is not an accident of parental love, but the natural *offspring* of union and a concrete sign of their love. When this is not communicated and substantiated, the meaning of one's existence is obscured or falsified. All other education follows upon this first truth, that we are loved and ordered unto love.

Necessarily then, education is personal. True education is the education of the whole person, heart and mind. For, to know in a human way is ultimately to know as we ought (1 Cor. 8:2; 1 Cor. 13). There are two implications: first, education ultimately depends on One who can form and instruct our hearts; second, in training up a child, one must know, love, and direct *that* child to his or her true end (Prov. 22:6). Educators must respect the tension between the common good at which every man ought to aim and the distinctive manner in which a given individual will receive and respond to that calling.

We can state it this way: the given conditions structuring human education include not only a received, objective framework, but a duty to incorporate that framework in a matter befitting the persons concerned, thereby respecting the subjective conditions of life. We are not just equipping children to "assume their place in the world." In fact, as we shall see, such a mechanical *placement* would conflict with the very nature and dignity of the human person.[11] We are creatures who must not only act but act accordingly to who we each are. We must therefore become aware and self-aware. Without this, our powers and vocations remain obscured.

---

[9] See Jacques Maritain, *The Person and the Common Good* (Notre Dame: University of Notre Dame Press, 1994).

[10] Josef Pieper, *Faith, Hope, Love* (San Francisco: Ignatius Press, 1997), 174. See also Hans Urs Von Balthasar, "A Resume of My Thought," *Communio* 15, no. 4 (Winter 1988): 468–73.

[11] See Luke 9:58; cf. also Walker Percy, *Lost in the Cosmos: The Last Self-Help Book* (New York: Picador USA, 2000), 57, 106–15.

We can now state something implicit about parenting, namely, that the education of a child is the radical right, privilege, and demand of parenthood. To bring a child into the world is to intentionally cooperate with God in the creation of someone who will live forever and who will live by what they know and love.[12] Education is therefore not a parental extra, alongside childbirth and physical care. Taken holistically, education is precisely what constitutes human parenthood. The whole life of a child takes its first direction toward love and knowledge or selfishness and ignorance, toward goodness and truth or evil and falsity, in light of education. By the very nature of parenthood, one receives a vocation. All formal education is merely a structured outworking of this fact and therefore has its own spiritual dimensions.

CHRISTIAN DISCIPLESHIP

The purpose of education is to aid the learner by directing him to a knowledge of that which is most needful: how to live well and attain true happiness.[13] All education must be in touch with and informed by the real ends we are to seek. Educators then must ultimately and primarily direct man to a knowledge and love of God (Mark 12:30). Christian education is in this respect the extension, rectification, and fulfillment of what is truly human—a declaration of our ultimate end, to know God (John 17:3).

Jesus Christ is the exemplar of education: the doctor and the supreme doctrine of God, our divine teacher and our teaching. He is the true teacher because he is God, but he communicates his revelation of God to man *as* a man. That is, he is the revelation of God to man and of man to man (John 19:5).[14] In him, the knowledge of God and knowledge of man converge.[15] By no means does he dispose of the personal dialectical structure of education;

---

[12] John Paul II, *Love and Responsibility* (Boston: Pauline Books & Media, 2013), 34–37, 244–45.

[13] See Plato, *Theaetetus*, 176a–e.

[14] See John Paul II, "Redemptoris Missio," December 7, 1990, para. 5, Vatican Archive, http://www.vatican.va/content/john-paul-ii/en/encyclicals/documents/hf_jp-ii_enc_07121990_redemptoris-missio.html. See also Pope Paul VI, "Gaudium et Spes," December 7, 1965, para. 22, Vatican Archive, https://www.vatican.va/archive/hist_councils/ii_vatican_council/documents/vatii_const_19651207_gaudium-et-spes_en.html.

[15] See Calvin's *Institutes* I.1.

rather, the material, familial, social, and spiritual aspects of education are uniquely incorporated and elevated in him. He teaches by living among us as friend and brother.

Jesus confirms that familial-friendship is characteristic of education. This presupposes that a teacher desires the true good of a student and that a student willingly seeks that good alongside and under a teacher. But in the Gospel, and in traditional education, to learn is not only to receive information but to become *like* one's Master. Education, exemplified in Christ's discipleship, is a communication of life, a way of coming to be one with God. Discipleship is therefore an educative, adoptive friendship which reveals that Christian education is to be ordered toward union with God, to an all-embracing friendship between the creature and the Creator.[16]

A NORM: MEANS AND ENDS

Two conclusions can be drawn out from these previous reflections. First, there is a norm for education. Authentic education contributes to the perfection of the person by facilitating and directing human freedom by revealing its proper end. This would be a "personalist norm."[17] It presupposes that man is himself a good (*bonum honestum*). Any treatment of man which falls short of this norm cannot respect the true goals of the person. Any mode of acting which so instrumentalizes, uses, or reifies the individual (denying value, interiority, freedom) is contrary to human dignity.[18]

Man is by no means the greatest good, but as a person, he possesses a radical and irrevocable dignity. By our very nature we are made to rejoice in truth, to use the language of St. Paul and St. Augustine (1 Cor. 13:6; *Confessions* X.23). Man possesses the dignity of being called by his nature to seek and love the Good intentionally, to participate in it interiorly. We are made to be living temples of truth, houses of an interior flame which burns with the light

---

[16] Both the Latin *discipuli* and the Greek μαθηταί express that a disciple is a *learner*.

[17] John Paul II, *Love and Responsibility*, 21, 24–28. See also Kant's *Groundwork for a Metaphysics of Morals*.

[18] A trade school or job does not do this unless it insists the man is *only* a "worker." It is only absolute subjugation to labor which is evil. An employer has an obligation to keep in mind the dignity of those they employ. The worker must continually recover the fact that they are not merely a worker, that they have an irrevocable dignity.

of love—our spiritual share in the divine nature, possessed consciously and gladly. We not only can rejoice in truth, but *are made true*, like God, by worshiping in Spirit and Truth (John 4:24).

A second conclusion is that education must be an education in both ends and means. Ends gives order to things. But without a knowledge of what contributes to that end, human education is incomplete. A welding college that only showed students what perfectly fused parts looked like would be a total cipher. Therefore, among other things, welders are taught about various materials, their applications, kinds of joints, their uses, their strengths and weaknesses, as well as about tools, and safety. To be a good welder means organizing and utilizing all these things in respect of an end. Similarly, a person must fundamentally coordinate a vast multitude of complex powers and conditions in order to realize his true end. These include psychological powers and attitudes, norms, relations, material objects and conditions. We must not only specify an end but also the means by which to realize it.[19]

The work of the educator is that of making known both the Good (the end) and that which is conducive to (good *for*, *bonum utile*) that end.[20] Education is, therefore, not primarily about a process or a product. It is a form of leadership (*e-ducare*) which draws men out of themselves and disciples them as men, communicating a *habitus*, a mode of relating to God, self, neighbor, and the world. This implies the development of virtue: moral, intellectual, and theological. It especially requires a habit of identifying both that which is good and the *respect in which it is good*.

For some, material wealth seems to be the greatest good, while for others wealth is only good for acquiring other things. For some physical pleasure, honor, or glory constitute happiness. For others, the greatest good is social work, service to neighbor, the intellectual life, or religion.

Within this horizon, we can see why the category of *use* belongs uniquely to man (and also *abuse*).[21] Use belongs to someone who ordains one

---

[19] We do not choose our ultimate end (happiness), but we must decide, rightly or wrongly, what constitutes that happiness, just as a bride does not marry a generic husband.

[20] Thus our Master reveals not only the Truth, but the Way (John 14:6; Luke 24:13–35).

[21] Augustine, *On Christian Doctrine*, trans. J. J. Shaw (Mineola, NY: Dover Publications, 2009), I.4.

thing to another. No other animal is intentional in this manner, judging ends and means. The bee does not decide whether it is good to gather pollen. While pollen is useful for the bee, it is known as desirable, rather than under the aspect of a *means*. The bee cannot grasp the *why* because it cannot abstract and judge whether it should do what it does. It therefore does not consider anything as true or good simply, but only as desirable. The bee never says, *I am a bee and therefore my true good is to collect pollen*. Collecting pollen is simply a fact for the bee. An end belongs to the bee by virtue of God, who moves it to act according to its nature. What else is instinct but God directing each creature to its good? An end belongs to other animals but without that end being known and loved for its own sake. Therefore, the *why* escapes every creature but man, to whom the end belongs in a special way.[22] Aquinas puts it thus:

> All other things concur in man's last end, since God is the last end of man and of all other things. If, however, we speak of man's last end, as of the acquisition of the end, then irrational creatures do not concur with man in this end. For man and other rational creatures attain to their last end by knowing and loving God: this is not possible to other creatures, which acquire their last end, in so far as they share in the Divine likeness, inasmuch as they are, or live, or even know.[23]

A corollary of this is that while God is our true good, we need not know him as such. We must learn to specify what and whom we shall love. There are two consequences: first, whatever falls outside a designated *end* can be considered as a means; second, a knowledge of means is indispensable. This is just as true for the craftsman as it is for man as such. We must develop a habit by which to take up that which is conducive to the good, a power of valuation and ordination. This is simply a way of speaking about wisdom—whether of the craftsman or the Christian. Wisdom is a kind of knowledge which values and orders things well by that which is first. This means we can definitively classify all servile arts as secondary. Servile (or productive) arts presuppose a more comprehensive order, a prior and more fundamental

---

[22] Angels also intentionally love God.

[23] Thomas Aquinas, *Summa Theologica*, trans. Fathers of the Dominican Province (Notre Dame: Christian Classics, 1981), II–I q.1, a.8.

education. Man requires a more comprehensive *why*. Why weld? Why paint? The servile arts have relevance only in light of *human* ends.[24]

It is in this light that the liberal arts, philosophy, and, most of all, religion can be said to belong to a human community. A true *polis* must include in it all those goods which are most fundamental and perfective of human nature.[25] A city must first of all therefore include God. This is because man has a necessary relation to that which is greater than him. He is a spiritual being whose perfection is not in himself. Without religion, we remain ignorant both of God and human nature, designating things other than God as ultimate. Without religious education, man necessarily instrumentalizes himself. Education therefore clarifies the kind of creature we are and the kinds of goods we are to seek.

USE AND ENJOYMENT

Scripture teaches us that we are saved by grace through faith by Jesus Christ (Eph. 2:8). We are God's workmanship, and we are to do all things to his glory (Eph. 2:10; 1 Cor. 10:31). We are to hate our life in this world and to love God above all things, love our neighbor as our self, and worship nothing that He has made (John 12:25; Mark 12:30–31; Exod. 20:3–5). We are pilgrims here, seeking a city with foundations (Heb. 11:10). We are servants, even as, and because, we are free (John 13:16; John 8:36). We are not slaves, but rather serve God as sons and friends who know what our Master is about (John 15.15). The Son himself is our pattern, having taken on the form of a servant (Phil 2:5–8). He clung not to his divine prerogative but, offering himself on our behalf in love, and for the joy before him, he endured the cross (Phil. 2:5–8; Heb. 12:2). Therefore, we too have a race to run, running not as if we have already obtained the prize (1 Cor. 9:24; Phil. 3:12). We are to count all things as loss in light of the prize set before us, setting our minds on that which is above (Phil. 3.8; Col. 3.2). We are to take all things captive to Christ so that all may be placed in subjection to God the Father (2 Cor. 10:5; 1 Cor. 15:28). In this way, we offer our reasonable worship, pouring our lives out in a thanksgiving to God (Rom. 12:1).

---

[24] Because man is a person ordained to God, to an end that surpasses all nature, there are times we may forgo natural necessities, sacrificing and subordinating even life to God and to our fellows.

[25] See again Maritain, *The Person and the Common Good*.

There are two conclusions here. First, Christians must grapple with means in light of the end, since all things should be hated, in respect of that love due to God (Luke 14:26). Second, the Gospel itself upholds the personalistic norm, implying that the human person has a special share in the final end, not as a mere instrument, but as a proximate and participatory good. This suggests that our hatred of family and friends, that all subjection and subordination of earthly goods, must be understood relative to our final end and not always as absolute opposition. Hatred, other than hatred of sin, must be understood as a willingness to subordinate a thing to God, as a readiness even to part with something, but not as the absence of affection or love simply. As will be shown, this *subalternation* will be the connecting point between faith and the liberal arts. This duality and the need to order is confirmed in the twin cause of our salvation: God has done and does all that he does for his glory (John 12:27–28); simultaneously, God has no need of glory, but rather acts out of love for us (John 3:16). This tension must be upheld wherever authentic Christian faith is proclaimed and practiced: God acts for his Name's sake; yet he also acts out of genuine love for us.

In *On Christian Doctrine*, Augustine reflects on this mystery by analyzing God's relationship to us through the categories of *use* and *enjoyment* (*uti* and *frui*). Augustine first states that we should not presume through pride to be instructed by the Spirit alone, but rather should humbly receive instruction from human teachers. God in no way disdains secondary causes (e.g., preaching) in communicating salvific doctrine. Augustine next argues that it belongs chiefly to Christians and to Christian instructors to distinguish between and order signs and that which they signify. Augustine views the distinction of sign and signified as parallel to that between ends and means, use and enjoyment, and ultimately between God and his creature. He believes this distinction is essential to the right interpretation of Scripture, one analogous to the distinction between Spirit and letter—that is, between life and death (*De Doctrina*, Book I, Book III.5; 2 Cor. 3). The act of interpretation is not merely analogical to but is itself part of the spiritual life. We are living epistles, written by God and made alive through the Spirit (2 Cor. 3). We are called to be interpreters of God's Word—priests and mediators of the knowledge of God which is written upon our hearts of flesh (2 Cor. 3).

Although Christians are instructed by the Spirit, we yet must learn through God and his ministers to read and to live according to that Spirit—to interpret rightly. Therefore, Augustine writes *On Christian Doctrine* chiefly to aid the Church in the spiritual-semiotic work of interpretation. The Christian life is a spiritual education concerning signs and their significance. Reading is therefore a means of spiritual formation. Augustine, says Alasdair MacIntyre, believes that "it is only the self as transformed through and by the reading of the texts which will be capable of reading the texts aright."[26] Augustine in fact proposes his well-known "rule of love" in *On Christian Doctrine*—concluding that love is the authentic measure of the bounds of Christian doctrine. He recognizes, however, that, much like the Scriptures themselves, love is manifold. Therefore, to rightly understand love (and thus the Word), we must reckon with letter and Spirit, with means and ends. This brings him to *uti* and *frui*.

Augustine introduces an analogy in Book I.4 by which he addresses both the intellectual and moral life, while also attempting clarify the crucial distinction between letter and spirit. Here, he places letter and spirit under the more general categories of use and enjoyment (*uti* and *frui*).

> For to enjoy a thing is to rest with satisfaction in it for its own sake (*Frui est enim amore inhaerere alicui rei propter seipsam*). To use, on the other hand, is to employ whatever means are at one's disposal to obtain what one desires (*Uti autem, quod in usum venerit ad id quod amas obtinendum referre*), if it is a proper object of desire; for an unlawful use ought rather to be called an abuse (*abusus*).[27]

Augustine then applies this principle to the world itself, casting humanity as pilgrims who must *use* travel as a *means* of returning home. The world is to be used as a means, not enjoyed as an end. Therefore, we need to be healed by Wisdom, so as to seek to enjoy God, who is himself Wisdom. Augustine initially concludes from this that it is not even lawful for man to have enjoyment in himself or another; we too are objects of use rather than enjoyment (I.10–14, 22).

---

[26] Alasdair C. MacIntyre, *Three Rival Versions of Moral Enquiry* (Notre Dame: University of Notre Dame Press, 2006), 84.

[27] Augustine, *On Christian Doctrine*, I.4, trans. Philip Schaff, https://faculty.georgetown.edu/jod/augustine/ddc1.html. Latin from "Augustinus Hipponensis – De Doctrina Christiana Libri Quatuor," accessed April 23, 2021, https://www.augustinus.it/latino/dottrina_cristiana/index2.htm

Next, Augustine proposes love as the broader genus under which both use and enjoyment fall. We can love means without treating them as ends. He then examines the special relationship God has with man through the categories of *uti* and *frui* (I.31–32), insisting that we should not hold that God enjoys us. That is, we cannot be God's end in which he finds rest (*frui*). God is in no way incomplete, unhappy, or needy. So does God use man? Use also implies need, being always for some end. Augustine's conclusion is "that use, then, which God is said to make of us has no reference to His own advantage, but to ours only; and, so far as He is concerned, has reference only to His goodness."[28] God uses us for our own sake, that we might be happy in him. His radical goodness is such that when we say that he has made us "for his glory," this is not so that he might be greater; rather, it is so that we might partake in his beatitude. We are made for his glory insofar as his glory is our good. God has made us for our own sake with reference to him as our end. Therefore, we can unequivocally declare God's work as a work of love. His *use* of us is more like the love of a parent for a child than the use of a tool. A tool is directed to a good external to itself (the good of the master). As instruments of God, we are directed toward our own good which is the Master himself (Luke 1:46–47).

This helps us understand what Augustine says next, which seems to be a surprising reversal of his prior position. He then says that it is in fact lawful to enjoy a human being (I.33). However, we can do so only if we enjoy them (i.e., love them) insofar as they are in God. Having clarified that God is our chief end, and how God uses us, we can now recognize something distinctive about man. That is, having read things spiritually (through their end), we can see that man is semiotically unique—he is a living letter. Man is a creature whom we may love in God, in whom our love may rest with satisfaction, insofar as that enjoyment is actually a repose in God. We may lovingly cleave to another man for his own sake (only because and insofar as our enjoyment does not ultimately stop in him (I.4). All love must be ordered with reference to God, but in man that reference passes through the mystery of the *imago Dei*. Human love is most *like* that love which is our end (Mark 12:31).[29]

---

[28] Augustine, *On Christian Doctrine*, I.32.

[29] Thus, we are prone to make an idol of this love and of our fellows.

ORDO AMORIS

We are called to subject all things to God in Christ Jesus, which implies ordering ends and means in the Christian life. Augustine places both ends and means (use and enjoyment) in the broader category of love (*amor*), insisting that we may love things which are beneath, equal to, and above us. In fact, all things may be loved with reference to God (I.27). Thus *uti* and *frui* are opposed to one another not as contraries, but as the imperfect mean is to the term (the perfect end), as proximate participation is to the ultimate unparticipated cause. This is why Augustine treats *frui* as a species of amor; it is a *love* which cleaves to a thing for its own sake.[30] In this regard, all love has an order.[31] Only insofar as a love falls short of order and ceases to be directed to God is it disordered and illicit; insofar as it is directed to God, it is lawful and good. Thus, all things having been made in and through the divine image, they may be loved in some respect.[32] All things can be loved, insofar as they are loved in God, but not all things may be loved in all ways.

Insofar as man is uniquely made in the image of God, insofar as seeing a human face "is like seeing the face of God," we approach a mystery; we can declare without equivocation that it is good to see someone's face, and therein find an imperfect rest (Gen 33.10). Man is rightly loved in this manner, not merely as an instrumental or conventional sign of God. We are not images of God in the manner that a red octagon signifies "stop," but in the way that the face of a child reminds one of his father, or that a kiss communicates an interior spiritual disposition. When we love our neighbor as we ought, we indeed, if somewhat secretly, act out the love of God, or a love most like it (Matt 22:39). We can conclude that man is simultaneously a *bonum utile* and *bonum honestum*.

---

[30] Throughout Book I of *On Christian Doctrine*, Augustine uses terms such as *frui, diligo, caritas*, and *amor*. *Amor* is used generically, including even charity (*agape*). However, charity (friendship with God—love of God for His own sake, and love of neighbor as self) is not just *another* love. Charity falls in the genus love only logically, not ontologically—it is the source, director, and exemplar of all love, not one among many in a logical class. Love (just as being, goodness, righteousness, unity) is an analogical and not a univocal term.

[31] This must exclude those things that are always and everywhere unlawful, such as adultery.

[32] It is in this respect God hates nothing He has made (Wisdom 11:24–25).

It is in reference to this mystery that our Lord says, "As you did it to one of the least of these my brothers, you did it to me" (Matt 25:40). Man, as a good in himself, is never to be treated merely as a useful instrument. Otherwise, we fall short of that love which God has for us and which we are to imitate (John 15:12). Paul reminds us of this when he argues that "'all things are lawful,' but not all things are helpful. 'All things are lawful,' but not all things build up'" (1 Cor. 10:23). He unites the personalistic norm with the ordering of ends and means. We are to look not to our own license, but to subordinate our freedom to love and union with our brothers and sisters in Christ. We are even to consider ourselves as less than one another, for we are being built up together into one body (Phil 2:3; 1 Cor. 10.24–33). In doing so, Christ's presence and our conformity to him is realized in each of us and in the whole.

LIBERAL ARTS AND SUBALTERNATION

The Christian tradition is shaped by the mystery of the *ordo amoris*. God infinitely surpasses his creature, and in him alone can we find rest. Yet he is not the only lawful object of love. Nevertheless, all other loves must come under the direction of this one. Now, as we turn to consider how the traditional liberal arts bear upon our discussion of education—the ordering of the heart and mind—an implicit theme of this essay emerges: the mystery of *the one and the many*. We have already considered how *one* love is to govern the *many*—the unity and order of the will generated by charity. But the one and many are by no means unique to ethics or moral theology. There are, after all, "as many forms of unity as there are kinds of being" and so the one and many concerns every science.[33] "Every science involves coming to know how a many is essentially one, how parts are essentially related to constitute a whole."[34] This expresses a governing human aspiration: the pursuit of unity, and this is why the traditional liberal arts are an exemplary mode of education.

While all sciences seek to unify a field of understanding, the liberal arts exemplify this by seeking the unity of the whole created order. They analogically seek to express the unity, not of a single subject, but of the cosmos. Therefore, they encourage a habit of inquiry by which the unity of a complex whole is discerned. Due to their method, clarity, and analogical

---

[33] Aristotle, *Metaphysics*, IV.2.
[34] Redpath, "The One and the Many."

character, they aid young minds (and old) who wish to seek wisdom. The liberal arts in no way can replace or cause Christian Wisdom, but they can serve as a tool of preparation and training for its development. One way that they engage us in the mystery of the one and many is through the principle of subalternation.

Subalternation refers to the manner in which various sciences (and thus things which exist) are understood as meaningfully and causally interrelated. Subalternation is a result of diversity and complexity, of the fact that the world can be divided into distinct subjects which are yet united in various ways. The principle is exemplified within the trivium and quadrivium, as well as in their relation to one another and to philosophy, and in philosophy's relation to theology. Subalternation will help us explore our questions about Christian education because it discloses something about the character of divine government.

Many medieval universities employed the threefold division of liberal arts, philosophy, and theology—a division which goes back further than recorded history. As evidenced in Plato's *Theaetetus* (set at a local gymnasium where arithmetic, geometry, music, and astronomy were taught), the subjects of the quadrivium were well established by Socrates's time. The remaining three arts of the trivium (logic, grammar, and rhetoric) were also extant in some form during this period, as evidenced by method and content in pre-Socratic authors, as well as Plato's dialogues.[35] However, Aristotle's *Organon* gives the first systematic exposition of the trivium. The earliest theoretical treatment of the quadrivium is in Book VII of Plato's *Republic*, which argues that it is a fitting preparation for philosophy.[36] The quadrivium, paired with dialectic, facilitates a periagogic education—the turning of the soul to underlying realities. The quadrivium can do this because of its relation to wonder, its mathematical character, and its cosmic scope.

Wonder, *aporia*, and education go hand in hand for Plato. Wonder is the experience of a creature who expects the world to make sense and to operate as an intelligible unity: someone who in fact knows something of that

---

[35] The grammatical and logical can be seen especially in *Parmenides, Cratylus, Philebus*, and *Sophist*, while the rhetorical is evident in *Gorgias* and *Phaedrus*. Logic is sometimes called dialectic. For a useful history of the trivium see: John Deely, *Introducing Semiotic: Its History and Doctrine, Advances in Semiotics* (Bloomington: Indiana University Press, 1982).

[36] Philosophy for Plato necessarily included and culminated in theology and ethics.

unity, but who nevertheless experiences apparent contradiction, as when that which is one is also in some manner two; when that which is big is also small; when that which *is*, in some respect, *is not*.[37] Wonder, coupled with hope, moves us to search into ultimate causes.[38] As a psychological source of science, it moves us to make a many one through some unifying principle.[39] In this respect, the quadrivium encompasses four potential subjects of wonder: number, shape, music, and heavenly motion.

The quadrivium's relation to wonder is further reinforced by its mathematical character. It is no random collection of sciences, but an architectonic order governed by number. Through number, it is an initial, albeit imperfect, step toward the unity of all science (imperfect because number is not the principle of being *per se*). Its comprehensive goal uniquely corresponds with our spiritual-psychological desires.

This accords with the character of our intellectual-volitional teleology. To unify the sciences by simply studying them all in one place (at a college) would be to unify them accidentally. To unify them by something external would fail to be scientific—something like uniting the study of trees, animals, and houses because they all have *coverings*. The quadrivium is unified by a principle which belongs properly (although distinctly) to each subject. Number happens to belong to each science because it analogically expresses the very structure of being.[40] Each thing, insofar as it *is*, is one, and from this substantial unity, quantity is itself abstracted. Thus, quantity is related to and expressive of the character of being.[41] Number is therefore a proper principle of the quadrivium. As both Aristotle and Thomas argue, quantity can be

---

[37] Redpath, "The One and the Many." See also Plato's *Republic*, 522e–526c.

[38] Redpath, "The One and the Many."

[39] Redpath, "The One and the Many." A principle of whole steps and half steps (w-w-h-w-w-w-h) unifies every major scale. Henry Moseley's 'staircase' shows that the governing principle of the periodic table is atomic number, not atomic weight.

[40] See Jacob Klein, *Greek Mathematical Thought and the Origin of Algebra* (New York: Dover Publications, 1992). See also Nicomachus's *Arithmetic*. Number concerns the division of being according to kinds, the one and the many, the psychological powers of knowing (collecting, ordering, dividing, apprehending). It is an analog, not only of the eidetic character of the world, but its elemental composition, our verbal expressions, and our mental conceptualization (thus to being and science universally).

[41] Thomas, *Summa Theologiae*, I–I q.11 a.1.

analogously predicated of substance.[42] Of all the categories (or accidents) predicated of being, "'quantity is the closest to substance'. . .Quantity is a *per se* accident of a material body because it necessarily inheres in, and emanates from, the body's natural matter. A quantitative body can thus be the proper subject of philosophical speculation."[43]

Number is the principle of arithmetic, the study of discrete quantity. Geometry, which studies continuous quantity, is related to arithmetic, insofar as it is numerically quantified. Music, which attends to arithmetic ratios, and astronomy, which concerns continuous motion in time and space, both have a relation to number. All three are subalternated or placed under arithmetic as quantifiable. One science thereby unifies four without subsuming them or their proper formalities.[44] The term "subalternation" is borrowed from logic, in the case when an "I" or "O" statement is related to an "A" or "E" statement, respectively (see Figure 1). For instance, "*Some living things are dogs*" (I) is related to "*All dogs are mammals*" (A). Insofar as *some* of the genus "living things" comes under or includes "dogs," we can apply the same conclusion in "A" to that *part* of "living things," just as there is a *part* of music to which number pertains.

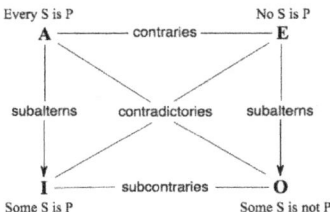

Figure 1. Traditional Square of Opposition, from Stanford Encyclopedia of Philosophy[45]

Each science of the quadrivium remains distinct in this manner, even as they are united. A strong Pythagorean reading would claim that shape, sound, and the whole cosmos are nothing but number. We need not affirm this to agree that quantity truly belongs in some manner to these subjects. Number is a

---

[42] Redpath, "The One and the Many."

[43] Redpath, "The One and the Many."

[44] One could never arrive at the perfect fifth by number alone, without the experience of sound, but could only discover later that its formal cause is a 3:2 ratio.

[45] Terence Parsons, "The Traditional Square of Opposition," n.d., https://plato.stanford.edu/entries/square/.

universal property, an accidental quality belonging to all matter. Arithmetic, the most abstract and universal, acts as an intelligible principle through which an integrated understanding of the whole is realized.

Further, because number is so basic, it is readily accessible to the young student, who can see that the cosmos is rational, whilst not being mathematical in itself.[46] Mathematical astronomy, like optics, is thus a mixed or subalternated science, borrowing principles from a higher or more fundamental study (arithmetic) which is not within the same subject-genus.[47] That is, the stars are not a species of quantity. What this means is that even as the quadrivium directs us toward a preliminary knowledge of the whole, it does so in an imperfect manner. It does not study the world by its essential principles.

It is the speculative sciences (philosophy proper), such as physics and metaphysics, which explore the proper principles of things. For this reason, physics and metaphysics are both more perfect and more difficult than the quadrivium. They require a more mature learner because they grapple with greater complexity. For instance, physics (natural philosophy) requires a consideration of form and matter, motion, time, and place, as well as three additional species of causality (mathematics has only the formal). In metaphysics, one considers being as such, substance, kinds of unity, act and potency, universals, composition, singulars, and ultimately God (natural theology).[48]

So, while students consider the unity of the entire created order in the quadrivium, the quadrivium is itself subordinate to philosophy, and philosophy to theology. But in each case, this subordination is not one which

---

[46] See Thomas Aquinas College, "Dr. Neumayr on the Order of the Arts and Sciences," YouTube, n.d., educational video, https://youtu.be/UNnirpxk0CI.

[47] "Just as optics is subalternated to geometry, so the science of the rainbow is subalternated to optics…it belongs to the naturalist who treats of the rainbow to know the 'quia', but to the expert in optics to know the 'propter quid'. For the naturalist says that the cause of the rainbow is the convergence of a visual line at a cloud arranged in some relation to the sun; but the 'propter quid' he takes from optics." Thomas Aquinas, "Commentary on the Posterior Analytics," n.d., trans. Fabian Larcher O.P., https://isidore.co/aquinas/PostAnalytica.htm, 1.25.

[48] Ethics, practical philosophy, is also more complex. One considers law, reason, conscience, passions, will, appetite, good and evil, habits (virtues and vices), and education. Christian ethics further requires a knowledge of revelation, salvation, the order of grace, the supernatural virtues, the gifts, and beatitudes.

eradicates the prior orders of causality or knowledge. For instance: in the *Physics*, Aristotle proves that motion is continuous, partly through mathematical reasoning; Copernicus uses the idea of proportion and ratio to argue for the organization of the heavens. In Christian theology, new principles are brought to bear—things we could not discover without special revelation. In fact, God himself is, in a unique way, the first principle of Christian theology. All that we know and love is to be incorporated into what we believe, into this highest science, by being placed under and informed by it, even as they, in part, set the conditions of reading and application. God is, after all, the one Author of creation and revelation. For this reason, something like subalternation is the means by which we learn to organize all that we know and preserve the real relations among things. We have merely used the quadrivium to make explicit something implicit in the traditional liberal arts and Christian theology—the fact that all that exists is somehow related. Subalternation therefore reflects the real diversity and unity of the sciences.

DIVINE GOVERNANCE: CAUSE OF CAUSES

Subalternation is an analog to divine government. God rules all things, but by diverse means. Through Wisdom, he causes all things to be precisely what they are. Yet he "gives other beings not only their existence, but also their existence as causes."[49] It is this which we have been exploring through our somewhat circuitous path: that God bestows reality and significance upon that which he creates. He bestows particular significance upon that creature who must discern order and situate himself within it, so that he might partake of and contribute to the realization of divine government. Jesus Christ is the definitive sign of this fact. The Incarnation signifies that God has accomplished our salvation precisely *as man*. Therefore, our image and likeness to God is restored and exalted *by* God *in* and through man, bringing all things into subjection to God. First and foremost, man himself is brought into this subjection. This makes possible an exemplary realization of divine government in us and through us.

Divine government is perfect, in part, because God comprehensively knows the end (himself) and the means by which that end will be realized

---

[49] Thomas Aquinas, "De Veritate," trans. Robert W. Schmidt S.J., n.d., https://isidore.co/aquinas/english/QDdeVer11.htm, q.11, 1.

(the creation). As seen in our reflection on *uti* and *frui*, the goodness of divine action has reference to God first, even as it redounds to the good of his creatures. Our reflections on subalternation served as an analogue to consider this hierarchical ordering through the framework of science. We turn now to consider the source of all order: how Wisdom moves all things.

A military analogy employed by Aristotle and Thomas is of some use here, clarifying the *ordo amoris*, subalternation, and the subjection of creation to God in Christ.[50] The general of an army directs each of its divisions and branches. But the general does not chiefly govern the cavalry, for instance, by telling them *how* to ride horses, but by directing them to his chosen end. Therefore, the Good exists chiefly in the general and secondarily in the army, insofar as the end is communicated to it.[51] While the cavalry employs the art of horseback, the general governs them by a higher principle which incorporates (without overriding) their art. The general has a knowledge of the universal good of the army (its final cause), as well as a knowledge of how to achieve that end by coordinating each of its parts. As the general *of an army*, he depends upon the excellencies of each part in order to dispose all things well. His architectonic wisdom includes and directs other forms of knowledge without obviating them.

In a like manner, God fashions and directs all things (Matt. 8:9), communicating his goodness to them by both simply creating them, and by directing them to their end. Because God is the end of all things, what he communicates to each creature is some specific likeness and tendency to himself, such that each creature, insofar as it pertains to their nature, strives to be like God through their proper perfections. All things *kindly* incline to him.[52] Further, as governor of the entire universe, he also arranges the order of things in relation to one another, in time, circumstance, and nature. The universe is in this respect governed by a universal providence, an eternal law which is Wisdom. Thus, God disposes all things by Love, and his Love moves all things, not by force, but by being lovely and loved. The Sun thus runs its course with joy, glorying to be like God, insofar as possible (Psalm 19:4–6).

---

[50] This appears in Aristotle's *Nicomachean Ethics* I.2 and *Metaphysics* 12.10, and in Thomas's commentaries on these texts, as well as various writings such as *Summa Theologiae* I–I, q.15, a.2, and *Summa Contra Gentiles* I. 42.

[51] Aristotle, *Metaphysics*, 12.10

[52] In sin, man seeks to be like God, though in a faulty way (without God). Yet even this contributes to the perfection of the universe. See *Summa Theologiae*, I–I, q.22, a.2.

If man is to be like God, he too must govern and must govern by a wisdom which knows both the End and the means (the creature).

There are significant implications to this doctrine for Christians and educators. God chooses to operate in and through his creatures in the ordinary course of the creation, as well as in his salvific work.[53] Salvation is the salvation of what has been made. God, therefore, brings all things into subjection by establishing himself in his creature.[54] He operates through the formalities and substantial character of all that he has made, even as he transforms the creature. Because he is the Author of all nature he, and he alone, can do this.[55]

This is realized uniquely in man, who, as vice-regent, is privileged with participating in divine government.[56] Through the gift of a spiritual soul, man has been made to know and to seek the Good as such. He too is moved by divine love, but in a unique way. God thus promulgates his will to man by making known his law: natural and divine. As Aquinas states: "Now among all others, the rational creature is subject to Divine providence in the most excellent way, in so far as it partakes of a share of providence, by being provident both for itself and for others."[57] Man can, with divine aid, freely respond to God with a rational-volitional love. He therefore requires, among other things, wisdom and direction. Our true wisdom is to seek out the friendship and aid of God, to seek God as our final end, and therefore to submit ourselves to the law of love. Only then will we, like the sun, run in

---

[53] This does not exclude miracles or specially directing some creature in a manner which exceeds its nature. Even miracles do not simply destroy or obviate the creature but establish it in a certain condition.

[54] Those subject to perdition alone will experience divine government as an external force, but indeed the judgment will be felt from within and thus as truly terrible.

[55] "The movement of the will is from within, as also is the movement of nature. Now although it is possible for something to move a natural thing, without being the cause of the thing moved, yet that alone, which is in some way the cause of a thing's nature, can cause a natural movement in that thing. For a stone is moved upwards by a man, who is not the cause of the stone's nature, but this movement is not natural to the stone; but the natural movement of the stone is caused by no other than the cause of its nature." *Summa Theologiae* I–II q.9 a.6. God, as the sole Author of spiritual life, can alone move (direct) the will.

[56] For all these reasons, we must reject Stephen Jay Gould's idea of a non-overlapping magisterium (NOMA) between faith and science; see Stephen Jay Gould, *Rocks of Ages: Science and Religion in the Fullness of Life* (New York: Random House, 2011).

[57] Aquinas, *Summa Theologiae*, I–II q.91 a.2.

nuptial delight according to the law of liberty. Man is for this reason most provident for himself when he places himself in the hands of God.

God's universal cosmic government is simple. His manner of governing is, however, complex.[58] Subalternation is simply one way of recognizing the character of divine wisdom. A Christian liberal arts education is thereby a mode of directing man to seek that wisdom which he needs in order to realize his calling.

VOCATION VS. PLACEMENT

Christian education is the education of one who is called to participate in divine government as prophet, priest, and king. Such an education must include God, the creation, and the individual learner—one who is to establish a relationship to the whole order of existence. If Christians are to take the works of God in hand, and if we are ourselves his workmanship, we need to know who we are and what we are about. We need to develop, through knowledge and practice, a personal habit of wisdom because "it is the office of the wise man to order."[59] This requires virtue, a mode of self-possession, whereby to continually place the self and all that is in one's power into the hands of God.

First and foremost, Christians take up a complex spiritual reality in themselves. Therefore, our calling is therefore not something which is merely external; it must be discerned from within. Hasty abstraction falsifies and does violence to the realities we must attend to. An individual who thinks God cares nothing about his desires, or that his talents, dispositions, and lot in life have no bearing whatsoever upon the direction he should take, who views God or the Gospel as a kind of impersonal law or force, has virtually excluded himself from friendship with God. He has closed off the pathways and conditions in which wisdom operates and falsely reduced the *many* to *one*. This is equally true of one who believes his situation, talents, or desires absolutely and unequivocally declare God's purposes. Both ultimately operate according to the elements of this world and do not enter into the rich cooperation with God which vocation implies. God's calling is not, however, ordered chiefly to realizing temporary goods, but to that which is everlasting.

---

[58] See Augustine, *City of God* 11.18; see also Boethius, *The Consolation of Philosophy*, IV.6 (n. 106).

[59] Aquinas, *Summa Contra Gentiles*, I.I.1.

Therefore, while pleasure is a sign of vocation, this does not imply we are to merely "follow our heart." Rather, pleasure is one of many conditions of discernment. Desires ought not be suppressed or ignored, even though they may need to be set aside, not as evil in themselves, but *as nothing* in *comparison* to our calling. Thus, the first rule of discernment is that we do not *chiefly* look to ourselves.[60]

But it is only by the fact of our spiritual interiority that we have a calling at all. As John Paul II says, vocation is something which belongs to us because we are persons, beings who can dedicate and direct ourselves to some realization of love.[61] Vocation is for this reason not chiefly about a career or a predetermined course of action. It is something creative, even co-creative. Wojtyla states, "Vocation means some main direction of love in a person."[62] He characterizes this discernment as "one of the decisive moments in the process of the formation of personhood."[63] This is because the purpose of human freedom is precisely that we might commit ourselves in love.[64] Our gift of self is the creativity *of self* in cooperation with God, that activity through which the love of God operates and is realized personally within an individual.[65] Finally, Wojtyla states that "by discerning the proper direction of one's development and main direction of love: each man knows at same time how to enter into God's action and respond to his love."[66] What else is this but friendship with God, with that Wisdom which reigns according to the order of love. All subjection, all subordination, even sacrifice is an expression of this. Until we grasp something of God's everlasting love for us, we remain incapable of response.

Christian education is to cultivate this friendship and cooperation with our Father, in order to know that Hhe intends to use us precisely insofar as we are persons, taking up what he has made to redeem it and direct it to its

---

[60] "Prudence is that illumination of moral existence which…is a thing denied to every man who 'looks at himself.'" Josef Pieper, *The Four Cardinal Virtues: Prudence, Justice, Fortitude, Temperance* (Notre Dame: University of Notre Dame Press, 2011), 36.

[61] John Paul II, *Love and Responsibility*, 241–43.

[62] John Paul II, *Love and Responsibility*, 241–43.

[63] John Paul II, *Love and Responsibility*, 241–43.

[64] John Paul II, *Love and Responsibility*, 241–43. See also Søren Kierkegaard, *Provocations: Spiritual Writings of Kierkegaard* (Plough Publishing House, 2014), 289.

[65] John Paul II, *Love and Responsibility*, 241–43.

[66] John Paul II, *Love and Responsibility*, 241–43.

fulfillment for his glory. He does not do this without us, and so we must know who it is we are cooperating with: one who gave his Son for us in order that the whole self might live unto God. Therefore, vocation follows the pattern of the cross: the total gift of self.

All this shows that vocational discernment requires attention both to divine revelation and to one's situation. Yet there must be a first principle of coordination, something first, without which one is left without direction. A spiritual principle alone can respect and direct all things. For instance, Christian counselors draw from a complex toolbox. A counselor must attend to physical, historical, financial, affective, valuative, moral-habitual, intellectual, and spiritual principles. Even while spiritual principles are first absolutely, a counselor cannot employ them mechanically, in a manner which ignores or does violence to other orders. An alcoholic needs to undergo change but may not do so very effectively while drunk. Further, it is God alone who changes the heart, but a good counselor will attend to client willingness. A man may be committed to change, but a situation may preclude transformation. The "how" and "when" of correcting or helping someone is not exhausted by a flow chart.

How does a counselor coordinate all these factors? In the manner of one who subalternates one order of being to another—by rising to a principle which governs and respects the whole.[67] This manner of *rising* is an act of wisdom, a spiritual act, a prayer which relies on all the providences of God. It is not a mathematical deduction but a personal dependency upon One who loves all that he has made. Joseph Pieper addresses something similar in his writing on prudence. Prudence is, after all, that virtue which characterizes virtue as human (a rational act). It precludes mechanization and even certainty:

> At this point the element of uncertainty and risk in every moral decision comes to light. In the decisions of prudence…there cannot be that certainty which is possible in a theoretical conclusion…the prudent man does not expect certainty where it cannot exist, nor on the other hand does he deceive himself by false certainties. The decisions of prudence and the 'intuitions' of *providentia* (which,

---

[67] For instance, to treat biology as absolutely determining behavior would fail to respect the spiritual freedom of man. Yet, to ignore biology would devolve into a kind of gnostic voluntarism or helpless fideism.

incidentally, Thomas considers to be the most important component of perfect prudence—he points out in fact that the name, *prudentia*, stems from *providentia*) nevertheless receive 'practical' assurance and reinforcement from several sources: from the experience of life as it has been lived; from the alertness and healthiness of the instinctive capacity for evaluation; from the daring and humble hope that the paths to man's genuine goals cannot be closed to him; from the rectitude of volition and the ultimate 'intention'; from the grace of direct and mediated divine guidance.[68]

If we are to respond to God's call, there is no escape from the human conditions in which we exist and therefore we cannot escape from a personal encounter with our God.

For all these reasons, when a college claims to make its students useful to God (just as when we purport to "*teach students to think*"), we should consider what this means. It is not our place to fit students into a career or solve these *problems* for them. Rather, we are called to invite and challenge them to engage in a process through which they can come to discover the possibility of authentically realizing that love which God is uniquely in them. It is no accident that Charity (Love) has been defined as friendship with God and also as that virtue which informs and governs every other virtue (making them true virtues).[69] Charity acts as the form of all virtues by directing them to their end.[70]

Further, because we are called to eternal communion with God, there is no earthly career which can be placed above us. "Servant" and "servant-leader," for this reason, need to take on a special meaning for the Christian. If we frame our whole vocational *problem* in light of "career," in the anxiety of identity, "we reduce [our]…search for…identity to a problem…[that] can be solved by diligent application of the techniques of the natural sciences" and this "denies the soul's true depth and so leads to the abolition of man."[71] A student whose one and only question in life is "What job should I do?" has

---

[68] Pieper, *The Four Cardinal Virtues*, 18.
[69] Aquinas, *Summa Theologiae*, II–II q.23, a.8.
[70] Aquinas, *Summa Theologiae*, II–II q.23, a.8.
[71] Carl Anderson and Jose Granados, *Called to Love: Approaching John Paul II's Theology of the Body* (New York: Image, 2009), 3–4.

reduced himself to a thing. We can return to the analogy of the family, in which our primary calling is not to a job, but to a life together with God.

But a man who merely seeks to place himself in the world will paradoxically find that he does not know who or where he is. Having lost sight of this, he cannot become who he is meant to be. Our Lord tells us that "foxes have holes, and birds of the air have nests, but the Son of Man has nowhere to lay his head" (Matt. 8:20). Man is not a creature who can merely *place* himself. *Things* have places. The waters fill the oceans, the air fills the sky, but man is not chiefly ordained to a place.

Remarkably, for Augustine, for John Paul II, and for Walker Percy, this problem of placement (of love and vocation) is concerned with interpretation and meaning, with signs.[72] Man seeks to find a place for himself, but because he is spiritual, he cannot do this—the world is not our home, no suitable helper is found (Gen. 2:20). We cannot place ourselves in the world without falsifying the spiritual-signification of our being and our *status viatoris*. We are pilgrims whose rest can be found in no creature. We are therefore ordained to that which surpasses work. But it is only in drawing near to God that we realize this radical calling, and only then do we find that our service to God is an expression of *sonship*, no matter our circumstance. Christian education therefore must chiefly foster a habit of dwelling with God personally. With this in mind, we can at last consider whether knowledge is to be treated only as a useful good or as something we might enjoy for its own sake.

KNOWLEDGE AND HUMAN DESTINY

Insofar as our Lord Himself calls us to serve Him, it remains to say a few words about the relation of the liberal arts to service, freedom, and work. This essay has argued that in order to live well, we must discover the character of divine government. The liberal arts are an instrumental means which aids us in this process of discovery. They are by no means necessary to the Christian life, and, in this respect, they are an unnecessary good. Nevertheless, this does not mean that they are not also good in themselves. The liberal arts (and more generally, knowledge) can indeed be useful. But because man is himself a *bonum honestum*, a non-instrumental good (albeit *per*

---

[72] Percy, *Lost in the Cosmos*, 106–12.

participation), knowledge, as something perfective of human nature, is truly a good.

We all know what it is like to be gladdened by knowledge, knowledge which will never be of use, or whose use is distant and subordinate to the good of knowing. A man who receives a word of blessing from a loved one does not leave with an *instrumental* good. On the other hand, knowledge of housebuilding is chiefly good insofar as it leads to the production of a house. The good of contemplating Euclid does not belong to one as a carpenter or an engineer. Delight of this sort resonates deeply with us because such knowledge is like coming home to that which we are made for. It is something like a pleasing familiarity with the governing power and plan of the universe. There is something personal and perfective in all contemplative knowledge. Such knowledge has been called 'contemplative' (also 'speculative' and 'theoretical') because it is exemplified in the act of seeing rather than in use. All contemplative knowledge has something of the lover's gaze about it.[73] Contemplative knowledge is a true good because it uniquely shares in our end, the very reason we exist. It uniquely participates in and signifies that "good portion" chosen by Mary (Luke 10:42). Jesus characterized this "part" (μερίδα) as a small but necessary and abiding whole, a good which would not be taken from her.

The liberal arts are an imperfect, proximate, preparatory good—a loving contemplation of created truth, which directs us to seek the uncreated Truth. Weil and Perrin describe them sacramentally: "The solution of a geometry problem does not in itself constitute a precious gift, but...it is a pure image of the unique, eternal, and living Truth....Every school exercise, thought of in this way, is like a sacrament."[74] So how does this clarify our initial questions about freedom, work, and knowledge?

Man is indeed free, yet is called to work by his Master. He is the free governor of what has been in some manner placed beneath him (Psalm 148). This governance, inseparable from his dignity and freedom, is founded upon and realized by being gathered into the rest of God—that Great Sabbath in which we shall rest in and delight (*frui*) in God Himself, in seeing his face.

---

[73] Josef Pieper, *Leisure: The Basis of Culture; The Philosophical Act* (San Francisco: Ignatius Press, 2009). See also Josef Pieper, *Happiness and Contemplation* (South Bend: St. Augustine's Press, 1998).

[74] Simone Weil and Joseph Marie Perrin, *Waiting for God* (New York: Harper Perennial Modern Classics, 2009), 112.

Contemplative knowledge and the liberal arts help preserve this fact by reminding us that labor is not an ultimate end. Work is by definition a means. It is leisure (*schole*) that functions as a sign and foretaste of our true destiny. Without such signs, we lose sight of who we are. Life becomes impersonal and utilitarian. It is no accident that Joseph Pieper wrote so passionately about this during the anti-religious period following WWII.[75] This is also why he understood the Sabbath and eucharistic worship/liturgy as the zenith of contemplative rest. Such a liturgy or work is not labor but delight and peace

Contemplation is a good which preserves that which is promised in every human face, sought for in every longing gaze, and veiled in all earthly beauty. It is a sign that God is our true beatitude. Insofar as any knowledge shares in and prepares us for happiness, it is a *bonum honestum*—something that can be loved in its own respect.

This essay's approach has been to take up the tension between freedom and service. In doing so, we have clarified a position long embraced by the Church. In attempting to argue that some things are simply worth knowing, one is immediately thrust upon the problem of faith and works, upon use and enjoyment, as well as the division between essence, property, and accident. None of these things can or should be utterly divorced in this life. Nevertheless, it is crucial that we distinguish between faith and works, ends and means, use and enjoyment.

From Plato to Pieper, we have been reminded that we work in order to *not-be-at-work*, in order that we might have leisure and be free to contemplate. Within the Christian tradition, we know of at least one knowledge which is good simply: "And this is eternal life, that they know you, the only true God, and Jesus Christ whom you have sent" (John 17:3) All work is ordered to that rest. If we keep in mind such knowledge is not possessed perfectly here, and that it need not and cannot mean the exclusion of work in this life, we will go far in recovering and preserving a core tenet of Christian wisdom: that there is indeed, here and now, a share in the enjoyment we shall one day possess without measure. There is only an imperfect contemplation available to us here of that perfect vision. It is this which all those who have argued for leisure, contemplation, and the preeminence of knowledge have had in mind. The pattern of the cross is the pattern of our life, the pattern of our thanksgiving, and the servant is by no

---

[75] See Pieper, *Leisure*.

means above his Master. But we must understand that even our Master called us to cleave first, above all things, to that one thing necessary (Luke 10:42). Even the cross is emptied of its power without this principle.

This can be sharpened if we recall that the Gospel is good *news*. News, first and foremost, pertains to the intellect (not exclusive of the heart or action). Thus the foundation of our salvation is not works but faith. The Gospel is the revelation of the love of God. What has been meant by all who have distinguished and prioritized the contemplative from the practical is simply that there is an order and an end. In heaven, we shall not labor, but we shall act, and our chief act shall be to behold the face of God. The Gospel is beautiful in itself. Yet it is also a beautiful way of life. It is first beautiful and secondarily practical. This is Christian Wisdom: practical, but first contemplative. Such knowledge becomes a principle of action, but without its intrinsic goodness, all our works are empty. It is this that our Lord meant when he said, "One thing is necessary. Mary has chosen the good portion, which will not be taken away from her" (Luke 10:42). St. Thomas, who argues that the contemplative life is yet more excellent than the active life, has this to say:

> Sometimes a man is called away from the contemplative life to the works of the active life, on account of some necessity of the present life, yet not so as to be compelled to forsake contemplation altogether. Hence Augustine says (*De Civ. Dei* xix, 19): "The love of truth seeks a holy leisure, the demands of charity undertake an honest toil," the work namely of the active life. "If no one imposes this burden upon us we must devote ourselves to the research and contemplation of truth, but if it be imposed on us, we must bear it because charity demands it of us. Yet even then we must not altogether forsake the delights of truth, lest we deprive ourselves of its sweetness, and this burden overwhelm us." Hence it is clear that when a person is called from the contemplative life to the active life, this is done by way not of subtraction but of addition.[76]

Lest we think he forgets the life of Christ, we can remember that it was only for the joy set before him that Jesus Christ endured the cross (Heb. 12:2). It

---

[76] Aquinas, *Summa Theologiae*, II–II, q.182, a.2, r.3.

was precisely through a vision of the final end that he lived, died, and glorified the Father.

This is signified at the transfiguration, when Christ manifests to his disciples a sign of his glory, in order to prepare them for the cross. Because Christ directed himself by a knowledge of the end, he manifested this end to those who were to follow after him.[77] What do we look upon when we see the transfiguration? What did Peter, John, and James see? They gazed, with Moses and Elijah, upon the end of all revelation. They glimpsed the end of Christ's work, a new heavens and new earth, a knowledge almost too terrible to behold. For they saw the true destiny of man. Our destiny in Christ is union with God, a union so profound that it will transform us through and through.[78]

Our destiny is to be like Christ, to gaze upon God in his temple, to *be* his living temple. A foretaste of this Sabbath vision, the incomprehensible and irrevocable friendship of God, gives Christian life its measure. Work is not opposed to contemplation; it is its result, ordained to a yet more perfect conformity to Christ, to our union with God. We are made like him that we might look with him and upon him, to see what he sees. We labor so that the whole body might be built up and together "behold the beauty of the Lord" (Psalm 27:4).

---

[77] Nate Shurden, "Transfigured: A Glimpse of the Glory of Jesus," sermon, 2021, https://www.cornerstonepresfranklin.org/sermons.

[78] "Christ's kingdom is the communion of the blessed with God (and with each other in God) through the inner bond of charity, a bond so strong that it transforms not only the souls of the blessed but also their bodies." Matthew Levering, *Christ's Fulfillment of Torah and Temple: Salvation According to Thomas Aquinas* (Notre Dame: University of Notre Dame Press, 2002), 72.

BIBLIOGRAPHY

Anderson, Carl, and Jose Granados. *Called to Love: Approaching John Paul II's Theology of the Body*. New York: Image, 2009.

Aquinas, Thomas. "Commentary on the Posterior Analytics." Translated by Fabian Larcher O.P. https://isidore.co/aquinas/PostAnalytica.htm.

———. "De Veritate." Translated by Robert W. Schmidt S.J. N.d. https://isidore.co/aquinas/english/QDdeVer11.htm.

———. *Summa contra gentiles*. Translated by Anton C. Pegis. https://isidore.co/aquinas/ContraGentiles1.htm#1.

———. *Summa Theologica*. Translated by Fathers of the Dominican Province. Notre Dame: Christian Classics, 1981.

Augustine. "Augustinus Hipponensis – De Doctrina Christiana Libri Quatuor." Accessed April 23, 2021. https://www.augustinus.it/latino/dottrina_cristiana/index2.htm.

———. *On Christian Doctrine*. Translated by J. J. Shaw. Mineola, NY: Dover Publications, 2009.

Aristotle. *Metaphysics*. Translated by W. D. Ross. http://classics.mit.edu/Aristotle/metaphysics.html.

Deely, John. *Introducing Semiotic: Its History and Doctrine*. Advances in Semiotics. Bloomington: Indiana University Press, 1982.

Gould, Stephen Jay. *Rocks of Ages: Science and Religion in the Fullness of Life*. New York: Random House US, 2011.

John Paul II. *Love and Responsibility*. Boston: Pauline Books & Media, 2013.

———. "Redemptoris Missio." December 7, 1990. Vatican Archive. http://www.vatican.va/content/john-paul-ii/en/encyclicals/documents/hf_jp-ii_enc_07121990_redemptoris-missio.html.

———. *The Theology of the Body: Human Love in the Divine Plan*. Boston: Pauline Books & Media, 1997.

———. "Urbi et Orbi." December 25, 1978. http://www.vatican.va/.

Kierkegaard, Søren. *Provocations: Spiritual Writings of Kierkegaard*. Plough Publishing House, 2014.

Klein, Jacob. *Greek Mathematical Thought and the Origin of Algebra*. New York: Dover Publications, 1992.

Levering, Matthew. *Christ's Fulfillment of Torah and Temple: Salvation According to Thomas Aquinas*. Notre Dame: University of Notre Dame Press, 2002.

MacIntyre, Alasdair C. *Three Rival Versions of Moral Enquiry*. Reprint. Notre Dame: University of Notre Dame Press, 2006.

Maritain, Jacques. *The Person and the Common Good*. Notre Dame: Notre Dame University Press, 1994.

Parsons, Terence. "The Traditional Square of Opposition." N.d. https://plato.stanford.edu/entries/square/.

Percy, Walker. *Lost in the Cosmos: The Last Self-Help Book*. New York: Picador USA, 2000.

Pieper, Josef. *Faith, Hope, Love*. San Francisco: Ignatius Press, 1997.

———. *Happiness and Contemplation*. South Bend: St. Augustine's Press, 1998.

———. *Leisure: The Basis of Culture; The Philosophical Act*. San Francisco: Ignatius Press, 2009.

———. *The Four Cardinal Virtues: Prudence, Justice, Fortitude, Temperance*. Notre Dame: University of Notre Dame Press, 2011.

Pope Paul VI. "Gaudium et Spes." December 7, 1965. Vatican Archive. https://www.vatican.va/archive/hist_councils/ii_vatican_council/documents/vat-ii_const_19651207_gaudium-et-spes_en.html.

Redpath, Peter. "The One and the Many." Course Notes. Holy Apostles College and Seminary, Cromwell, CT, Fall 2019.

Shurden, Nate. "Transfigured: A Glimpse of the Glory of Jesus." Sermon. 2021. https://www.cornerstonepresfranklin.org/sermons.

Thomas Aquinas College. "Dr. Neumayr on the Orders of the Arts and Science." N.d. Educational video, 6:46. https://www.youtube.com/watch?v=UNnirpxk0CI&ab_channel=ThomasAquinasCollege

Weil, Simone, and Joseph Marie Perrin. *Waiting for God*. New York: HarperPerennial Modern Classics, 2009.

MORE FROM DAVENANT PRESS

RICHARD HOOKER MODERNIZATION PROJECT
Radicalism: When Reform Becomes Revolution
Divine Law and Human Nature
The Word of God and the Words of Man
In Defense of Reformed Catholic Worship
A Learned Discourse on Justification

INTRODUCTION TO PROTESTANT THEOLOGY
Reformation Theology: A Reader of Primary Sources with Introductions
Grace Worth Fighting For: Recapturing the Vision of God's Grace in the Canons of Dordt

VERMIGLI'S *COMMON PLACES*
On Original Sin (Vol. 1)
On Free Will and the Law (Vol. 2)

LIBRARY OF EARLY ENGLISH PROTESTANTISM
The Laws of Ecclesiastical Polity: In Modern English, Vol. 1 (Preface–Book IV)
James Ussher and a Reformed Episcopal Church: Sermons and Treatises on Ecclesiology
The Apology of the Church of England
Jurisdiction Regal, Episcopal, Papal

DAVENANT GUIDES
Jesus and Pacifism: An Exegetical and Historical Investigation
The Two Kingdoms: A Guide for the Perplexed
Natural Law: A Brief Introduction and Biblical Defense
Natural Theology: A Biblical and Historical Introduction and Defense

DAVENANT RETRIEVALS
A Protestant Christendom? The World the Reformation Made
People of the Promise: A Mere Protestant Ecclesiology
Philosophy and the Christian: The Quest for Wisdom in the Light of Christ
The Lord is One: Reclaiming Divine Simplicity
A Protestant Christendom? The World the Reformation Made

CONVIVIUM PROCEEDINGS
For the Healing of the Nations: Essays on Creation, Redemption, and Neo-Calvinism
For Law and for Liberty: Essays on the Legacy of Protestant Political Thought
Beyond Calvin: Essays on the Diversity of the Reformed Tradition
God of Our Fathers: Classical Theism for the Contemporary Church
Reforming the Catholic Tradition: The Whole Word for the Whole Church
Reforming Classical Education: Toward A New Paradigm

DAVENANT ENGAGEMENTS
Enduring Divine Absence: The Challenge of Modern Atheism

OTHER PUBLICATIONS
Without Excuse: Scripture, Reason, and Presuppositional Apologetics
Being A Pastor: Pastoral Treatises of John Wycliffe
Serious Comedy: The Philosophical and Theological Significance of Tragic and Comic Writing in the Western Tradition
Ad Fontes: A Journal of Protestant Letters

ABOUT THE DAVENANT INSTITUTE

The Davenant Institute supports the renewal of Christian wisdom for the contemporary church. It seeks to sponsor historical scholarship at the intersection of the church and academy, build networks of friendship and collaboration within the Reformed and evangelical world, and equip the saints with time-tested resources for faithful public witness.

We are a nonprofit organization supported by your tax-deductible gifts. Learn more about us, and donate, at www.davenantinstitute.org.

Made in the USA
Middletown, DE
20 October 2022